Humanities, Religion, and the Arts Tomorrow

Edited by Howard Hunter
Tufts University

Holt, Rinehart and Winston, Inc.
New York   Chicago   San Francisco   Atlanta   Dallas   Montreal   Toronto

To Amos Niven Wilder

Cover: Picasso's "Crucifixion." Permission S.P.A.D.E.M. 1971
by French Reproduction Rights, Inc.

Library of Congress Catalog Card Number: 77–186568
ISBN: 0–03–085391–5
Printed in the United States of America
2345   038   123456789

Preface

"All of the arts, poetry, music, ritual, the visible arts, the theatre, must singly and together create the most comprehensive art of all, a humanized society, and its masterpiece, free man." These words of art historian Bernard Berenson serve well to introduce this book on contemporary culture, religion, and the arts. Like Berenson, the contributors to this volume view their respective disciplines as means to achieve authentic humanity and to enhance the quality of individual and social life.

The authors are specialists on subjects known in the academic world as humanities: philosophy, theology, literary criticism, art history, pedagogy, the novel, poetry, painting, drama, and film. They are concerned with problems found in every humanistic specialization and thus suitable for interdisciplinary investigation. These include determining the method of study and the principle of interpretation appropriate to each area, the method of validating claims to truth, and the images of authentic man, his place, and his destiny.

This book has been designed to serve as a basic resource for students in the humanities, in religion, and in the arts. A distinctive feature of the book is its usefulness to students and instructors seeking new primary sources for interdisciplinary studies. This book raises critical, philosophical, religious, and pedagogical questions which afford student and general reader alike an effective introduction to major issues in the humanities today.

I wish especially to thank Professor Arthur M. Eastman of Carnegie-Mellon University for his discerning comments on the manuscript of this book. An editor is fortunate to have the assistance of so keen a critic and I am happy to acknowledge my gratitude to him. I wish also to express my appreciation to my colleagues at Tufts University for assistance through a Summer Faculty Fellowship. The contributors to this book have been invariably gracious in their response to my editorial requests and to them I express my thanks. I speak for them as well as for myself in acknowledging our profound appreciation to Amos N. Wilder, whose life and work are an inspiration to students of religion and the arts. This book is dedicated to him.

Medford, Massachusetts   H. H.
February 1972

Acknowledgments

Grateful acknowledgment of the publisher and the editor of this book are extended to the following for permission to quote from their works:

Abingdon Press, *Contours of Faith*, John Dillenberger; Alfred A. Knopf, *Collected Poems of Wallace Stevens*, Wallace Stevens; Brandon International Films, *Monsieur Vincent*; Charles Scribner's Sons, *Religion, Revolution, and the Future*, Jurgen Moltmann; Chilmark Press, *The Anathemata*, David Jones; Church Society for College Work, *Parable, Myth & Language*, "A Personal Approach," Denise Levertov; Farrar, Straus & Giroux, Inc., *His Toy, His Dream, His Rest*, John Berryman; Farrar, Straus & Giroux, Inc., *Homage to Mistress Bradstreet*, John Berryman; Farrar, Straus & Giroux, Inc., *77 Dream Songs*, John Berryman; Robert Steele, Federico Fellini, *8½; Film-Makers' Cooperative Catalogue*; "For the Hundredth Birthday of Robert Frost," Galway Kinnell; Four Seasons Foundation, "Above Pate Valley," Gary Snyder; French Reproduction Rights, Inc., Picasso plates; Harper & Row, *The Gospel According to Thomas*, tr. by A. Guillaumont; Houghton Mifflin Co., *Body Rags*, "Testament of the Thief" and "The Porcupine," Galway Kinnell; Houghton Mifflin Co., *Flower Herding on Mount Monadnock*, "For Robert Frost," Galway Kinnell; Kayak Books, Inc., *Animae*, W. S. Merwin; Liveright Publishing Corp., "The Bridge," Hart Crane; New Directions Publishing Corp., *A Coney Island of the Mind*, Lawrence Ferlinghetti; New Directions Publishing Corp., *Collected Earlier Poems*, "The Flower," William Carlos Williams; New Directions Publishing Corp., *Relearning the Alphabet*, Denise Levertov; New Directions Publishing Corp., selections from *The Cantos of Ezra Pound*, Ezra Pound; New Directions Publishing Corp., *The Jacobs Ladder*, "Overland to the Islands," Denise Levertov; *The New York Times*, Air France advertisement; Random

House, *Autobiography of Alice B. Toklas*, Gertrude Stein; Random House, *The Man With the Blue Guitar*, Wallace Stevens; *Time* magazine, Air France advertisement; University of Michigan Press, *New England Saints*, Austin Warren; Vantage Books, *No Exit and The Flies*, Jean-Paul Sartre.

Contents

1

Religion and
the Arts Tomorrow

Howard Hunter

The critical study of the arts and religion holds promise of being a personally fulfilling and socially significant field of inquiry in the remaining decades of this century. For whoever seeks to participate in the critical dialog between the arts and religion must take into account issues fundamental to the style and even to the survival of life in the future. The closely connected crises of man's relationship to his own technology and his ability to establish a viable culture are integral to the arts and religion. It is unlikely that any work of art or expression of religion will be thought adequate if it fails to communicate awareness of modern man's plight.

While the need for sensitivity to environmental and cultural conditions is perhaps unprecedented in its intensity, the requirement is as old as the beginning of art and of religion alike. The expression of man's will toward his environment has always involved his ability to make judgments involving esthetic and religious discrimination. Choosing among possibilities for appreciation and for action, determining the implications of paths chosen, reckoning with the results of the choices of previous generations—man has discovered himself to be both maker and, at times, victim of his making. If man is to retain or, in some cases, to regain control over his technology and to establish viable cultures he has to gain perspective on himself and his situation. He is required to have more than an idea but a full picture or "image" of both man and nature as they are and as they might be. To gain perspective and to specify the nature of man and his world are tasks which involve inextricably intertwined esthetic and religious factors.

The word "image" is used here rather than "concept" because it connotes more fully the subjective dimension of knowledge. "Image" involves ideas and knowledge but is more than these: It is the picture one has of himself and his situation. This picture may be altered with new ideas and revised understanding, but it is the image that largely determines the way new experiences and new ideas are received and interpreted. Thus the image is vastly important in determining one's behavior. History affords innumerable examples of images of man and the world that have expressed and determined man's life during the period of their power. It is possible to read history in terms of the rise and fall of powerful images. Western man, for example, has had his prevailing images significantly altered by the changes associated with men like Copernicus, Darwin, Marx, and Freud. Once man had the image of his world as the center of the universe. His intellectual and artistic activities related to and reflected this fundamental picture. After Copernicus this image was no longer implicit and the implications of the new knowledge forced a crisis in the imagination of man. Once man saw himself as the center of life on this planet, but after Darwin this image was profoundly questioned with a resulting crisis of the imagination. Once the picture of man as having the ability and thus the responsibility to control his own fortunes socially and individually was widely accepted. After Marx and Freud this image of man was severely challenged by new theories of the role of economic and psychological factors in determining man's life.

One does not have to turn to history to note the presence and the power of images. One may look into his mirror or about his room. The cut of his hair, the manner of his dress, the style of his furnishings—all testify to his prevailing self-image. A glance outside the window in any city affords further illustration, for the landscape is crowded with representations in mortar and steel of man's image of himself as a child of God, explorer of space, maker of things, perpetuator of tradition, or iconoclast. Thus images are in evidence throughout the wide range of human experience from cosmology to individual style of dress. Throughout this book the matter of "images" recurs, for they are crucial for the understanding of the arts, religion, and human culture in every age.

It is, of course, impossible to know now what images of man and nature will be required in the future. But it is quite desirable to consider what tasks and obligations responsible artists and religionists are likely to have to accept. We may venture the suggestion that future images will need to make clear to man the timeless, and thus always timely, power of religious criticism of any man or society guilty of despoiling the gift of life by upsetting the conditions that make the sustained enjoyment of that life possible. Such images will, therefore, not suggest sentimental versions of times and places that never were nor ever will be, but will point to a fecund Source whose nature it is to deal disinterestedly with those who respect it or who violate it. They will help make clear to man his potential felicity and the enormity of the consequences of his waywardness. They will point to the supporting order which may be discerned in the immutable regularities or laws which man may only illustrate but never abrogate. In short, images deriving from religious sources will offer a perspective on man as a remarkable but nonetheless significantly limited creature whose situation requires responsible stewardship from him.

It is likely that future images deriving primarily from esthetic experience will be found most acceptable when they give evidence of having the power to bring significant illumination upon the general condition of man and his culture. This is not to suggest that they be in the nature of philosophical illustrations but only that they give signs of having moved beyond being rootless individualistic privacies effectively invulnerable to critical assessment precisely due to their being arbitrary and isolated. What is called for in the next decades is a recovery from the sense of separation from the past and the joining of forces of kindred spirits from many traditions and epochs. As William Kane observed:

> It is an oversimplification to suggest that, historically, the processes of transformation of cultural values, including such concrete manifestations as works of art, have been carried on mainly by a success of enlightened "younger generations" during the past century or so, while conservation of traditional values has been the preoccupation of security-conscious, nostalgic, establishment-bound elders. History, including the history of modern art, reveals that the most profound transformations of form, meaning, and value in cultural enterprises have been brought about through interaction between generations, between traditional and innovative forces rather than through the opposition of these elements and the suppression of one over the other.[1]

Both artists and religionists have behind them and about them all too readily accessible, and even aggressive, exponents of mystiques whose position—not to say argument—is that art and religion are self-authenticating experiences and thus beyond criticism. Such a position, profoundly nonintellectual if not antiintellectual, is no novelty within higher education. But if this is accepted, it means the end of critical discrimination, for there is no longer any foundation for it. It is not difficult to find those who insist that such is the case, regrettable or not, and that it is only taste or personal experience which determines commitment and evaluation. They argue that in the final analysis one cannot with propriety criticize the actions of another in any absolute sense. This position allows its defender the psychological sense of certitude while denying him the possibility of establishing in a general and objective way the conviction of certainty.

One does not have to accept as self-authenticating truth whatever an artist or religionist offers, nor be rigid in defense of one or another set of

---

[1] William Kane, "Toward a New Aesthetic," *Tufts Review* 1, no. 1, (Spring 1970), p. 22.

a priori standards when confronting the works of artists and religionists. Rather, one may approach statements and actions emanating from religious conviction in much the same way that William Kane suggests as appropriate for assaying art: ". . . the viewer tries to make of his experience of a new and unprecedented expression something which may function to enlarge or expand his intellectual understanding of and to intensify his emotional responses to the object itself and to its cultural context."[2]

Those images which deserve to be called both radical and relevant and which deserve to be considered authentic expressions from the creative wellsprings from which both individuality and community flow will be as rare as they will be wonderful. Nothing less, however, than the generation of such images ought to be the goal of every religionist and every artist. And it should be the task of the academician to see to it that every person, insofar as everyone is intimately involved with the fundamental questions with which both art and religion deal, should be given basic direction in both these fields for the purpose of making more appropriate critical judgments about them. It is, of course, easier to welcome such images than to give infallible advice regarding their cultivation.

We are not without direction, however, and the dialog between the arts and religion will be enriched tomorrow by the contributions of such scholars as Harvey Cox. In this volume he extends his continuing analysis of the complex interrelationships of the arts, technology, and religion. It has been clear since the phenomenal reception afforded *The Secular City* that in Cox a generation has found an articulate spokesman, guide, and goad. Cox has an unmistakably contemporary style which makes his work accessible to many who would not otherwise become acquainted with the theory and criticism of culture. As his essay in this volume indicates, Cox is concerned to make manifest the perennial nature of man's technological and cultural crises.

Students concerned with the relationship of humanities, religion, and the arts tomorrow will have to take into account the work of many theorists of culture from the earliest times to the present. Since the orientation of the present volume is toward the future, there is value in considering a theorist of culture other than a contemporary one for the assurance that the problems facing us today are scarcely unprecedented. Friedrich Schiller wrote eloquently of culture inflicting a wound upon the essential harmonious unity of human nature by its causing rigorous dissociations of ranks and occupations and its encouraging the rise of the separate disciplines centering either on the intuitive or on the formalizing impulses. Schiller did not view the fateful separation between disciplines of thought and of feeling as a new development in his own 1795; rather it was a legacy from the very

---

[2] Kane, pp. 24–25.

success in ancient times of enlarged experience and more precise reflection which came from using the intuitive and the speculative faculties.

It might give a composer of contemporary jeremiads pause to realize that Schiller was writing in his time of conditions whose roots he saw as ancient and yet whose description would be applicable today and, no doubt, will be so tomorrow:

> Eternally chained to only one single little fragment of the whole, Man himself grew to be only a fragment: with the monotonous noise of the wheel he drives everlastingly in his ears, he never develops the harmony of his being, and instead of imprinting humanity upon his nature he becomes merely the imprint of his occupation, of his science.[3]

For all the benefits—and they are real—of specialization, they are bought at the cost of the lost unity of man within himself. Schiller foresaw that it was a task of more than a single century for man to recover from degrading servitude to Nature or to sensuality in one place and to return to her simplicity, truth, and fullness in another. His advice was to echo Horace: *sapere aude,* dare to be wise! An unedifying banality if not expounded in some explicit detail, but Schiller proceeded to elaborate as he advised the artist, whom he saw as inevitably a child of his time, not to be his time's disciple or even its favorite but rather its redeemer. His view of vocation has a strong religious dimension:

> he will indeed take his subject matter from the present age, but his form he will borrow from a nobler time—nay, from beyond all time, from the absolute unchangeable unity of his being.[4]

Securing himself against the corruptions of his time, the artist will "look upwards to his own dignity and to Law, not downwards to fortune and to everyday needs."[5] Surely his advice to the artist could be taken well by both artist and religionist tomorrow:

> Give the world on which you are acting the DIRECTION towards the good, and the quiet rhythm of time will bring about its development. You have given it this direction, if by your teachings you elevate its thoughts to the necessary and the eternal, if by your actions or your creations you transform the necessary and eternal into the objects of its impulses. . . . Live with your century, but do not be its creature; render to your contemporaries what they need, not what they praise.[6]

Schiller's advice is peculiarly appropriate for students of the humanities, for it delineates forcefully the intensity of the individual and the social

---

[3] Friedrich Schiller, *On the Aesthetic Education of Man* (New Haven: Yale University Press, 1954), p. 40.

[4] Schiller, p. 52.

[5] Schiller, p. 52.

[6] Schiller, pp. 53–54.

dynamics relating to man's esthetic and religious experience. It roots these dynamics in profound personal experience common to men in all ages. His work connects us with our past and yet does not ask us to become slaves to it. He clarifies culture's ambivalent contribution to art and religion: simultaneously inhibiting unfettered flights of fancy which attempt to authenticate themselves merely by the fact of their being and resisting the confining rigidities to which the formalizing impulse is prone. His statement of culture's task with regard to the impulses to sense and to form is especially valuable:

> To watch over these two impulses [form and sense], and to secure for each its boundaries, is the task of *culture*, which therefore owes justice equally to both, and has to uphold not only the rational impulse against the sensuous, but also the latter against the former. Thus its business is twofold: first, to secure the sense faculty against the encroachments of freedom; secondly, to secure the personality against the power of sensation. The former it achieves by the cultivation of the capacity for feeling, the latter by the cultivation of the capacity for reason.[7]

The task of the student of interdisciplinary studies in the arts and religions could still be so described with little change.

What will be needed tomorrow, as always, are theorists of culture who will not only take into account the technological and cultural environments and their related problems but will also develop keen and informed specialized critical abilities appropriate to the several artistic and religious modes. Despite the inevitable and, in part, proper reaction of some that such culture critics are not necessary and that only the practicing artists and the practicing religionists "doing their own thing" are ultimately important and authoritative, the need continues for serious and strenuously scrupulous criticism. It is no derogation of either artist or mystic to suggest that he may, in fact, be least well prepared to exercise the kind of judicial discrimination about areas of human experience in which he is so intensely involved.

In our own time students of the complex issues of religion and culture have been aided and greatly stimulated by the work of Paul Tillich. Like Schiller, Tillich was drawn to the polarities in Western thought between the absolute of being and the absolute of knowing. He saw Western humanity attempting to overcome the age-old bondage of "powers" by religious subjection to the universal God and by philosophical subjection to a universal principle.

> The problem created by the subjection of absolute principle is "*the problem of the two absolutes.*" How are they related to each other? The religious and the philosophical Absolute, *Deus* and *esse,* cannot be unconnected! What is their connection from the point of view of being as well as of

---

[7] Schiller, pp. 68–69.

knowing? In the simple statement "God *is*," the connection is achieved; but the character of this connection is the problem of the philosophy of religion.[8]

As did Schiller, Tillich emphasized the necessity for man to come to terms with the question of his relationship to his culture. In words which repeat Schiller's analysis and thus, regrettably but accurately, also fulfil his negative prophecies, Tillich wrote:

> Man is supposed to be the master of his world and of himself. But actually he has become a part of the reality he has created, an object among objects, a thing among things, a cog within a universal machine to which he must adapt himself in order not to be smashed by it. Out of this predicament of man in the industrial society the experiences of emptiness and meaninglessness, of de-humanization and estrangement have resulted. Man has ceased to encounter reality as meaningful. Reality in its ordinary forms and structures does not speak to him any longer.[9]

There are exceptions, however, for there are those who still have the gift of meaningful encounter with reality and who strive to communicate the actuality and the meaning of such extraordinary experience. For Tillich, the key to understanding contemporary culture was through the "great works of the visual arts, of music, of poetry, of literature, of architecture, of dance, of philosophy which show in their style both the encounter with nonbeing and the strength which can stand this encounter and shape it creatively."[10] To these we may add here the expressions of men and women of profound religious sensitivity and, not least of all, persons trained in the disciplines of criticism. For the task of religion and the arts tomorrow will not be simply to encourage but to discriminate among the variant expressions deriving from what is perceived or purported to be the depths of artistic and religious experience. There is likely to be no dearth of experience of the "ineffable" but more than a dearth of expert exercise of the critical faculty.

Responsible participation in the developing dialog between religion and the arts will require familiarity with the efforts of those interpreters whose work both reflects and influences the direction of the present, and thus to some extent, the future in this field. In any field so diverse and so vast it would be possible, of course, for each observer to draw up a different and valuable list of those scholars whose work he would consider necessary for an adequate introduction. With this qualification in mind, one way to gain understanding of the literature and the major issues is through study of the essays in this volume.

[8] Paul Tillich, *Theology of Culture* (New York: Oxford University Press, 1959), p. 12.

[9] Tillich, p. 46.

[10] Tillich, pp. 46–47.

It is required of the serious student in the field of religion and the arts that he make a careful scrutiny of the theological positions and the principles of interpretation employed by leading scholars. In his essay for this volume Nathan Scott, Jr., widely recognized as one of the most productive and influential scholars concerned with theology and literature today, discusses in careful detail a central problem of the theology of culture, that of the principle of interpretation or hermeneutic. Beginning students seeking to become acquainted with major issues occupying present and, one may be assured, future studies in this field are well advised to familiarize themselves with this fundamental statement as well as with Scott's other works. Experienced students and fellow scholars will see this essay as especially timely in view of recent lively exchanges between Scott and a commentator on his work. The commentator wrote from the standpoint of what he terms "radical theology" with its self-imposed imperative of drastic methodological reconception centering on acceptance of contemporary cultural expressions as proper standards for theologizing in what he considers a post-Christian era. It is not feasible here to enter the discussion in progress, but it seems clear enough that critical discussion of fundamental positions is ultimately to the good of the discipline. Scott's essay in this volume is a gracefully articulated statement of theory and practice in interdisciplinary studies in literature and theology. It is based less on commitment to a particular theological model and "methodology," and more on a passion for the integrity of the art under scrutiny combined with a respect for the integrity of the critical intellect.

Charles Kegley, well known in the academic community for his editorship of the valuable series of volumes called the *Library of Living Philosophers*, speaks to the issues raised in Scott's essay from the vantage point of a philosopher and esthetician writing in the spirit of linguistic and conceptual analysis. Kegley insists upon fundamental definitions and is willing to confront common usage when he forces us to consider precisely what is meant by "religious interpretation." For, as his analysis shows, this apparently innocent and common phrase is, in fact, very ambiguous. Faith, hope, and clarity, and the greatest of these is clarity—Kegley might well accept this view of the analytic philosopher's ordering of values, for he asks for clarity with regard to the basic questions.

It is well to enlist the support of those among us who have most assiduously dedicated themselves to the task of clarifying issues. Such analysts do not find a paucity of work in the field of religion and the arts. Is there "religious" interpretation? If so, which religion is being used as a model? Religions differ. And, if that problem be settled, whose religion is central: that of the artist? the fictional character? the critic? How useful is the notion that any work, intense enough, may be considered "religious"? As an esthetician Kegley rehearses the dimensions of the intentionalist fallacy without a knowledge of which no one should venture into the difficult realm of criticism in the field of religion-and-the-arts today or tomorrow. He persists in asking for precision from those who gloss over difficulties with easy generalizations such as there being more faith in honest doubt than in some belief. Kegley wants to know when it is that doubting is religious and what view of religion is being held.

The novice would do well to consider Charles Kegley's demand for precision in terminology. Is Kegley right in rejecting the descriptive phrase "negative theology" for atheistic and agnostic literature? Is it correct to argue, as he does in this volume as well as elsewhere, that no formal definition of art or religion is possible? Is Tillich's interpretation of religion as a "matter of ultimate concern" so broad as to be practically useless, as Kegley believes? Is it appropriate to argue with James and Wieman for "essential factors" in religion such as the ultimate ascendancy of good in view of Kegley's rejection of definition? However one responds, it is certain that each person will have to do something similar to what Kegley does here if he is to enter the dialog between religion and the arts. Not only does Kegley introduce the reader to literature in the field and to major problems, he offers a basic approach in discrimination, distinguishing among themes, theses, and symbols, in works of Sartre, Camus, and Beckett. His essay leaves the reader, as it should, to answer the question as to what makes a work of art religiously significant. Should one hold that religion is inherently affirmative and redemptive?

A disciplined appreciation of the past is required of those who will contribute most to the developing dialog between religion and the arts. It is scarcely novel to stress the need for solid historical knowledge, but the need continues to be fundamental—in fact, it is accentuated in a time of rapid social and intellectual change.

This is not to say that every budding artist or saint ought to be discouraged from acting until he has undertaken the task of rigorous self analysis. The freedom of artists and religionists for self-expression has been won at too great a cost and is entirely too precious to lose. Assuredly it is better to accept this freedom at the cost of enduring aberrations, excesses, and the indulgences of the self-deluded than to abandon it. But it is nonetheless vastly important for someone to be in the position of trying to learn more about the artistic and religious temperament and its various manifestations throughout history than any given artist or religionist may have either time, ability, or interest to know. This is one of the tasks of the critic who will understand best the dialog between religion and the arts. He, if anyone, may preserve us from the banalities of the "Like Wow!" school of criticism and the arrogancies of the doctrinaire "true believer." As profoundly different as our present may be from the past and as unprecedented as much of the future may appear, there is still need for awareness of history's lessons. The essayists in this volume display within their areas of concentration a concern for the lessons of history and for the intriguing problem of determining the relationhips of the esthetic and the religious dimensions of man's consciousness.

Writing from the perspective of a specialist in the field of drama-and-theology to which he has made a distinguished contribution, Tom Driver reflects on the situation of that amazingly resilient but chronically ailing artistic institution, the theater. Driver's essay moves quickly to the heart of the matter for the dialog between religion and the arts. Given the all but totally unprecedented present cultural situation, how can one most effectively prepare for a future whose shape cannot be known and for which no past models are thus adequate? Driver is clearly too well informed about and appreciative of the achievements of the past to be satisfied with being merely modish about viewing the present as revolutionarily different from anything that has been known before. Yet he is too much aware of today's realities and too much involved in current thought about religion-and-the-arts to gloss over the insistent actualities of a deracinated culture.

It is instructive to consider the work of scholars like Driver who have roots in a past which they are certain no longer exists, who are free from vested interests in attempts to revive the past, who are not afraid of an adventure into the unknown, but who have some responsibility for the direction the trip into the future will take. They know that the past, for all its failures, had its hardwon good, and that the future simply as future is no guarantee of resolution of present problems. Even the present was once a future. To ponder the implications of what Driver terms the current culture's "seismic changes in sensibility" can be a deeply felt personal experience with profound moral and intellectual dimensions. For what is at stake in such reflections is the determination of a way to live and to think. Is it the main task of religious thought to concentrate on the effort to translate received traditions into current language or should it instead focus on understanding those experiences out of which new theologies may arise? Readers will find it especially instructive to compare Driver's analysis with those of Cox, Scott, Dixon, and Hazelton and Austin in this volume.

Turning to the area of religion-and-poetry, Tony Stoneburner, himself a poet as well as a scholar of literature and religion, moves the discussion to a detailed examination of the images of man in a number of contemporary poets, including Galway Kinnell, John Berryman, David Jones, and Denise Levertov. Stoneburner is not sanguine about the likelihood that any one image-of-the-life-of-man will emerge in the coming decade. While in his view there are obvious movements in the history of poetry, and at any one period dominant and receding emphases, there are a limited number of archetypes or original forms with which man has to work. Stoneburner sees the present as "special" not in its being totally revolutionary but in its being the scene in which "All the human options address and beckon us." Here again the reader must conclude that what is required is careful consideration of the fundamental problem of discriminating among claims upon us by competing models of authenticity.

John Dixon, Jr., demonstrates in his essay for this volume the felicitous manner in which a connoisseur's expertise may combine with the academician's and religionist's concern for fundamental values. A scholar and teacher in both art and religion, Dixon makes his case for the essential unity of art and religious experience by means of an investigation of Tuscan theology through the art of Giotto and Duccio, which he then relates to twentieth-century art. By precept and by example Dixon makes clear that, whatever one may say about the current cultural situation, it is not without roots in a past whose shape and whose dynamics may be understood through application of scholarly and critical diligence. Though concluding that none today can know what the images of the future "can be or ought to be," Dixon offers a procedure by which new images might emerge. Especially pertinent to the continuing discussion within college groups concerned to relate appropriately to the changing cultural conditions is Dixon's charge against what he sees as the unspoken dogma of the liberal academy. "Under the only real statement of it—scholarly objectivity—it is rigourously forbidden to enter into profound commitment to the objects of study."

It is this attitude which Robert Bellah scored in his article, "Confessions of a Former Establishment Fundamentalist." Writes Bellah:

> The establishment view of religion in American universities today is what I have called "enlightenment fundamentalism." This is the view that science and historical scholarship have effectively disposed of fallacious religious beliefs. If the study of religion has any place in the university at all, which is doubtful to enlightenment fundamentalists, it is to disclose the true reasons why religious believers have been so misguided.[11]

However, as Bellah knows: "The present student generation is not at all prepared to accept these presuppositions. In fact many students feel that there is probably more of importance in primitive shamanism than in all the cut-and-dried rationality that college professors serve up to them."[12] Bellah has moved away from conventional teaching with its development of carefully articulated conceptual schemes leading to consideration of concrete examples. He now attempts "to get the students to face the religious dimension of existence directly, to some extent chaotically and without concepts."[13] To this end he quite naturally employs the arts. Dixon would not find this development surprising—only sadly still newsworthy. Bellah's "confession" is the lead article for the *Bulletin* of the Council of the Study of Religion, for December 1970. For Dixon argues not that an essential

---

[11] Robert N. Bellah, "Confessions of a Former Establishment Fundamentalist," *Council of the Study of Religion* 1, no. 3 (December 1970), p. 3.
[12] Bellah, p. 3.
[13] Bellah, p. 4.

unity exists *between* art and religion but rather that there is already an essential unity *of* art and religious experience.

The explosive increase in the number of books and articles on film subjects is one index of the recent growth of general and scholarly interest in this most popular art form of the twentieth century. Since film is both art and commerce and involves an extraordinary range of interests, it is not surprising that most persons involved with it have a specific and limited interest in the subject. Even now there are relatively few scholars whose interest in film is broad and general. I say "relatively" in comparison to the numbers of scholars devoting careers, say, to literature or to philosophy. It is still apparently the all but unthinkable thought to imagine a university, a theological school, or a consortium of theological schools where the number of specialists in contemporary communications media is more than a very small fraction of the number in the conventional media of biblical, literary, and philosophical studies. Too typical, even today, is the recent response of a theological student to the suggestion that there should be more work in the arts in theological school: "I am not an artist, I'm a divinity student!" It is instructive to consider the difference between the amount of money spent yearly to support the hosts of professional scholars interpreting religion in works of literature and that invested in professional interpretation through such other art forms as cinema. Yet, is it not a legitimate question whether one medium so much more profoundly expresses and influences contemporary man's moral, intellectual, and religious life?

Robert Steele is one scholar who has pioneered in the effort to bring religion and cinematic studies into a more fruitful relationship. As with most scholars who approach their work in a thoroughly interdisciplinary manner, Steele does not find the boundaries between religion and the arts holding firm. Himself the holder of graduate degrees in both films studies and theology, he has made films professionally, has written and taught extensively on film subjects, and has directed workshops in cinema and religion. His essay in this volume reflects his critical view of those filmmakers who attempt to substitute technical competence for vision and of those laymen who focus solely on artistic failures in the attempt to excuse their ignorance of the genuine achievement of a small but significant number of film artists.

As we have emphasized, dialog requires rigorous attention to the terms of the dialog and all should know that the meaning of any term is not constant. The developing dialog between religion and the arts may turn out to be most successful, paradoxically enough, to the extent that it makes itself unnecessary. Roger Hazelton and Dorothy Austin caution that insistence upon building semantic-conceptual bridges between the arts and religion may lead one to forget that their (proper) relationship is not external but internal. "Both have their roots tangled in the rich subsoil of man's feeling and awareness." Hazelton and Austin see the arts as especially appropriate for theology at a time when its situation seems more precarious than ever before. They ponder the situation in which it appears to them that the theological way of thinking and being is threatened by extinction and it is an open question as to whether it can be reinvigorated or reexpressed. If ever it is, it will be only when the theological profession of which the seminary is, classically, the intellectual center, broadens and deepens, with the aid of artists, its understanding that more is required than rational criticism and conceptual abstraction. Tautness, rigorous attention, and excitement are required if theology is to fulfil its proper task. With Driver and Dixon they emphasize the absolute necessity for religious experience without which theology is dead.

All those interested in the growth of scholarly research and practical programs of education in religion and the arts find encouragement in evidence of increasing concern shown for this area in the profession of the ministry. Significantly, among the authors of essays in this volume are faculty members of several of the major seminaries and directors of two centers of theological learning.

Walter Wagoner, Director of the Boston Theological Institute, here considers facilitating the concerns expressed by Dixon and Hazelton and Austin. Wagoner has long been championing the cause of a much closer and more fruitful interrelation between the arts and theological studies and the present article reflects his eagerness to have more positive action in this area.

Picasso's *Crucifixion* is the subject of a collaborative essay by John Dillenberger, President of the Graduate Theological Union of San Francisco, and Jane Dillenberger of the faculty of that institution. Their study shows concern for detailed esthetic analysis set in the context of theological reflection. The Dillenbergers demonstrate that the work of a great artist is a mine whose riches are not always apparent on the surface. In the instance of Picasso there is the special thrill of becoming acquainted with unfamiliar dimensions of one whose work is at once secure in history, thoroughly contemporary, and not yet completed.

Stanley Hopper, with whose essay the volume concludes, has devoted much of his career as scholar, teacher, and administrator to the study of theology and the arts and to the encouragement of both students and colleagues to undertake similar studies. His essay reflects his concentration in the specific area of theology and literature. Hopper, as the others, has found it necessary to pay careful attention to the matter of the principle of interpretation.

During the preparation of these essays Amos Wilder's *Early Christian Rhetoric: The Language of the Gospel* became available in a new and enhanced edition.[14] In this seminal book, which treats issues germane to

---

[14] Amos Wilder, *Early Christian Rhetoric* (Cambridge: Harvard University Press, 1971).

those considered in this volume, Wilder delineates dimensions of the contemporary crisis in communication, noting that we are no doubt enduring a period of the death and birth of language itself. His analyses are made with reference to the rhetoric employed in an earlier time of profound crisis, that of the writing of the New Testament Gospels. The message of these present essays confirms Wilder's insights into the pervasiveness of the contemporary crisis in vision, value, and personal and social life. They confirm his teaching that, distressing as they are, our times are not without precedent, and that men in the past found a way they called the Way.

It is encouraging to find Wilder, himself so sensitively aware of the present and informed of the past, holding to a conviction regarding the persistence of a remnant whose values serve to sustain authentic man in every age. In his *The New Voice* Wilder takes a positive view of "that whole Western exploration and continuing revolution which had led to our present disarray and anomie." Appealing over and beyond the long view of the humanist to the "remnant," Wilder sees this remnant "in incognito in all levels of society" and enduring in witness to justice and freedom. He discovers "a cable or life-line of survival and promise running through the years." He takes occasion for hope in what he perceives as "some aboriginal increment of health from the beginning, some prior fiat of life itself."

> In man's conscious history it can be recognized as an archetypal covenant, not only between man and man but between man and the stones of the field—as in Job—and between man and the stars: that is, a covenant between man and the powers. Earthly hopes as well as spiritual are sustained by this diffused and anonymous remnant which not only suffers with the miscarriages of time but is served by them.[15]

Wilder's thought on this "fiat of life" serves as a bridge from this introductory essay to those that follow.

[15] Amos Wilder, *The New Voice: Religion, Literature, Hermeneutics* (New York: Herder & Herder, 1969), p. 15–16.

2

The Virgin and
the Dynamo Revisited

An Essay on
the Symbolism of Technology

Harvey Cox

The Legacy of Henry Adams

In 1900 Henry Adams visited the Great Exposition with its famous forty-foot dynamo. For Adams it was an unforgettable experience. He at once became fascinated, almost obsessed with the dynamo. As a medieval historian he was then already mulling over his classic *Mont St. Michel and Chartres* which was to appear a few years later, a book in which he penned lyrical antiphons to the spiritual power of the Virgin, the spirit, he said, that had built Chartres. Now this same Henry Adams, his attention riveted to the great soaring dynamo, came to an insight which has intrigued the twentieth-century sensibility ever since: the Virgin was gone, but the Dynamo had taken her place. "To Adams," he wrote, referring to himself as always in the third person, "the dynamo became a symbol of infinity . . . he began to feel the forty foot dynamo as a moral force, much as the early Christians felt the Cross. . . . Before the end, one began to pray to it."[1]

Adams was a modern man with a medieval heart, or maybe the other way around. He was one of America's most perceptive analysts of symbols. As such, he was only secondarily interested in the great dynamo's capacity to produce electric power. He was even less interested in its eventual impact on domestic lighting, consumer value choices, productivity, or even social change. Adams was intrigued by the dynamo as a symbol. He saw it as a cultural or indeed a religious symbol, an emotionally vivid image organizing and codifying consciousness.

[1] Henry Adams, *The Education of Henry Adams* (Modern Library), New York: Random House, p. 380.

15

Technology as Symbol

Since the days of Henry Adams, few historians, to say nothing of sociologists, have delved into this enticing but elusive field of inquiry. Yet today we need the sensibility of a Henry Adams to understand ourselves. If he was that prescient about the dynamo, what could he have told us about those throngs of hushed pilgrims gathered around the blistered American space capsule at Expo 67? Why that air of reverence? What could he have told us about our feelings toward our automobiles (family escutcheons?), the hydrogen bomb (apocalypse?), the computer (delphine oracle?)? To understand ourselves and our technologies today we need an Adamsian fusion of Yankee shrewdness and gothic fantasy.

This is not to say that the symbolic meaning of technology has gone wholly unexplored in our time. Journalists, poets, social critics, and others thread their way into the labyrinth periodically and return to tell us something about the machine-as-god theme. Take for example the work of the American poet Hart Crane, for whom the subject had a continuing interest. In his long poem, "The Bridge," completed in 1930, Crane sings of a man who, of a morning, walks across the Brooklyn Bridge (which Crane could see constantly from the window of his room on Columbia Heights) and returns at night. The walker, and then the poet, begin to see the great bridge not just as a means of conveyance but as a link between the empirical and the spiritual world, that elusive spiritual world which Crane, like Henry Adams and Crane's great contemporary T. S. Eliot, saw as eroding away. Near the end of Crane's poem the bridge itself is addressed in a canticle like St. Francis, in an age before steel suspension bridges, addressed to the sun, or like the ancient Hebrew Psalmist sang to God. Crane's psalm says:

> O Thou steeled Cognizance whose leap commits
> The agile precincts of the lark's return;
> Within whose lariat sweep encinctured sing
> In single chrysalis the many twain,—
> Of stars Thou art the stitch and stallion glow
> And, like an organ, Thou, with sound of doom—
> Sight, sound and flesh Thou leadest from time's realm
> As love strikes clear direction for the helm.[2]

Poets and critics have not avoided probing the powerful symbolism of technology. Not all, of course, have followed Crane in transubstantiating technological artifacts into altars. Many, if not most, at least in recent decades, paint technological creations in somber or lurid colors, depicting them as destructive, demonic or poisonous. W. H. Auden, for example, sees the wrecked and abandoned effluvium of technology as an augury of dis-

---

[2] From *The Complete Poems and Selected Letters and Prose of Hart Crane.* Copyright 1933, 1958, 1966 by Liveright Publishing Corp., New York. Reprinted by permission of publisher.

aster. For other poets it is technology itself that crucifies the grass and soil on a cross of concrete.

But the important thing to notice is that whether technology is seen as saviour or satan, its *power* is recognized and respected. This awe before the power symbolized by the bridge or the dynamo is in one sense more important for our purposes than the question of whether the power is good or evil. William Carlos Williams catches this insight with simple clarity in his poem, "The Flower" which, like Hart Crane's focuses on a great bridge, this time, however, on the feelings aroused in Williams by its amazingly fast construction. Here the poet is talking to a "woman of 38" he has just described as "worth looking at both for her body and her mind."

> She it was put me straight
> about the city when I said, It
>
> makes me ill to see them run up
> a new bridge like that in a few months
>
> and I can't find time even to get
> a book written. They have the power,
>
> that's all, she replied. That's what you all
> want. If you can't get it, acknowledge
>
> at least what it is.[3]

Fools and poets rush in where sociologists and theologians, albeit for different reasons, fear to tread. But poets, painters, sculptors, and filmmakers, all of whom "acknowledge at least" the fearsome power symbolized by technology, should not be expected to do the more pedestrian, analytic, and descriptive work of the less muse-inspired callings.

Theologians and social scientists have steered clear of the inquiry into the symbolism of technology, no doubt for very different reasons. The reasons indeed are almost the opposite of each other. For the sociologists it has no doubt been the acknowledged inadequacy of properly precise conceptual tools that has prevented the inquiry. For the theologians, on the other hand, whose methods might at first appear to be more serviceable in scrutinizing the death and birth of deities, one suspects it was the odor of heresy that discouraged investigation. Also perhaps the theological and symbolic significance of technology probably seemed, to practitioners in both fields, at best remote from the main issues, at worst a trivial or even distracting consideration.

Henry Adams would never have agreed that the symbolic analysis

---

[3] William Carlos Williams, *Collected Earlier Poems*. Copyright 1936 by William Carlos Williams. Reprinted by permission of New Directions Publishing Corporation.

of technology was trivial. He believed that about the year 1600, the year of the burning of Giordano Bruno, Western civilization had gone through an epochal transition. It was a sea change from what he called the "religious" to what he called the "mechanical" age. Adams describes this transition in terms of "energy," a popular if somewhat loosely used word in his day. But he was really talking about how a culture orders and symbolizes its meanings and aspirations, how it sanctifies its values and celebrates its hopes. Adams saw, in short, what so many commentators on technology since then have missed. He saw that the dynamo (read jet plane, computer, automobile, nuclear accelerator) was not only a forty foot tool man could use to help him on his way, it was also a forty foot high symbol of where he wanted to go.

This paper is written in the spirit of Henry Adams. In it I shall inquire into the symbolic significance(s) of technology and into the closely related question of how such an inquiry should in fact be conducted. In so doing my modest hope is to bring into fuller consciousness some current cultural attitudes toward technology, to ask about the possible import of these attitudes and then to register a few implications for future work.

Symbolism and Technology

> The great mythological themes continue to repeat themselves in the obscure depths of the psyche. . . . It seems that a myth itself, as well as the symbols it brings into play, never quite disappears from the present world of the psyche; it only changes its aspect and disguises its operation.[4]

Should we begin this foray with a crisply clear definition of each of the central terms? Maybe ordinarily we should. But I do not believe instant clarity of definition always facilitates a discussion. Especially where meanings are in dispute, as is the case here, resorting to the dictionary may settle interesting questions *ab initio* instead of in the course of the argument itself. I can say at the outset that by "technology" I shall merely mean the tools and procedures, in their nearly infinite variety, that men utilize to observe, cope with and modify their environment. I realize that even this simple definition is not likely to escape dispute. By using it I am quite consciously rejecting the kind of definition advanced, for example, by Jacques Ellul in *The Technological Society*. "Technique," says Ellul, "is the totality of methods rationally arrived at and having absolute efficiency in every field of human activity."[5] I regard this definition as at once too sweeping and too imprecise. Also I do not think it is particularly clear. Some definitions of

[4] Mircea Eliade, *Myths, Dreams and Mysteries* (New York: Harper & Row, 1967), p. 27.
[5] Jacques Ellul, *The Technological Society* (New York: Random House, 1964), p. xxv. (Italics are Ellul's.)

technology are too narrow, identifying the term wholly with "the machine." Others, including I fear Ellul's (and perhaps Lewis Mumford's) are too inclusive and therefore render precision, hard enough to attain in this murky field, even harder. I also understand that by "technique" Ellul appears to mean something different from "technology," although his English-reading supporters rarely make the distinction. In any case, I am trying here to avoid making "technology" mean either too little or too much and to stay fairly close to an ordinary-speech meaning.

Before defining "symbol" I want to say something about the ambiguous status of that term in sociology and thereby to defend my particular usage in the present paper.

The lack of clarity in defining the concept of "symbol" in social science today is related to the weakness of methods for studying whatever symbols are. It would be overly gentle to say the analysis of the relationship between symbols and society has *not* been a strong point in American sociology. It has, in fact, been a nearly fatal weakness. In introducing Part Four of *Theories of Society*, the part dedicated to "Culture and Social Systems," for example, Talcott Parsons writes that the neglect of this nexus "was the major sin of omission committed by the early theorists" in scientific sociology. Parsons admits the interrelationships are complicated but argues that this complexity should not exclude such a vital consideration from social science. "On the contrary," he continues,

> taking them into account will prove to be one of the main bases on which social science can advance beyond its present state—which in certain theoretical respects, seems to be stuck on a dead level.[6]

Parsons himself has tried to correct some of this lamentable underemphasis but has not really done much to improve the picture. American scholars who have dealt with symbolism, such as Suzanne Langer, Kenneth Burke, and Hugh Dalziel Duncan have often been viewed as offbeat or peripheral. Consequently, because the theoretical edifice is so shaky and because the subject itself is so complex, much American sociological writing has simply ignored the question of symbols. This is certainly true of recent writing on technology.

Duncan, in *Symbols in Society*, suggests some reasons for the traditional American neglect. For example, he recalls the old American philosophical bias that defines all values and symbolic meanings as "subjective" and says this bias is partially to blame. It tends to exile symbols into an inner realm of the self, unobservable by scientific means. Duncan also believes that the popularity of what he calls "mechanistic models" in sociology has worked to the detriment of symbol analysis. He also puts the blame on theories of symbols as mere "masks" behind which "real interests"—

[6] Talcott Parsons, *Theories of Society*, vol. 2 (Glenville, Illinois: Free Press, 1965), p. 988.

political, economic, sexual—act. These theories, he says, reduce symbols to transient epiphenomena, unworthy of really sustained analysis. Who wants to waste time on the masks and the mystifications when we need to know about the "real"actors?

It is beyond the scope of this paper to speculate further on the sources of the disability to deal with symbols, a disability that does seem to infect most American sociology, or to say for sure whether Duncan is correct. I simply agree that the weakness is *there* and is regrettable.

There is one brief point advanced by Duncan however which is unavoidable here because it touches on the question of what we mean by a symbol and therefore on the heart of our theme. Duncan rejects very force-ably the notion, commonly held among many sociologists, that symbols are completely arbitrary, that their meanings have nothing to do with their *inherent* content but are bestowed entirely by social convention. Thus he disagrees totally with the assertion by Professor Joyce A. Hertzler that there "is nothing *in the nature* of any of the signs . . . used as symbols that gives them the meanings they carry, these meanings we human beings bestow upon them by agreement or convention."[7]

This is a tricky problem. It has to do with the relationship between "signs" and "symbols" and therefore is integral to our inquiry here. Just what do we mean by the word "symbol"? What makes a symbol a symbol (and not a sign, image, metaphor, emblem)? Hertzler herself says that symbols are ". . . the instrumentalities whereby men codify experience, or create a map of the territory of experience. Their utility depends upon the fact that all group members are conditioned to react more or less uniformly to them."[8]

What I want to do here is to define "symbol" in such a way that I do not "settle" this important dispute by fiat. I accept the first part of Professor Hertzler's statement but raise a question about the second part.

Yes, symbols as I am about to define them do facilitate, perhaps even make possible cognitive experience. All cognition and communication pre-suppose social existence, and social existence is made possible through mutually appreciated words and gestures. Symbol thus suggests the intrinsic sociability of human existence. Symbol is the medium of oneself's partici-pation in the selfhood of others. Symbols must, by their very nature, be shared. Even dream symbols, as Freud pointed out, have a public side. We can agree with Hertzler that a symbol can be anything (a word, object, person, gesture) that has a certain common significance and that helps to order or make sense out of raw experience. That can serve as a kind of defi-nition. But must we "react uniformly" to symbols? I think not. The American

[7] Joyce A. Hertzler, *Sociology of Language* (New York: Random House, 1965), p. 28.

[8] Hertzler, p. 28.

flag is in some senses a symbol, but there are a variety of different ways that people react to it. Our *appreciation* of an important symbol, that is our *feel* for it as something with a powerful meaning, precedes our particular *attitude* toward it. At least those who tussle over whether to burn or salute the flag both believe there is something important at stake. They share a symbolic orientation toward the flag. Neither saluters nor burners see the flag as a mere piece of cloth. They see it symbolically but they do not act toward it uniformly.

But we have still not asked whether there is anything *intrinsic* in a symbol that gives it meaning, as Hertzler says "in its nature." Of course, what constitutes the "nature" of something is itself an enormously difficult question. But even if we sidestep that and simply ask whether all symbols are completely arbitrary, and could just as well have been something else, we come no closer to settling the issue. Presumably, if Betsy Ross had fashioned a green flag with yellow stripes, it would eventually have accrued to itself all the meanings of Old Glory, and people today would be burning or saluting a green and yellow flag with the same gusto they now direct toward the red, white and blue. That would score a point for Professor Hertzler's side, that is, that a symbol, here a flag, is an arbitrary, conventional symbol.

But is that true of *all* symbols? Is it even sensible to ask whether the central symbols of Christianity *could* have been something other than body and blood, or bread and wine? Are there symbols that are not merely conventional? In a brilliant new study entitled *Natural Symbols*, Mary Douglas, a British anthropologist, argues that some symbols are *not* merely conventional.[9] The human body itself she contends is a "natural symbol" of society. In addition, blood, breath, and milk are natural symbols that express the kind of relationships that tie various kinds of people to each other and to society. Without rehearsing Mrs. Douglas's reasoning here I wonder myself whether other contenders could be added to her list of natural symbols. What about fire, light and darkness, water, the sky, etc.? And finally what about tools, technological devices and machines? Are they arbitrary signs, or natural symbols, or a little of each?

Before I respond to this series of questions I cannot resist mentioning, at least, that one of the most universally recognized symbols of our age consists of tools: the interlocked hammer and sickle of communism. But what about "natural" symbols? Can we speak of such things with any accuracy?

Again without dodging this important issue I would say that for the purposes of this paper, whether the symbolic qualities of an entity are "intrinsic" or "bestowed" is not crucial. The question may in fact not be answerable since man, as a culture creating being, never (after his first days of infancy, and maybe not even then) experiences anything completely

[9] Mary Douglas, *Natural Symbols* (New York: Pantheon, 1970).

untouched by cultural meanings that were already there before he came onto the scene. Indeed the argument between Hertzler and her colleagues on the one side, and Duncan and Douglas on the other, and between other theorists who talk about the "bestowing" of meaning and those who identify "natural symbols," has a familiar ring. It is very reminiscent of the venerable Medieval debate between the "nominalists" and the "realists." Although the nominalists triumphed in that altercation, and much of modern science stems from their victory, the argument was never fully closed. It has reemerged recently, for example, in the case advanced by people concerned about ecology to the effect that natural phenomena have a meaning and value of their own, a significance *an sich* which is quite apart from anything they may mean to man.

Perhaps now it is clear why I did not proceed at the outset of this paper to a sharp definition of "symbol." I wanted first to allude to some of the philosophical issues that lurk just below the surface of what appear to be mere "definitions." But having identified the debate, I do not at this point wish to pursue it. Rather I will simply state my own opinion rather boldly: namely, that "meaning" as I use the term, including value and symbolic significance, originates with man. Meaning and value and symbol are categories of the *human* world. But I would add that meaning does not originate in *one* person, nor is it simply invented. It emerges out of the corporate history of the race and is altered by mankind's ever-changing experience.

Although this would seem to put me on the side of the "nominalists," I want to add that the "realists" such as Douglas have a point. Certain phenomena, such as the body for example, *do* lend themselves more readily to symbolic uses than others. I would not argue however that because certain symbols are *in this sense* more "natural" they are any more authentic or any more valid, whatever that might mean. It has not been demonstrated that because a symbol has a longer history or a more universal distribution that it is more powerful, its disciples more humane, or its impact more constructive than a more recent or even a more provincial symbol.

For me, a symbol is anything which has a cultural significance beyond mere utility. It can be literally anything from dirt to the most abstract idea of deity. Furthermore it can be relatively rich or poor in the power of its symbolic significance, and it can be universally recognized or it can be appreciated by a very small group. What makes it a symbol is that it signifies something beyond itself, something in some measure different from itself, and its "meaning" is shared by a group.

Now putting together the definitions of the two key terms in this essay becomes possible. By the "symbolism of technology" I have in mind those meanings technologies have above and beyond their merely technical function or use. Technological artifacts become symbols when they are "iconized," when they release emotions incommensurate with their mere utility, when they arouse hopes and fears only indirectly related to their empirical content, when they begin to provide elements for the mapping of cognitive experience. The dynamo becomes a symbol when it begins to designate the self-understanding of a people or of an epoch, when it is placed on view at an exposition, when, as Adams said, one begins to pray to it.

Technologies and Religious Symbols

> High from the central cupola, they say
> One's glance could cross the borders of three states;
> But I have seen death's stare in slow survey
> From four horizons that no one relates.[10]
> > —Hart Crane, "The Bridge"

If Henry Adams's insight was correct it means that in the past two centuries or more, certain technologies have begun to acquire an aura that is not only symbolic but religious. The dynamos and their assorted metallic kinsmen have stolen fire from the saints and virgins. But to support this assertion it is necessary first to make clear what a "religious symbol" is, and then to show how certain technologies have begun to acquire sacred significance. To aid us on our way we turn first to the work of the great pioneer in the study of religious symbols, Emile Durkheim.

In *The Elementary Forms of Religious Life*, in a classic passage, Durkheim describes what he calls "the ambiguity of the notion of sacredness." He argues that religious phenomena are of two contradictory sorts. Some are beneficent, dispensers of life and health; others are evil and impure, the sources of disorder, disease, and death. The good ones elicit feelings of love and gratitude, the evil call forth attitudes of fear and horror. The two sentiments, although both are "sacred," are very far apart, and are often separated from each other by rigid ritual rules. "Thus the whole religious life gravitates about two contrary poles," Durkheim declares, "between which there is the same opposition as between the pure and the impure, the saint and the sacrilegious, the divine and the diabolic."[11]

But then Durkheim goes on to make a masterful observation, one that is borne out by the study of any religious system. He shows that while these two contrasting attitudes seem at first disparate and even contradictory, in practice there is a *close kinship* between them. Both the positive as well as the negative are *sacred*, as opposed to profane. In more recent

[10] From *The Complete Poems and Selected Letters and Prose of Hart Crane.* Copyright 1933, 1958, 1966 by Liveright Publishing Corp., New York. Reprinted by permission of publisher.

[11] Emile Durkheim, *The Elementary Forms of the Religious Life* (Glenville, Illinois: Free Press, 1954), p. 456.

terms, both have a highly charged, symbolic character, rather than a merely empirical or instrumental one. As Durkheim says

> . . . There is a horror in religious respect, especially when it is very intense, while the fear inspired by malign powers is generally not without a certain reverential character.[12]

He goes on to remark that the shades by which these two attitudes are differentiated are so slight that sometimes it is not possible to distinguish one from the other. In fact an impure thing or evil power often becomes, through a simple modification of circumstances, a source of healthful power and goodness. "So the pure and the impure," concludes Durkheim, "are not two separate classes, but two varieties of the same class." This "class" includes all sacred (that is, symbolic) things and

> There are two sorts of sacredness, the propitious and the unpropitious, and not only is there no break of continuity between these two opposed forms, but also one object may pass from the one to the other without changing its nature. The pure is made out of the impure, and reciprocally. It is in the possibility of these transmutations that the ambiguity of the sacred consists.[13]

Later on Durkheim hints at, but never really makes explicit, still another facet in the ambiguity of sacred symbols. He suggests that it is precisely the most powerful symbols that exhibit the most ambiguity. Lower level symbols and those functioning in a more restricted geographical area can more easily be classified as simply positive or simply negative. High order, very potent and more universally recognized symbols, on the other hand, exhibit a much more ambiguous character. The local patron saint can help us with special problems. Almighty God, however, can grant us eternal bliss or cast us into the lake of fire. Durkheim's thesis is confirmed by other scholars. Malinowski, for example, in his famous studies of the Trobriand Islanders, shows that a dead man is viewed with horror and fear, but that ingesting part of his flesh is also the source of incomparably potent health-giving and tribe-sustaining energy. In Hindu and in some other iconography, important sacred figures are often depicted with more than one head so that the malevolent and the beneficent aspects can clearly be shown as belonging to the same divinity. The Christian cross is not only the "emblem of suffering and shame." It is also the assurance of God's love for man and life's victory over death. Wherever symbols reach a degree of intensity and power that could be called "religious" (and the borderline is always fuzzy), the devil turns out to be a fallen angel.

[12] Durkheim, p. 456.
[13] Durkheim, p. 458.

Symbols of the sacred then are characterized by a *high degree* of *power* and *ambiguity*. They arouse dread and gratitude, terror and rapture. The more central and powerful a symbol is for a culture, the more vivid the ambiguity becomes. A symbol becomes religious or sacred when it reaches such a degree of priority or ultimacy that it begins to sanctify and legitimate other values, symbols, and meaning definitions. This is an important point: a "religious symbol" is defined not by its *content* but by its *relative degree of cultural power*. At least this is the way, in the manner of Durkheim and other students of symbols, that I shall define them.

Naturally, this definition could easily be criticized by those who would like to restrict the term "religious" or "sacred" to symbols now accepted by recognized "religious institutions" such as churches. This could of course be done. The disadvantage is that it turns over to the society's presently recognized religious institutions the rather considerable power to decide what is and what is not religious. This not only restricts investigation unduly; it also systematically prevents us from recognizing the appearance of new religious symbols and practices as yet not blessed with ecclesiastical legitimation. Churches notoriously try to prevent religious change by declaring what is and is not religion, or "true religion." We need a wider scope. I believe my definition does this without making quite the whole world its parish. Clearly there is nothing to prevent technologies of any kind from functioning as sacred symbols in Durkheim's sense. Our question now is whether this is in fact happening.

In his book *Symbolism of Evil* the French phenomenologist Paul Ricoeur discusses, among others, two principal axes on which religious symbolism develops. The first is that of *bondage* and *extrication*. The second is *defilement* and *purification*. Both Ricoeur's axes suggest dynamic symbols and are consequently classifiable as "rituals." There is another category of religious symbols, however, those that provide the material for "placing" man and society in a larger network of meanings. These we could call myths.

The case that some technologies are beginning to function as sacred symbols could be made for either of these types of symbols. Take the ritual of defilement and purification, for example. Who could deny the enormous interest in sterilization, purification, and cleansing that characterizes our society today, and we have developed highly refined technologies—sanitary, medical, prophylactic—to aid us in our self-purification. Our fascination with detergents alone, which any evening of television advertising will amply demonstrate, should prove that. We also know however that obsessive cleanliness reveals a deeper-stated anxiety ("Out, damned spot . . .") and that our technologies have also become symbols of defilement. The billowing smoke stack, the auto graveyard, the oil slick—all have turned into icons of pollution. But the irony is delicious. The very detergents we churn out to cleanse us, end up defiling our lakes. Vishnu is also Shiva.

I plan now to deal with two classes of technological religious symbols, one from the "ritual" side, one from the "myth." On the ritual side, instead of exploring the purification-defilement theme, I have selected the bondage-extrication one. After that I will move on to the technological symbolism of man-in-society.

Bondage and Extrication

Evidence is accumulating that many people in industrial-bureaucratic societies, today experience themselves as trapped, powerless, and immobilized. Ordinary speech abounds with phrases like "stuck," "trapped," "hung-up," "rat race," and "dead end" to describe work, marriage, and everyday life. The theme also appears in artistic creations. In a play ironically entitled *Happy Days,* by the Nobel Prize winning playwright Samuel Beckett, both characters sit mired uncomfortably in piles of sand up to their waists. As the play proceeds, each act finds them more deeply buried in the sand until, in the final act, only their heads remain visible. The same writer ends his play *Waiting for Godot* by having Estragon say to Vladimir, "Let's go," and Vladimir answering, "O.K. Let's go." The stage directions then read, "They do not move." Curtain. In his *Endgame* the characters sit in garbage cans. Themes of powerlessness, immobility, and miredness are not new in contemporary cultural expressions. Jean-Paul Sartre's play *No Exit* is a classic statement. Another is Luis Bunuel's film *The Exterminating Angel* which depicts a group of people who for some eerie reason seem unable to get out of the salon where they are having a party. The American sociologist Ernest Becker discusses the striking frequency of such images in his book of essays *Angel in Armour* and attributes it in part to the perception, felt by large numbers of people, that they are powerless to influence the vast and baffling social institutions they live in. Whatever the social and historical circumstances that induce in a society an ethos of bondage, symbols of bondage recur constantly in the history of religion. One can be a prisoner in his own body, as Socrates says he is in *The Apology*, or a slave of the great Wheel of Fate, or chained to a rock, or a captive in hell, or possessed by demons, or in slavery, or entombed. Whatever the symbolism, the feeling conveyed is of powerlessness, that is, the inability to exert significant influence over one's own life and destiny.

The symbolic solutions offered to this crisis are of four major types: first, one can *escape* the bondage oneself by exerting enough energy or guilt—operation bootstrap; second, one can learn to accept the enslavement and to live with it with dignity and *resignation*; third, one can be *extricated* from it by a power greater than oneself; fourth, one can cooperate with powers greater than oneself to *struggle* against, and eventually defeat the conditions imposing bondage. Escape, resignation, extrication, and struggle are the four major alternative solutions to the curse of confinement. It should be added that each of these four possibilities can occur either individually or corporately. One pervasive theme in the traditional stories of the great religious "founders" is that they refuse to be satisfied with *individual* escape or extrication. They all "return" either to teach others the solution they have found (the Buddha) or to lead captives into some form of liberation (Moses).

I would like to argue that one important symbolic meaning of technology for numberless people today, especially in the U.S.A., is that of *extrication.* Technological devices and procedures become the *deus ex machina* we look to, to lift us out of our trapped and immobilized condition and thereby deliver us from bondage. This is not however a corporate salvation. Technologies save us individually or in small groups. To demonstrate this symbolic use of technology fully would require more space than is available here. I prefer rather to be satisfied with *suggesting* this pattern with two examples, one rather commonplace, one somewhat bizarre. The first is the way jet tourist travel is increasingly sold with images of "escape" (meaning really extrication). The second is the infant (pseudo?) technology of cryonics, the quick-freezing of human beings for possible resuscitation later, when cures for the diseases they have died of have presumably been discovered.

Extrication from the Ordinary: Jet and Bikini

> The high white contrails of cruising jets are bright symbols of the promise and pleasure of air travel.
>
> —*Time*, January 19, 1970[14]

The secular iconography of the travel pages of any large newspaper invariably features a juxtaposition of bikini clad women and jet airplanes. This is not really surprising. The majority of the night dreams of people in industrial societies center on themes of sex and violence, or so clinicians tell us. These dreams reflect, they say, our hunger for community and power. The admixture of woman-and-jet planes conjures both feeling clusters at once. The scantily clad girl smiling invitingly poolside tells us we are loved, welcomed, nurtured—delivered from isolation and frustration. The soaring jet plane tells us it is all within our grasp. Technology extricates us, as the Air France ad proclaims, "from the ordinary." The airlines' omnipotent wings bear us aloft to an elysium where, in contrast to our daily experience, we can either be as "deeply involved" or as "left alone" as we want. So says the ad.

The theme of deliverance from the woes of this ordinary world to a very extraordinary world, albeit even temporarily, through the powerful intervention of a benevolent savior is an old one. Some shamans who are

[14] From an Air France advertisement.

capable of going into trances describe the experience as one of feeling picked up and borne away to the magic land by a huge bird. Of course the woes from which one is delivered vary to some extent from culture to culture. Philip Slater in *The Pursuit of Loneliness*[15] shows how Americans today seem to feel frustrated by our conflicting quests, at one and the same time, for both privacy and community. We produce technologies designed to insulate us from human contact (cars versus trains, housing design, self-service devices), then we consequently miss the human relationships. But when human beings do touch our lives, the experience seems intrusive, competitive, irksome, or otherwise unpleasant. It is a vicious circle. We are on a pilgrimage in quest both of deeper involvement *and* more privacy. No wonder then that one travel ad assures us that on the sun-drenched enchanted island to which the huge bird will carry us one can have "all the involvement you want" or "none at all." The text of a recent advertisement for Escape Unlimited, a tour organization, in the Sunday *New York Times* includes the following:

> Escape Your World. Embrace Ours.
> *Abandon the Ordinary.* Fly with us to our exciting European resort-villages. Where Internationals play. And total involvement is up to you. *Join Escape Unlimited.* Let yourself go. Embrace the uninhibited. Escape to any of three private and privileged resort villages in the azure Mediterranean. . . . Now a limited number of Americans may join Escape Unlimited and savor the freedom of our continental Escape-Aways. . . .
> *Total Involvement is Up to You.* Escape Unlimited involves you in everything . . . or nothing.[16]

The ad goes on to promise companionship with "Fellow bons amis" who are "lovers of the free and uninhibited life" and "young in spirit" (if not always, I suppose, in chronology). The key words are "involvement," "escape," "experience," "freedom," and "excitement." The picture shows a generously endowed woman frisking in the surf with a less clearly seen man. Both appear to be young in years as well as in spirit. The sexual overtones of the word "involvement" are underlined by the pictures, the insulation from intrusion by the island's isolation. Whereas in *this* vale of tears we lurch between loneliness and intrusive, bothersome interruptions, *there* we will experience both perfect community and perfect privacy. No revivalist hymn ever promised more. Sweet Beulah Land!

The link between our hungry search for authentic community and the extraordinary hopes we pin on technology deserves further exploration. The big bird is still swooping to save us in our need. But beware! When we concentrate hopes so heavily, if the cure fails, the disappointment, anger,

---

[15] Philip Slater, *The Pursuit of Loneliness* (Boston: Beacon Press, 1970).
[16] From a February 8, 1970, *The New York Times* advertisement for Escape Unlimited.

and scapegoating of the false savior sours into righteous rage. The automobile, which promised to give us privacy and mobility, freedom, and community (or so we hoped) has let us down. So now it becomes the object of our hatred, that of a lover abandoned or, worse still, a devotee betrayed. A group of college students recently dug a grave and buried an automobile. But all this suggests that even a universal *auto da fé* of all our cars and pets would not really get at the heart of our malady, which is our inability (related, I think, to our compulsive acquisitiveness and consequent fear of others) to fashion a more human form of community.

Extrication from Death: Cool and Cure

> No one can escape from the machine. Only the machine can enable you to escape from destiny.[17]
>
> —Tristan Tzara

"The last enemy," St. Paul says, "is death." Although the fear of death and punishment after death does not haunt twentieth-century man as it did his medieval forebears, it still lingers in the recesses of the modern imagination. We fear death today not because dying entails physical pain—thanks to medical technology that can be minimized. Nor do we fear hell fire. Rather we fear death because it removes us from the human community. When we say that perpetual solitary confinement would be "worse than death" what we mean, I suppose, is that in both conditions we are deprived of human relationships, but that in death we are at least unaware of the deprivation. All this is what makes the alleged science of "cryonics" so interesting, admittedly in a somewhat ghoulish way. If death is the last enemy, then cryonics is surely the ultimate "technological fix." The theory is simple enough. Immediately after death, the body is frozen in a chemical solution to await the future discovery of cures for whatever caused the patient's demise. "Cryonics" comes from the Greek word for ice, krystallos. Cryonics societies meet in New York and in California. The small journal of the movement, begun in 1966 as *Cryonics Reports* was rechristened in 1970 and is now called, simply, *Immortality*. Several individuals are already stored in cryonic suspension awaiting the secularized last trumpet of a white coated Gabriel in whose porcelain tureens presumably, the first antidote to angina pectoris has just sprouted.

Alas, it is far too easy to hold up the cryonics crowd to ridicule, as I am even now tempted to do. It is true that organismal death (unconsciousness due to heart and lung stoppage) often precedes psychic death (destruction of cerebral cortex cells through lack of oxygen) and vegetative death (destruction of other cerebral cells). It is also true that animals have been

---

[17] K. G. Pontus Hultan, *The Machine as Seen at the End of the Technical Age* (New York: Museum of Modern Art, 1968), p. 13.

suspended and returned to normal. Nor are the questions of cost of maintenance and the eventual ration of caretakers to cryonically suspended souls in liquid helium purgatory the really significant ones. Not even the seemingly overwhelming problem of simply finding space for all the bodies should detain us, especially since one Robert Schimel, identified in *Cryonics Report* for December 1969 as "an experimental designer . . . employed as an instructor at Kent State University," has drawn up plans for a storage facility on the moon that would accommodate 1,437,696 patients. He calls it a "cryosanctorum." (The primitive religious parallels to Mr. Schimel's scheme, the belief that the spirits of the dead go to some nearby but relatively inaccessible place and return when appropriate conditions are ripe—I think especially of Malinowski's work on the Balema—are tempting to describe here but I will resist.) Once death is defined as a problem for which there is a technological solution, then there is always at least a *theoretical* answer to every bug in the system.

But I do not intend merely to dispose of the cryonics people with a laugh. The laugh can often be a way of avoiding deep-seated and threatening issues, just as raising technical queries about cryonics is often a way to escape the philosophical questions it raises. I find cryonics interesting because it provides the clearest posisble example of the refocusing of a perennial human hope (the conquest of death) from one symbolic object to another. There are obvious similarities between the two. In one of the most familiar Greek orthodox icons, Christ is seen striking open the caskets of the dead and consigning the now awakened corpses either to bliss or to oblivion. In medieval theology, the place the resurrected ones spend eternity is dependent on their comparative virtue. In Calvinism it depends entirely on God's grace. In cryonic eschatology, I suppose, virtue has nothing to do with who gets resuscitated although money does. At present the cryonics specialists must have a down payment of $500. After ten days $2000 more is required for the initial rites and following that, $6000 for the encapsulation, a rather crass commercialization of the right to immortality which recently sparked a science fiction novel. In *Bug Jack Barron*, by Norman Spinrad, a fearless TV commentator takes on the powerful topdog of the freeze business.[18] Luther Versus Tetzel? Cryonics gives man a new basis for an old, old hope.

The cryonics movement is not now very widely known. It may never be. The suspension theory is not even very new. The Egyptians apparently believed that their pharoahs preserved in pyramidal cryosanctorums would eventually come alive again, not just in a superterrestrial sphere but here where they would need their bowls and dogs. Cryonics is interesting to me mainly as a singularly dramatic example of a problem that theologians have steadfastly avoided. If not nitrogen freezing, what about aging deterrents?

[18] Norman Spinrad, *Bug Jack Barron* (New York: Walker and Co., 1969).

If not in the next 100 years, what about the next 1000, or 10,000? The theological issues fairly swarm over the subject. Do the cryonics people realize, for example, just how *Western* (even Christian) their operation is? There are some religious traditions in which coming back from the dead into *this* world is not at all a desirable goal. Preservation of the body and the rekindling of consciousness are also not hoped for in religious traditions that view the body as evil and consciousness as illusory. For a white male of twenty-five in the U.S.A. today, suicide is the second most probable cause of death (auto accidents are first). Presumably only people who choose to do so would be frozen, and suicides would not. But should they be condemned to an eternity of oblivion for one impulsive act? Or should they be frozen and revived, when the cure is found, to give them another chance? Not to give them such a second chance would seem to perpetuate the traditional Roman Catholic view (now almost wholly inoperable) that a suicide dies in mortal sin and goes to hell, forever.

There are numerous other theological questions. Let me avoid them at the moment simply by hazarding my guess that if cryonics grows into a more widely practical art, the rituals and symbolic overtones attached to its equipment, practitioners, and procedures will be fascinating to watch. But, and this is my real point, the obviously symbolic-religious dimensions of cryonics differ only in degree, not in kind, from the same dimensions of other technologies.

In this section of the paper, I have tried to show how certain technologies are beginning to achieve a *ritual* significance. They touch our fears and our fantasies at levels that lie much deeper than we usually think. They crystallize our hopes. They sanctify values in terms of which crucial decisions are made and provide the ritual means by which the desired state may be attained.

Now I turn from technology as *ritual* (means of grace) to technology as *myth*, as the symbolic definition of man's place and purpose in the scheme of things.

The Machine as Symbol of Man in Society

The use of machine language and images to symbolize man has a long history, the classic written statement of which is probably Julien LaMettrie's *L'Homme Machine* first published in 1747. Although his book shocked many of his contemporaries it really should not have since LaMettrie was merely extending insights that had already been in wide intellectual circulation since the previous century. During Descartes's time (1596–1650) there was a lively interest in comparing men with machines and in making life-size mechanical replicas of people. Some contemporary observers thought the practice sacrilegious. Descartes however expressed his disagreement with anyone who should regard discussing man in mechanical terms as impious.

He drew the familiar analogy between man who makes automation and God who makes man. The human body, he declared, "is a machine made by the hands of God, which is incomparably better arranged, and adequate to movements more admirable than in any machine of human invention." Descartes added, of course, that the mechanically superior human body was also differentiated from the animals in that God had placed within it a rational soul through which man could participate in the spiritual world.

Since Descartes and LaMettrie there has been a continuing tradition —now defended, now attacked—of viewing man *sub specia machina*. Aram Vartanian has traced the origins of this stream of interpretation in his book *La Mettrie's "L'Homme Machine:" A Study in the Origins of an Idea*.[19] Sometimes man is seen as a machine, sometimes machines are endowed with human qualities. Sometimes the symbolization is negative, at other times positive. But in any case it remains a significant tradition and an important root metaphor. Its influence can be seen in as widely disparate places as psychoanalysis with its hydraulic images of man and recent cybernetic theories of human knowledge and perception. Arthur Koestler both uses and criticizes the imagery in *The Ghost in the Machine*.[20]

The symbolization of society as a machine however is not as easily traceable a tradition. The seventeenth- and eighteenth-century deists, influenced by some of the same currents that touched Descartes, liked to refer to the universe as a clock God had created, wound up and left to its own devices. But I can find few poetic or iconic images of the society as a machine until the nineteenth century. Poets then began to use technological images, especially factories and locomotives, to represent the entire new age that seemed to be rushing in. Leo Marx has made a good deal of Thoreau's feeling that the shriek of the locomotive whistle was the harbinger of a new and undesirable age.

One epochal example of the machine-as-society motif is Charles Chaplin's classic film *Modern Times* made in 1936. In this film the factory and its machines clearly represent the society Chaplin and many others were beginning to regard with suspicion and distrust. Charlie is a worker who is driven insane by the monotony of endlessly tightening bolts and is finally drawn into the machine as a helpless victim. (Interestingly, he later escapes by skillfully using the machine against his pursuers.)

There is a subtle connection between the depiction of society as a machine and the perennial fear that man may be turned into a machine. As Chaplin himself said, *Modern Times* was an effort to "say something about the way life is being standardized and channelized, and men turned into machines—and the way I felt about it."[21] In a more recent film, Stanley

[19] Aram Vartanian, La Mettrie's *"L'Homme Machine:" A Study in the Origins of an Idea* (Princeton, New Jersey: Princeton University Press, 1960).

[20] Arthur Koestler, *The Ghost in the Machine* (New York: Macmillan, 1968).

[21] Theodore Huff, *Charlie Chaplin* (New York: Henry Schuman, 1951), p. 253.

Kubrick's *2001,* a computer named Hal takes command of a space ship until a determined astronaut disconnects his circuits. In the *Forbes Project,* released in 1970, the computer wins, making all the people on earth his subjects.

The fear that man could be dehumanized or enslaved by the machine reflects some of the same discomfort and ambivalence we have noted in the age of Descartes. No wonder many people still have an uneasy feeling when they watch machines performing humanoid tasks, a feeling of fascination tinged with fear. The uneasiness is the obverse of the feeling experienced when we observe muscles or joints and see how they resemble machines. This feeling is not unrelated to our theme since it resembles in some measure the mixture of fascination and horror of the sacred described in Rudolph Otto's *The Experience of the Holy.* It is a theme which, in the history of cinema, ties together two of the major varieties of horror films. In the one, an invention of either a well-intentioned or a "mad" scientist gets out of hand and threatens to destroy all of life: technology as demon. In the other type, human beings are deprived of their souls by vampires or zombies. In a more recent cross-breeding of these two streams, the scientist employs his technology to make docile slaves out of people usually through injections or electrical control. In either case the loss of "soul" or conscious selfhood is portrayed as the ultimate threat, worse even than death (zombies would *rather* be just plain dead instead of the "living dead").

The loss of soul through demonic technology is a fascinating theme still very much alive today. We cannot pursue it here. We can only say that there are obvious theological roots to the very modern notion that loss of soul is even worse than death. The other facet of the fear, however, is germane to our discussion. Terror of the machine's and/or the society's capacity to deprive us of our essential human personhood is always mixed with a fascination for that very power and the possibility of using it for one's own purposes. "Machinaphobia," the fear of the machine, is always a complex compound in which a certain amount of fascination is usually present. The standard line at the end of a hundred horror movies, as the monster dies or the laboratory goes up in flames, is that with just a little different luck or a little more virtue the whole thing might have gone the other way.

The symbolization of man or of society as machine thus turns out to be one particularly dramatic example of our general thesis. We experience technology today in ways that go far beyond cognitive or utilitarian categories. Machines are now invested with our deepest hopes and terrors. They play an active role in the life of the modern imagination. They deliver us from danger, threaten to destroy us, steal our souls, trick us into serving them, bewilder, and enrage us. In the dream of the Golem or of Hal in *2001* they become men and help us or tyrannize us. In other instances they lure us or coerce us into becoming like them. Whatever else they may be, however, at least in the all-too-real world of fantasy and human symbol, the artifices of technology are certainly *not* lifeless and neuter tools waiting docilely to be picked up and used.

Third rate horror movies, science fiction novels, and other items of popular culture may not be worth examining with any real seriousness. Their images of technology may be superficial, transient, or trivial. On the other hand, popular culture may be saying something to us about our civilization's deep ambivalence regarding technology, something we ignore at our peril.

In the previous section I discussed technology as *ritual*, as the means of grace. In this section I have focused on technology as *myth*, as the symbolization of man's place in the scheme of things. One obvious question, however, remains: why?

Cur Deus Machina?

Toward the end of the eleventh century, St. Anselm of Canterbury, perhaps the greatest medieval theologian, St. Thomas excepted, wrote his masterpiece *Cur Deus Homo* explaining how God had become man. In our time, the question might better be why the divine substance seems to be flowing away from human representations, virginal or otherwise, and toward technological ones.

In thinking about this question I want to turn first to that group of psychologists and cultural critics that makes use of the term "identity" in its theories. Among these are Eric Erickson and Alan Wheelis. Wheelis, for example, says that in his clinical experience the original idea, that therapy helps a client resolve conflicts between the elementary urges of the id and the constrictions imposed by the superego, simply isn't true anymore. The problems that bring most clients to a psychiatrist today, states Wheelis in *The Quest for Identity*, spring not from such conflicts at all but rather from the disappearance of those superordinate cultural symbols that once formed the superego. Our problem today, he says, is not neurosis and inner conflict but yearning and fear arising from the disappearance of those firm cultural and religious verities that once bounded and checked the elemental drives. Rather than anguished guilt, the therapist deals with what Wheelis calls "intense, preoccupying yearning." This yearning, he says further, has no particular focus or object. It is "formless and diffuse." This is an important clue. Any student of the history of religion knows that a yearning without a focus is a set-up for a new messiah.

In his book *Theology After Freud*, Pete Homans relates this disappearance of the superego with what some theologians have referred to as the "death of God."[22] Both suggest the collapse of "transcendence," of any culturally or psychologically operative sense of an objective realm of reality

[22] Peter Homans, *Theology After Freud* (New York: Bobbs-Merrill, Inc., 1970).

toward which man is drawn, against which he revolts, or by which he is governed, punished or saved. In this reading, however, the death of God has not turned man into a liberated Ubermensch as Nietzsche expected. Nor has it made man himself into a god. The death of God, in so far as it symbolizes the dissolution of the cultural superego, has turned man from a penitent into a pilgrim. Now instead of looking to the gods for rules of conduct and for punishment and grace, he looks rather at the void, at the empty throne where God once sat, and gives himself over to "intense preoccupying yearning."

How does this relate to the iconography of technology? When the mountain of the gods is emptied, men usually search for other mountains and other gods. When the Virgin begins to lose her charisma, they look somewhere else. But why to the dynamo?

Whatever the reasons underlying the dissolution of the cultural superego in our time, the fact is that it has been going on just as technology has accomplished some of its most dramatic and highly visible successes. Without going too much further into the question, this is certainly one of the most obvious answers. The coincidence of these two movements explains why technological symbols have been *among those* that have replaced traditional religious symbols in the cultural imagination.

I say "among those" and "replace" (rather than "displace") for very conscious reasons. It is important to remember here that technological symbols are not the only ones that have rushed into the vacuum. Race, party, blood, soil, class, and sex symbols have also staked claims to the turf vacated by the retreating saints and heroes of Christendom. Although in this particular paper I am discussing the role of technological symbols in this regard, I in no way wish to suggest that they are without peers in populating the symbolic universe. The new gods are many.

Also, when I say that in some ways technological symbols have begun to replace traditional religious ones, I avoid the term "displace" for a good reason. To me, "replace" suggests a process whereby something *fills* a place once occupied by something else but does not necessarily *contribute* to the dislocation that caused the vacancy. We *replace* a burnt out light bulb. *Displace* suggests that the new entity contributes to forcing the elimination of the previous tenant. A fat man *displaces* the water in a very full tub forcing it onto the floor.

To say that technological symbols may be *replacing* traditional religious symbols avoids precisely the technology-versus-religion fallacy that has obscured so much of this sort of discussion in the past. To say that technology *displaces* religion oversimplifies the issue by attributing to technology a kind of causal potency and direct agency that goes far beyond anything I am suggesting here. In fact such simplified causal statements fuzz over what I am convinced is a much more complex series of social and cultural patterns.

Technological change may even be *one* of the factors contributing to the decline in the power and influence of traditional religious symbols. In my own view it probably is such a factor. But there are many other factors, some of them more significant than technology, such as population growth, urbanization, the appearance of heightened historical consciousness, internal problems in the development of Christian theology itself, and the rise of revolutionary ideologies. The obvious fact that some of these were also partially released by technological change only shows again how complex and how resistant to simplification the whole picture is. By using *replace* rather than *displace* I am saying in effect that there are very important forces, outside technology, which have contributed to the present decline in the influence of traditional religious symbols and that either "blaming it on technology" or "giving the credit to technology" (depending on how one feels about the process) loads too much praise and blame on technology itself. It represents the Luddite fallacy, blaming machines for something men have done.

Adams, then, did not get the whole picture. Perhaps he looked at it too soon. The dynamo today has not just replaced the Virgin of Chartres. The Virgin is always merciful, health-giving, benevolent. The dynamo has also replaced the gargoyles of Chartres, those leering and frightful reminders of the Evil One. And that is a lot of symbolic weight for any single cluster of symbols to incarnate.

I have not tried to answer in this paper the Adamsian version of the Anselmian question. I have restricted myself to showing why I believe divinity has, for many, assumed the form and visage of the machine. But to contend *that* God has done something is not the same as saying why. The "why?" will have to be postponed for another discussion.

The Return of the Virgin?

What would Henry Adams have thought if he had lived to witness the ritual burial of an automobile, the "die-in" in protest against jet noises at Logan Airport, the astronaut in *2001* ripping the cells out of the rebellious computer? At the very least he would surely have seen that many of the complex hopes and fears we have directed toward technologies in the past have become more intense and more visible. At the most we could be entering a period in which the Western attitude toward technology becomes much more negative, in which the demonic side is emphasized much more than the divine.

But how can we even discuss such an issue critically and with any degree of precision? Adams visited the great exposition in 1900. By 2000 will the Virgin or some other more recognizably "religious" symbol, in the more conventional sense, have replaced the dynamo? Are there trends in our present cultural consciousness that point that way?

Further, are there any normative statements that theologians explicitly rooted in the Judeo-Christian tradition should make about either the rise or the decline of the symbolism of sacred technologies?

I believe there is evidence that our culture may be shifting its attitude toward technology and that the result could be momentous. In my own view some corrective of our attitude toward technology is needed, but it would be too bad if what happened turned out to be a kind of twentieth-century Ludditism. Nor do I greet the onrush of mystical, nature and anti-machine themes in recent years with unmixed approval. Confronted with a machine in the midst of our garden we are tempted to seek salvation first in one and then in the other. But, especially when viewed from the perspective of biblical thought, neither the garden nor the machine can save man. The Hebrew prophets knew this somehow. There were two major temptations against which they warned the errant children of Abraham. One was the sweet lure exuded by the sacred grottoes of the Canaanites—nature religion. The other was the temptation to fall down and worship the things made with their own hands—idolatry. Yahweh expects man to enjoy and tend the garden, but not to offer sacrifices to it; to make things for his own use, but not to pray to them. In other words, the cardinal sin of Hebrew man was to attach an inappropriate degree of religious feeling to inappropriate objects (idolatry). His effort to avoid idolatry produced at once the earthy Hebrew appreciation for food and flesh, but also the constant refusal (albeit with periodical episodes of backsliding) to divinize either. It also produced a healthy capacity to use the things men could make without investing them with excessive hopes.

The conflict between the nature baals of Canaan and the man made idols on the one side, and the transhistorical creator-redeemer God on the other provides the unique dynamic to Hebrew religion and, to some extent, to its Christian daughter. It has reappeared in various forms throughout Western history: in the medieval conflict between the Cathedral and the Desert, in the American version of the City and the Wilderness, in today's alternative life-style images projected by the astronauts and the flower children.

But in each instance the biblical tradition at once rejects and affirms both options. It never sanctifies one at the expense of the other. It supports both when they are seen and appreciated as the provisional, limited human creations they are. It condemns both insofar as they escalate themselves into paths to salvation. Theologians (mainly Protestant) have seen some of the same dangers in the Virgin that the Hebrew prophets saw in the baal: the illegitimate sanctification of merely natural impulses and processes. Other theologians (many Catholic) have viewed with distrust the confidence modern man places in his technical prowess. It is understandable, in these terms, why Protestants should have welcomed and endorsed "artificial means" of birth control while Catholics have resented the intrusion of technology into the "natural." What both sets of arguments have tended to overlook is still, to my mind, the central issue: not the contraceptive machine versus the garden of the womb, but how man can best exercise responsible freedom in view of an open future.

Further theological evaluation would now take me on to another paper. I do think such evaluative work is right and proper. Theology, unlike many other disciplines, make no secret of the fact that it *is* a normative undertaking. Christian theology is critical and normative reflection of the religious (in the broadest sense) aspects of life. Unfortunately, too much theology restricts itself unduly to reflection on religion in only the narrowest and most ecclesiastical sense of the word. The kind of theological inquiry I am calling for here should survey a wider horizon without sacrificing either its critical rigor or its normative premises.

In recent years our minds have been inundated by a wave of writing about technology and society. Some of it has been excellent, some poor, most just mediocre. But in this ocean of print I have been able to find almost nothing about the symbolic and perhaps even sacred significance that technologies acquire. Yet in one sense, simply because symbols do exercise such massive power, especially in the long run, few areas of investigation are more crucial. If, as I believe, man is to take responsibility for his world, including its symbols, then the question is too important to be left undiscussed or ignored. I do not believe, with Tristan Tzara, that the machine can save man from destiny. But that is because I believe man's only destiny is to use his God-given freedom to shape and achieve his destiny for himself. If he refuses this destiny, then nothing can save him at all.

3

Criticism and
the Religious Horizon*

Nathan A. Scott, Jr.

A very large amount of activity in recent years—in the form of numerous conferences and symposia, and of a remarkable spate of publication—has been devoted to the consideration of the various ways in which the study of literature may necessarily trench upon orders of valuation that are essentially religious; and the discipline of theology has occasionally been held forth as one in which criticism may find a useful resource. It is, however, a fact of the case that the conventional English-department mentality in university circles has regarded this development with scepticism, and the average don can be counted on to render something like the kind of judgment that Mrs. F. R. Leavis once handed down, that

> There is no reason to suppose that those trained in theology, or philosophy for that matter, are likely to possess what is essential to the practice of literary criticism, that "sensitiveness of the intelligence" described by Matthew Arnold as equivalent to conscience in moral matters. A theological training seems to have a disabling effect and has subsequently to be struggled against when literary criticism is the concern.[1]

Its subaltern position in the modern *studium generale* doubtless makes particularly easy the supposition that theology will have a corrupting effect on the student of literature. But the animus with which it will normally be regarded by the academic literary man deserves to be understood as merely one expression of a more fundamental hostility. For the approved theory of our period is perhaps intolerant of nothing so much as the notion

[1] Q. D. Leavis, "Charlotte Yonge and 'Christian Discrimination,'" *Scrutiny*, 12, No. 2 (Spring 1944), p. 158.

that literature may be entangled in extramural affiliations of a kind that require collaboration between literary study and other humanistic disciplines. The young aspirant to success in the world of criticism is told that his great task is that of learning to read literature simply "in and for itself." His duty is said to be that of performing an act of strict attention before the *donnée* which is presented by the unique structure of *this* poem, of *this* novel. He is informed that he will behave responsibly toward his text only in so far as he undertakes meticulous specifications regarding a given pattern of imagery and meter, or of plot and character and point of view. And he is assured that any departure from a rigorously inductive procedure is calculated only to make room for some kind of mischievous obscurantism, for the introduction into the literary order of one or another kind of "extrinsic" consideration. "The axioms and postulates of criticism," says so prestigious a spokesman as Northrop Frye, "have to grow out of the art it deals with"[2]—for this, as he declares, is "the way of scholarship."[3]

The way of scholarship was, of course, differently conceived a generation ago. For in what now seems (as the affairs of literary study proceed) a very remote time indeed, when the examples of a Grierson and a Kittredge and a Livingston Lowes still formed the academic conscience, the task of the humanistic scholar was commonly assumed to be that of producing definitive texts, of reconstructing the cultural matrix in which the sundry phases of our literary inheritance were originally embedded, of charting the kind of documentation literature provides of social and intellectual history, and of doing various other related jobs. The life of literature was considered to have something to do with the kind of carpentry that went into the construction of Elizabethan playhouses and with the intricacies of Dr. Johnson's club world, with Coleridge's indebtments to a half-dozen Germans, and with the repeal of the Corn Laws. And it was onto topics in this mode that the labors of ambitious young professors were often directed. But, then, the advent of what we long ago learnt to call the New Criticism—which was in full force by the early forties—brought a great change in all this. And, thereafter, *Hamlet* and *The Prelude* and *The Princess Casamassima*, however interestingly they may lend themselves to the kinds of measurements that are taken by specialists in social-intellectual history and literary genetics, seemed to require, finally, a different sort of measurement—in terms appropriate to their distinctive reality not as biographical or historical or political documents but as works of art. It was toward such an acknowledgment of the poem *qua* poem[4] that the new insurgency of thirty

[2] Northrop Frye, *Anatomy of Criticism* (Princeton: Princeton University Press, 1957), p. 6.

[3] Frye, p. 72.

[4] The term "poem" is used in its broad, traditional sense as the comprehensive term for works of verbal art.

years ago was pressing, and its major proponents[5]—though often making up an exceedingly diverse group—did all find a common place of meeting at the central point of their intention to honor the fact, as T. S. Eliot had announced in his uniquely dry and ironical tone, that "poetry is poetry and not another thing."

The New Criticism is not, of course, today still in the ascendancy, but this is so because its basic doctrines have become so much a matter of common assumption in the academy that they are no longer often felt to require any sort of assertive exposition. And the unquestioned premise of the literary curriculum is that literature can be fruitfully reflected upon only "in terms of a conceptual framework derivable from an inductive survey of the literary field."[6]

The highly praised book which René Wellek and Austin Warren first issued in 1949, *Theory of Literature*, presented so complete a codification of the New Criticism as to have been widely hailed as the Novum Organum of its period, and it has steadily exerted a broad and generally wholesome influence over the past twenty years. But, in one particular, it has noticeably had very little impact on scholarly opinion. For, in its final chapter (on "The Study of Literature in the Graduate School"), it proposes that the revitalization of literary study in the American university awaits departments being built up not around professors of French and English and German but professors of literature—men who value and understand literature as an art and who, possessing "intellectual and literary distinction," are able significantly to relate belles-lettres to the generality of culture. They say:

> Instead of staffing a department in terms of "Shakespeare men" and "Wordsworth men," we should, better, invoke types of mind and method. . . . Have we a literary theorist? Have we a man of strong philosophical interests and training who can analyze the interrelations of literature and philosophy in the "history of ideas"? . . . Have we a teacher who has active social and political interests without ceasing to be a literary man? Have we a "Catholic intellectual"? Have we a man versed in modern psychology and psychiatry?[7]

And they make it plain that the appointment policy they have in view would be calculated not to convert an English department into an outpost of social science or religion but to make it something, indeed, more genuinely literary. They anticipate, of course, the rejoinder being offered by Chaucerians and Miltonists that such a policy would make for a lowering of standards. But they reply:

[5] It is such men as I. A. Richards, William Empson, Yvor Winters, R. P. Blackmur, Allen Tate, Cleanth Brooks, and John Crowe Ransom who are being recalled here.
[6] Frye, p. 7.
[7] René Wellek and Austin Warren, *Theory of Literature* (New York: Harcourt Brace Jovanovich, Inc., 1949), p. 291.

All such laments, it is important to see, are not statements of fact but judgments of value. If, in 1930, Kittredge had retired and T. S. Eliot had been appointed in his stead, most Harvard Ph.D.'s would probably have said that Harvard standards had declined. They would obviously have changed. When our standards for professors grow more literary, we shall surrender some things once thought imperative while we shall also make new exactions.[8]

Many of the other lessons inculcated by the critical movement Messrs. Wellek and Warren were methodizing had been learned so well, however, that, in their recommendations regarding the Graduate School, they were striking against head winds well-nigh irresistible. For—to borrow a phrase that Saintsbury applied to European neoclassicism of the eighteenth century[9]—the *Catholic Faith* prevailing now in the academy is that the life of literature is something essentially autogenous, breeding itself in a manner not unlike what André Malraux conceives to be the normal mode of creativity in the life of visual art. In his great books on art of the forties and fifties—in *Le Musée imaginaire, La Création artistique, La Monnaie de l'absolu, Les Voix du silence*—he is contending that what is most decisively formative of the artist is not any vision he wins of the environing reality of his world but, rather, the pressure exerted upon him simply by the funded tradition of art itself. It has often been noticed that he has a great fondness for the verb *arracher* (to uproot, to wrest, to tear away), and it figures so largely in his lexicon because he deems the process of self-definition for the artist to be, at bottom, an affair of his wresting himself loose and tearing away from the art that constitutes his received tradition. Artistic creation, in Malraux's account, is never consequent upon the artist's simply submitting himself to the causality of the "real world," for, in the space between the artist and the world, there is always inserted some anterior custom of usage by which the painter's or sculptor's vision is oriented, even if only negatively—so that the idea of an artist uninfluenced by other artists and simply attempting by himself to deal with the given factuality of the world is for Malraux an idea virtually inconceivable. He is unwilling to grant even that primitive art presents any sort of exception, for here, too, as he insists, the work of the individual artist will always be found to express certain established conventions that bear the stamp of a folk culture. In short, Malraux's is a vision of art as its own progenitor, and, in its own kingdom, he nowhere descries its hegemony to be fundamentally qualified.

Now it is something of the same kind of autonomy that the prevailing Catholic Faith in criticism today attributes to literature. Numerous surveys[10]

[8] Wellek and Warren, p. 292.

[9] *Vide* George Saintsbury, *A History of Criticism*, Vol. 2 (Edinburgh and London: William Blackwood & Sons Ltd., 1949, 6th Impression), pp. 407–421.

[10] *Vide* Hyatt H. Waggoner, "The Current Revolt against the New Criticism," *Criticism*, 1, No. 3 (Summer 1959), pp. 211–225; Mark Spilka, "The Necessary Stylist:

in the last several years have been designed to measure the distance at which we presently stand from the insurgency of a generation ago represented by such documents as *Seven Types of Ambiguity*,[11] *The Double Agent*,[12] *The World's Body*,[13] and *Modern Poetry and the Tradition*.[14] And, unquestionably, the many new tacks that have been taken since the mid-fifties have now the effect of making the halcyon days of the New Criticism appear to be very much a thing of the past. Yet, for all of the new experiments in mythography and historical studies, there is a basic residue of that earlier time which provides the period's bench mark in theory of literature. For critics so different from one another in stratagem as W. K. Wimsatt and Northrop Frye, Roy Harvey Pearce and Marius Bewley, Murray Krieger and Richard Poirier will be found taking it for granted that the literary work is an autonomous structure any one of whose constituent elements derives its meaning not from its relationship to the ordinary universe but from that system of "intramural relations"[15] wherein, within the work itself, it is fused into a total fabric of language and symbol. Which is to say that literary structure is conceived to be "organic." And, since the meaning of a work's component parts is wholly determined by the ensemble which results from their interaction, literary value is held to be terminal: tenor and vehicle are one and indivisible, making up a "new word" which has the power of trapping us within the unexampled universe that it calls into being. "The true father or shaping spirit of the poem is the form of the poem itself. . . ."[16] The executive principle of the poetic process is wholly immanent within that process. "Literature shapes itself, and is not shaped externally. . . ."[17] And thus the only habitat for the literary work is such an infinitely capacious space as T. S. Eliot was avowing long ago in his famous postulate about Tradition. For, given the essentially autogenous nature of the life of literature, the given poem dwells nowhere but in that universe wherein "the whole of the literature of . . . [the West] from Homer . . . has a simultane-

---

A New Critical Revision," *Modern Fiction Studies*, 6, No. 4 (Winter 1960, 1961), pp. 283–297; Murray Krieger, "After the New Criticism," *The Massachusetts Review*, 4, No. 1 (Autumn 1962), pp. 183–205; Walter Sutton, *Modern American Criticism* (Englewood Cliffs, New Jersey: Prentice-Hall, Inc., 1963), Chap. IX; and René Wellek, *Concepts of Criticism* (New Haven: Yale University Press, 1963), pp. 316–343.

[11] William Empson, *Seven Types of Ambiguity* (London: Chatto & Windus, 1930).

[12] R. P. Blackmur, *The Double Agent: Essays in Craft and Elucidation* (New York: Arrow Editions, 1935).

[13] John Crowe Ransom, *The World's Body* (New York: Charles Scribner's Sons, 1938).

[14] Cleanth Brooks, *Modern Poetry and the Tradition* (Chapel Hill: University of North Carolina Press, 1939).

[15] Krieger, p. 188.

[16] Frye, p. 98.

[17] Frye, p. 97.

ous existence and composes a simultaneous order."[18] It dwells in something like Malraux's *le musée imaginaire*—where, now that modern photography has created essentially one visual space for the entire artistic tradition, simply by leafing through the pages of Skira folios, we can encounter all works of visual art on terms that have the effect of decontaminating them of their historicity, of their involvement in all the extraneous particularities of religious and cultural history. In Malraux's view, the uniquely privileged perspective that modernity affords is that of being able to regard the great painting and sculpture and architecture of the past not as "icons" of a particular time and place but as essays in world transformation through plastic expressiveness that belong to the timeless and eternal present of *le musée imaginaire*. And thus African fetishes and Oriental landscapes and Byzantine madonnas can, by dint simply of their power of plastic eloquence, be felt to coexist simultaneously in *one* museum, an "imaginary museum," along with Gothic *Pietàs* and Rembrandt portraits and Cubist abstractions.

Now it is a similarly kaleidoscopic boundlessness which belongs to that interminate space wherein literature—"the whole of . . . literature . . . from Homer"—is thought to dwell. The literary universe is a "synchronic present" which is conceived in the terms of an "open-ended historicism."[19] And one can readily imagine a representative of academic *lettres* today being prepared to alter the famous word in Donne's *Devotions* and to say that, finally, no poem "is an Iland . . . [but] a peece of the Continent"— which is "the whole of literature." So it is this great Continent which is made the object of study in university departments. And the result—at once in terms of pedagogy and of the despair it breeds in the young—is savagely reported in a recent essay by the gifted young Berkeley critic, Frederick Crews. For, given the prevailing academic vision, what tends to be supremely valued is "sheer acquaintance" with the "great phalanx of works aligned by genre and period"[20] that constitute the tradition. Since literary works can only be made out of other literary works and since the poetic process is wholly shaped from within itself, it is considered a breach of critical decorum to employ any sort of interpretative principle that is formed by a philosophical or a theological interest, for it will only "have a disabling effect and . . . subsequently [will have] to be struggled against." The regimen offered the young apprentice in graduate school is one of learning the requisite bibliographical techniques and "working up" the set primary and secondary texts—for this is "the way of scholarship." An Edmund Wilson, to

[18] T. S. Eliot, "Tradition and the Individual Talent," in *Selected Essays*: 1917–1932 (New York: Harcourt Brace Jovanovich, Inc., 1932), p. 4.

[19] The terms "synchronic present" and "open-ended historicism" are Fr. Walter Ong's: *vide* his *In the Human Grain: Further Explorations of Contemporary Culture* (New York: Macmillan Co., 1967), pp. 17–41, p. 123.

[20] Frederick Crews, "Anaesthetic Criticism: I," *The New York Review*, 14, No. 4 (26 February 1970), p. 33.

be sure, has written brilliantly on Dickens and Kipling from a psychological perspective;[21] a Kenneth Burke studies the various ways in which literary works may become "strategies" for encompassing social reality;[22] an Irving Howe takes a lively interest in the relations between literature and politics;[23] or a Hillis Miller investigates the kind of religious inquiry being conducted by the Victorians.[24] But "the idea that we positively ought to . . . [make 'extraliterary' sense of literature] is conceived as a threat to scholarly balance."[25] And, as Professor Crews reminds us,

> . . . students who reject this consensus must either feign acceptance of it or drop out of school. The survivors and inheritors of literary training tend to be those best adapted to dull, safe provincial work, while the more creative and inquisitive students, having squandered valuable years on the graduate regimen expecting that it *must* have something to do with the life of the imagination, are mastered at last by despair.[26]

It has not, of course, gone unremarked that the reigning dispensation in literary study of the past thirty or forty years, when not pressed to foolish extremes, has yielded an extraordinarily vital body of theory and practical criticism. Certainly for the foreseeable future, it has quite fortunately redefined the terms in which discourse about literature is possible. And virtually no one any longer wants to return to the time when "the assembling of footnotes and the culling out of charming little anecdotes about the foibles of authors"[27] constituted an acceptable style and idiom for the classroom and for the printed page of published criticism, when the literary work was taken merely as document of a life or of religion or the "history of ideas" or of something else. Today—whether it be George Herbert's *The Temple* or Emily Brontë's *Wuthering Heights* or Nabokov's *Pale Fire*—it is the living poem that engages us, and (as a result of the lessons we have been taught by the great masters of criticism in this century) we now take it for granted, with all the exactions entailed, that "the study of literature ought not to be merely a tour through a kind of refined Madame Tussaud's."[28]

[21] Edmund Wilson, *The Wound and the Bow: Seven Studies in Literature* (New York: Oxford University Press, 1947).

[22] Kenneth Burke, *A Grammar of Motives* (New York: Prentice-Hall, Inc., 1952).

[23] Irving Howe, *Politics and the Novel* (New York: Horizon Press, Inc., and Meridian Books, Inc., 1957).

[24] J. Hillis Miller, *The Disappearance of God* (Cambridge: Harvard University Press, 1963).

[25] Frederick Crews, p. 33.

[26] Crews, p. 34.

[27] Cleanth Brooks, "Metaphor and the Function of Criticism," in *Spiritual Problems in Contemporary Literature*, Stanley R. Hopper, ed. (New York: Harper & Row, 1952), p. 130.

[28] Cleanth Brooks, "The Quick and the Dead: A Comment on Humanistic Studies," in *The Humanities*, Julian Harris, ed. (Madison: University of Wisconsin Press, 1950), p. 5.

But, though a wax-works kind of museum may no longer be considered the appropriate setting for literary reflection, there is another equally sterilizing museum—a kind of *musée imaginaire*—into which we are often by way of being thrust by the mystique of *tradition* and *the text* that frequently controls the academic study of literature. And thus it comes to be that some attempt at breaking out of this cage[29] is being represented, in one way or another, by many of the more significant proposals that have been offered to American criticism in recent years.

In, for example, his brilliant book of 1954, *The Burning Fountain*, the late Philip Wheelwright proposed that the crucial dimension to which criticism must be finally attentive is that of what he called "depth meaning." On the opening page of his book he cites the Estonian legend which recalls how

> . . . the god of song Wannemunne once descended onto the Domberg, and there, in a sacred wood, played and sang music of divine beauty. All creatures were invited to listen, and they each learned some fragments of the celestial sound: the forest learned its rustling, the stream its roar; the wind caught and learned to re-echo the shrillest tones, and the birds the prelude of the song. The fish stuck their heads as far as the eyes out of the water, but left their ears below the surface; they saw the movements of the god's mouth and imitated them, but remained dumb. Man alone grasped it all, and therefore his song pierces into the depth of the heart, and mounts upwards to the dwellings of the gods.[30]

And it is Wheelwright's contention that, when men aspire "to imitate the god worthily and sing the full song," theirs is an utterance that deserves to be called *expressive language* or *depth language*—the kind of language that is being used in the Psalms of the Old Testament and in *Hamlet* and *Moby Dick* and *The Man with the Blue Guitar*. Which is not, of course, "the language of plain sense," or what Wheelwright calls "steno-language." For, when we want logical clarity and denotative precision—for the sake of efficient enterprise in the marketplace or the scientific laboratory—we employ language in ways that stipulate certain constantly stable and exact meanings. But, when the aim is to speak at once referentially and emotively, with a "humanly significant fullness" of statement, then, inevitably, language becomes "plurisignative," the meanings of its symbolic components being at once multiple and so fused into one another as finally to surpass *in toto* the sum of their ingredients. It is the language of the full song—whose aim is to express (with an immediacy so eloquent that it commands imaginative

[29] I am not unaware of the small paradox which is made by my use of this term, for, of course, *le musée imaginaire*, in André Malraux's description, is "without walls." But, in so far as the literary universe as conceived by recent Anglo-American criticism makes a kind of analogue of Malraux's conception, it is, as I would contend, by no means unshuttered.

[30] Philip Wheelwright, *The Burning Fountain: A Study in the Language of Symbolism* (Bloomington: Indiana University Press, 1954), p. 3.

assent) the poet's experiential encounter with whatever reality it is that has claimed his concern. And it is a language whose "depth meanings" are inseparable from the fundamental loyalties to which we are implicitly being invited to acquiesce when these particular meanings are given embodiment in imaginative statement. So what is implied by the whole drift of Philip Wheelwright's argument is that the rigor with which criticism attempts to study the particular pattern of "plurisignation" distinguishing a body of literature is undertaken for the sake of finally clarifying the special quality of "depth-experience" to which that literature gives rise.

Or, again, Fr. Walter Ong was suggesting a few years ago in a series of fascinating essays[31] that there is a "jinnee" in "the well-wrought urn" of literary art. He was calling into question the approved modern theory of the poem-as-object with its emphasis on the work of art *as such*, the whole notion that "it is neither the potter who made it nor the people, real or fictional, to whose lives it is tangent, but the well-wrought urn itself which counts. . . ."[32] And he wanted to declare his own sense of how imperfect is the justice done the actuality of esthetic experience by this modern idolatry of the art-object. Fr. Ong is careful to acknowledge that the artistic situation does itself claim for the work of art the kind of autonomy which modern theory has insisted upon: he knows it to be the case that the poem bids for the kind of attention which Eliseo Vivas calls "intransitive."[33] But he contends that, precisely in the degree to which the object is taken with ultimate seriousness, our contemplation of it inevitably involves us in a very profound disappointment. For, given the essentially personal orientation of our humanity, we cannot finally perform a genuinely intransitive act of attention before anything less than a person. Contemplation of this sort requires that someone else be *there*, for it involves love—which cannot be "projected into an unpeopled void." Yet, curiously, the end of the esthetic transaction is not psychological disaster, since, as Fr. Ong maintains, "in proportion as the object of art pretends to be serious," it drives us to the point of considering it, indeed, as "a surrogate for a person"—as a surrogate not (as I take him to mean) for the actual scribe who wrote the sonnet or the story but for him whom Wayne Booth calls "the implied author"[34] and whose real profile is to be found not in the biography of the historical person but in the texts

---

[31] Walter J. Ong, S.J., "The Jinnee in the Well Wrought Urn," *Essays in Criticism* 4, No. 3 (1954), pp. 1–12; "A Dialectic of Aural and Objective Correlatives," *Essays in Criticism* 8, No. 2 (1958), pp. 166–181; and "Voice as Summons for Belief," in *Literature and Belief*, M. H. Abrams, ed. (New York: Columbia University Press, 1958), pp. 80–105. These essays are included in Ong's *The Barbarian Within* (New York: Macmillan Co., 1962).

[32] *The Barbarian Within*, p. 15.

[33] *Vide* Eliseo Vivas, *Creation and Discovery: Essays in Criticism and Aesthetics* (New York: Noonday Press, 1955), pp. 93–99.

[34] *Vide* Wayne Booth, *The Rhetoric of Fiction* (Chicago: University of Chicago Press, 1961), pp. 71–76 and *passim*.

which he created. "In proportion as the work of art is capable of being taken in full seriousness," says Fr. Ong, "it moves further and further along an asymptote to the curve of personality"[35]—or at least of a person behaving "enough like one to betray the bias of the human heart."[36] Which is to say that the world of literary experience is a personalist universe, a world of dialogue—where the poem is a word spoken and a word heard, this speaking and hearing enabling us to reach the interior not of an "object" but of a personal vision of reality.

Now, from those younger critics who have recently been responding to that Continental circle of the so-called Geneva school (including such figures as Georges Poulet, Marcel Raymond, Albert Béguin, Jean-Pierre Richard, and Jean Starobinski), we begin to get examples of what a criticism that concerns itself with the jinnee in the urn will look like. And, of this group, the Johns Hopkins scholar, Hillis Miller, who specializes in Victorian and twentieth-century studies, makes a representative example. Like his master Georges Poulet (and like Poulet's associates in the French Swiss tradition to which he belongs), Hillis Miller conceives literary art to be a transcription of the writer's consciousness and criticism to be an analysis of the subjectivity expressed in literary texts. He is not primarily interested in the single poem or novel in its individual autonomy but in the reverberative pattern of meanings which knits together the entire body of a writer's work and reveals the essential "structure of consciousness" wherewith a given universe of experience is constituted. Whether his subject be Matthew Arnold or Charles Dickens or William Butler Yeats, he is searching always for that most fundamental bias of vision and sensibility which "persists throughout all the swarming multiplicity of . . . [an artist's various creations] as a view of the world which is unique and the same."[37] He does not regard the literary work as a "mere symptom or product of a pre-existent psychological condition, but as the very means by which a writer apprehends and, in some measure, creates himself."[38] And thus, as he says (in an adaptation of Gerard Manley Hopkins's term), it is the "inscape" of a body of writing toward which critical inquiry ought to be directed—that is, the "organizing form which presides over . . . [an author's] elaboration of each of his works."[39] The assumption is that the consistencies and coherences defining a given body of literature are established by a particular perspective of valuing, and that the gradual evolution of this perspective through the developing history of an *oeuvre* constitutes a drama of consciousness,

[35] Walter J. Ong, S.J., p. 24.
[36] Ong, p. 25.
[37] J. Hillis Miller, *Charles Dickens: The World of His Novels* (Cambridge: Harvard University Press, 1959), p. viii.
[38] *Ibid.*
[39] J. Hillis Miller, *The Disappearance of God: Five Nineteenth-Century Writers* (Cambridge: Harvard University Press, 1963), p. x.

the spiritual adventure of the artist's search for his own deepest selfhood. But it is not any sort of speculative psychoanalysis which is being pursued, for the concern is not with the psychic condition of authors but with the structure of literary art. And a critic like Hillis Miller is always fully engaged with the public data presented by literary texts, and fully committed to verbal-stylistic-formal analysis. Yet, for him, "each sentence or paragraph of a novel, [say, by Dickens,] whether it is presented from the point of view of the narrator or of some imagined character, defines a certain relationship between an imaginary mind and its object"—"a certain relation between the mind and its world."[40] The work of art, in short, is an icon of *presence*: which is to say that the literary experience—the reader's transaction with the poetry of a Hopkins or the fiction of a Conrad—is itself a form of communion. And thus the critical effort—the attempt to identify and interpret the form of consciousness which a given canon of literature incarnates—is conceived to be an effort at retracing, with the greatest possible empathy and vividness, the artist's theological biography (in the sense of those ultimate beliefs and values wherewith he reckons with his own humanity and makes sense of his world).[41]

The French phenomenological tradition of the Geneva school does not, however, offer the only alternative to that objectivizing interpretation of literature against which Fr. Walter Ong was protesting so eloquently a few years ago. There is also another alternative which is presented by that German line of hermeneutical theory running from Wilhelm Dilthey (and more distantly still from Friedrich Schleiermacher) through Martin Heidegger to Hans-Georg Gadamer and to such contemporary theologians as Rudolf Bultmann, Gerhard Ebeling, Ernst Fuchs, and Heinrich Ott. Here, the view of the literary text as an "object" is refused because it is felt that such a perspective makes the work of art something lifeless and atemporal and thus betrays the essential historicity of the literary experience. But, in distinction from the Geneva school, the central emphasis in this German line falls not so much on the drama of consciousness incarnate in the literary work as on that drama of interrogation which involves our own personal existence being addressed and called into question by the work. What is

---

[40] Miller, *Charles Dickens: The World of His Novels*, p. ix.

[41] My own work, unlike Hillis Miller's, has not been directly influenced by the Geneva school, but it represents what is in many ways a parallel program. *Vide,* for example, the account of "vision" as the end of critical inquiry in Nathan A. Scott, Jr., *Negative Capability: Studies in the New Literature and the Religious Situation* (New Haven: Yale University Press, 1969), Chap. 5. And, in the terms of practical criticism, the following studies of mine are essentially essays in definition of a form of consciousness: *Albert Camus* (London: Bowes and Bowes Ltd., 1962), *Samuel Beckett* (London: Bowes and Bowes Ltd., 1965); *Ernest Hemingway* (Grand Rapids, Michigan: William Eerdmans, 1966); *Craters of the Spirit: Studies in the Modern Novel* (Washington and Cleveland: Corpus Books, 1968); and *The Wild Prayer of Longing: Poetry and the Sacred* (New Haven: Yale University Press, 1970), Chap. 3.

insisted upon is the basically dialectical character of the relationship in which one stands with respect to a literary text. For the work of art, in so far as it lights up the world in some significant way, is no merely neutral object to be attacked and manipulated and dissected and mastered. It does, to be sure, confront us with a certain otherness: to face *The Cherry Orchard* or *A Passage to India* or the *Four Quartets* is to face a "world" which has its own inner rhythm and dynamic, its own structure, its own authentic autonomy. And, since the work lives and moves and has its being within its own horizon, it would be manifestly a breach of tact for the interpreter to try to impose upon it his own categories, his own perspectives and values. But, then, a literary text does not simply stand over against us as something unimplicated in our own historical reality. On the contrary: in so far as it presents an ordering of experience which has richness and depth, it *speaks* to us, it asks how things are with us. The encounter between the reader and the text is thus one which presents the possibility of a kind of dialogue. For the interpreter stands in his own world: he has his own horizon—he approaches the work of art with his own conceptions of how the world is ordered, and they cannot somehow be suddenly suspended by an act of will. But the text is in effect challenging the interpreter to consent at least to submit his own perspectives to interrogation; and he, if he is intent upon a truly serious conversation, does indeed unreservedly enter into the exchange: he submits himself to the full claim of the text, undertaking to be as sensitively alert as possible to wherein it is that the world of the work illumines and enlarges and completes his own world. Which is to say that he allows the text to address him, while at the same time confronting it in turn with his own history, his own self-understanding, his own living present. And it is this dialectical interplay between the interpreter and the text that a theorist like Hans-Georg Gadamer calls the "hermeneutical" situation.[42]

From the perspective of hermeneutical theory, then, the "hermeneutical event" may be said to be that transaction which occurs when an interpreter of a text begins himself in turn to be so interpreted by his text that he discovers the whole dialogical occasion proving to be a sort of "homecoming" which prompts in him the sense of having found (as Max Weber predicted of the profoundest esthetic experience) "an answer to one's seeking self."[43]

The German theorists—whether it be a Gadamer or an Ebeling[44] or

---

[42] *Vide* Hans-Georg Gadamer, *Wahrheit und Methode: Grundzüge einer philosophischen Hermeneutik* (Tübingen: J.C. B. Mohr, 1965, 2d ed.).

[43] Quoted in Lawrence W. Chisolm, *The Far East and American Culture* (New Haven: Yale University Press, 1963), p. 231.

[44] *Vide* Gerhard Ebeling, *Word and Faith*, James W. Leitch, trans. (Philadelphia: Fortress Press, 1963), pp. 305–332.

a Fuchs[45]—are careful, of course, to insist that the hermeneutical event is a "word-event" or "language-event." The kind of self-seeking to which the literary experience gives rise does not, in other words, legitimize any sort of sovereignty of the interpreter over his text. For the interpreter's received *donnée* is the text itself, and the hermeneutical process can begin only when the interpreter consents to be utterly docile before the radical specificity of the given art-work: we must seek fully to take into ourselves this specificity and otherness, and with all the cunning that the most refined procedures of verbal-stylistic-formal analysis make available. Which means that the discussion of literature can never soar off into any supra-verbal sort of ether. But the critic's final concern is not with the "performance" of the work of art *as performance*, for its true function is to light up some space in the human universe. And thus the text, as Professor Gadamer says, must be brought "out of the alienation in which it finds itself"[46]—as document—in order that it may be *seen through*. Which may, of course, entail a certain violence being done to the text, for its horizon can in no way be merged with *my* horizon, its deliverance can in no way be brought into *my* life, if nothing more is risked than what recent American theory calls "explication." Merely to have produced a "reading" of Keats's great odes or of Joyce's *Portrait*, as though one's text were nothing more than a very subtle kind of exercise in dialectic, is not to have appropriated the work of art in a way that permits it to enter into one's own *Lebenswelt*. Indeed, it cannot begin to "thematize" *my* existence until I go forward to meet it as a real partner in the dialogue which it wants to initiate. The text itself must, of course, be permitted to say what it wants to say. But in all true dialogue, when the partners are listening to each other with the strictest attentiveness, what is said is accompanied by, and opens up a kind of access to, much that remains unsaid, the common horizon of the partners indeed being resident within this latter dimension (of deeply shared, but unspoken, mutual understanding). And so it is in the hermeneutical situation involving text and interpreter: which means that the interpreter must not only read the printed page but must also read "between the lines," if the full meaning of what his text discloses is to be retrieved—and he must do this even at the risk of appearing to handle his text with a certain violence. For it is only in this way that the otherness of the work and the otherness of the interpreter can finally be so joined as to enable the hermeneutical event to become a moment of revelation.

So it is that the New Hermeneutic conceives the nature of the critical effort. Outside the circles of theological discussion and specifically biblical criticism, this German tradition, however, has not had till now any considerable impact on American theorists. E. D. Hirsch's brilliant book of 1967,

[45] *Vide* Ernst Fuchs, *Hermeneutik* (Bad Cannstatt: R. Mullerschon Verlag, 1963).
[46] Gadamer, p. 350.

Validity in Interpretation,[47] made the first occasion of its receiving any substantial notice—though Professor Hirsch's response (to Gadamer particularly) was doubting and very largely hostile. But Richard Palmer's recent book, *Hermeneutics*, presents an account that is not only acute and comprehensive but fervidly advocatory: it concludes with a "Manifesto to American Literary Interpretation" which bristles with eagerness to launch a new program, and Mr. Palmer's Introduction assures us that his book is, indeed, only a first venture toward the larger project of "moving toward a more adequate approach to literary interpretation."[48] So it may well be that, before long, a fresh impulse will have begun to germinate in American literary studies.

In the ways, then, that have been noticed here—and in numerous others that might be specified, were a fully comprehensive inventory being aimed at—efforts are being made now in criticism to break out of the kind of cage in which it has been enclosed by the reigning academic tradition of our period. It begins to be possible to discern a growing movement of resistance against the conception of literature as something autogenous and self-contained, and the correlative theory of criticism as unessentially related to any other humanistic discipline begins also to receive an increasingly adverse estimate. What we are told that criticism must be after is that "depth-experience" into which we are beckoned by the poem, or the artist's theological biography (which is conceived, of course, in some Emersonian sense to be "representative"), or the possibility which the hermeneutical event offers the self of expanding its own horizon, of entering more deeply into its own *Lebenswelt* and of mitigating its own fragmentariness. But so to define the ultimate focus or direction of literary study is to involve the enterprise of criticism in precisely that region of thought with which modern theorists have least wanted it to have any alliance. For if "religion is more than a system of special symbols, rites, and emotions directed toward a highest being,"[49] if it does not pertain exclusively to any particular sphere of human life alongside other spheres or to any special psychic or cognitive function but if it has to do, rather, with the direction of the human spirit —in all provinces of life and culture—toward that which concerns it *ultimately*, then it is clearly the case that literary criticism is moving into the universe of religious meaning when it begins to address itself to those determinative values and root beliefs on which an artist's vision is most basically reared, or when it undertakes to interpret those depth-meanings

[47] New Haven: Yale University Press, 1967.

[48] Richard E. Palmer, *Hermeneutics: Interpretation Theory in Schleiermacher, Dilthey, Heidegger, and Gadamer* (Evanston: Northwestern University Press, 1969), p. 4.

[49] Paul Tillich, *The Protestant Era*, James Luther Adams, trans. (Chicago: University of Chicago Press, 1948), p. 59.

that arise out of some fundamental reconstitution of our selfhood which is a consequence of the hermeneutical experience.

Matthew Arnold's notion, that the great books save us[50]—which was being strangely reasserted a generation ago in that primer of modern positivist poetics, I. A. Richards's *Poetry and Science*[51]—has not of course, as it were, survived Buchenwald and Belsen, as George Steiner was in effect eloquently reminding us a few years ago.[52] For a long time, to be sure, it has been a matter of good form and almost of automatic reflex for the fashionable academic tradition to repudiate what is grossly evangelical in Arnold's humanism; but it is no doubt something like the Arnoldian doctrine that has supported the whole mystique in our time of the literary universe as autotelic and self-enclosed. For, the erosion of the religious landscape having left nothing behind but poetry, at least this—as it has seemed in these post-Arnoldian days of our desperation—must be itself converted into an absolute. But even though, to our astonishment, the most aggressively secular poetry may on occasion by some circuitous and dialectical route lead us into the outer precincts of blessedness (as, on his account, Claudel was so engaged by the poetry of Arthur Rimbaud[53]), the office of literature is at best in this regard Virgilian: for, at last, something better than poetry, some Beatrician agency, must "our steps befriend"—unto the innermost regions of the Holy City.

Quite apart, however, from the Arnoldian doctrine, when it is occasionally found permissible to acknowledge that religious meanings may be a part of the freight of implication carried by literary art, the established tendency in the academic study of literature is to assume these meanings to be an affair of explicitly elaborated themes and symbols and issues belonging to some historic tradition of faith. Such a conception of the matter has, of course, its obvious convenience, in the quick precision with which it permits religious meaning to be separated out as an easily isolatable quantity of a total literary fabric—which may then be handled in the terms of some kind of iconology or historicist account of the particular age whose religious style is reflected in the given pattern of theme and symbol and myth. But though much distinguished scholarship in this mode has been produced in our time—in the manner, say, of Leo Spitzer and Ernst Curtius, of E. M. W. Tillyard and Louis Martz, of Basil Willey and A. P. Woodhouse—when it legislates itself as the sole standpoint from which religious meaning in literature may be conceived and studied, it then becomes a kind

[50] *Vide* Matthew Arnold, "The Study of Poetry," in *Essays in Criticism*, 2d ser. (London: Macmillan and Co., Ltd., 1896), pp. 1–55.

[51] *Vide* I. A. Richards, *Poetry and Science* (London: Kegan Paul Ltd., 1926).

[52] *Vide* George Steiner, *Language and Silence: Essays on Language, Literature, and the Inhuman* (New York: Atheneum, 1967) pp. 3–11.

[53] *Vide* Paul Claudel, Préface aux *Oeuvres de Rimbaud* (Paris: Mercure de France, 1924).

of prophylaxis against genuinely serious inquiry. For what is most essentially distinctive of the religious imagination is not its embrace of this or that particular religious system or its quest of some other world but its concern to understand *this* world in relation to issues of ultimate meaning and value. The drama of our worldly life may, of course, be found to be illuminatingly "thematized" by the myths and symbols of a particular religious system; but what is of the essence of the religious consciousness is not an affair of its symbology but of its concern to apprehend the realities of our human world in relation to a region of things where all value and meaning are ultimately grounded. It might well be said perhaps that, in so far as man is a "religious" creature, he is so by virtue of his preoccupation with "the dimension of ultimacy."[54] Which is precisely what the English philosopher, Stephen Toulmin, is suggesting when he proposes that we consider reflection to be moving into a "religious" dimension just in the degree to which it focuses on "limiting questions," on questions having to do not with particular aspects of our moral or political or intellectual experience but with the ultimate foundations of all our valuing and acting and thinking —for this, as Professor Toulmin maintains, is most essentially the field of religious thought.[55] Indeed, as Paul Tillich declared again and again, to think religiously is to do nothing more nor less than to think about our experience in relation to that which concerns us ultimately because it is conceived itself to have the character of ultimacy: religion, as he liked to say, "in the largest and most basic sense of the word, is ultimate concern."[56] So wherever ultimate meaning, wherever truly ultimate concern, is expressed in the forms and materials of culture—whether in art or in philosophy or in theology itself—there, something is being set forth about our human reality which involves a basically religious order of valuation. It is not, of course, being proposed here that all serious literature is somehow itself "religious," for this is quite manifestly not the case. But the literary imagination, in the degree to which it envisages any large perspective on human experience, is, inevitably, guided by some scale of ultimacy; and thus it can be said that all serious literature may have at least the effect of dramatizing issues and posing questions that are of an essentially religious order and that invite from criticism an essentially theological response. For religion is not primarily an affair of some special sphere of myth and cult and devotion and ecclesiastical institutions: it is, rather, that entire effort of the imagination to take hold of its world *in the dimension of ultimacy*. And thus when we conceive the sole locus of religious meaning in literary art to be such

---

[54] The term is Langdon Gilkey's: *vide* his *Naming the Whirlwind: The Renewal of God-Language* (Indianapolis and New York: Bobbs-Merrill Co., 1969), pt. 2.

[55] *Vide* Stephen Toulmin, *An Examination of the Place of Reason in Ethics* (New York: Cambridge University Press, 1950), Chap. 14.

[56] Paul Tillich, *Theology of Culture*, Robert C. Kimball, ed. (New York: Oxford University Press, 1964), pp. 7–8.

iconological material deriving from a particular tradition of faith as may be present, we are simply shutting ourselves off from any possibility of making the really important discriminations that may be required by that structure of ultimate concern which knits together the poetic economy (and of which the iconological material—if any be present, and even if it be there in abundance—may furnish no reliable index at all).

Nor does this whole issue find any less restrictive definition in those proposals which assert that literature may be considered to embody religious meaning only "when and if it exhibits the visible or invisible presence or potency of the divine."[57] For in this perspective "the divine" is regarded not as the inexhaustible and mysterious *depth* of nature and history, not as "the dark backward and abysm of time"—not, in Dietrich Bonhoeffer's phrase, as "the 'beyond' in the midst of our life"[58]—but as some sort of *deus ex machina* from "out there," as a *being* who, having come into the natural order from some other realm, can become an element of a literary situation as "a member of the dramatis personae," making his appearance "visually, auditorily, tactilely, or as hidden but logically certain manipulator of scenery and events. . . ."[59] But, of course, this kind of crude supernaturalism is but one concretion of the religious consciousness. And, though a certain kind of secular scepticism (which is more "fundamentalist" than the most primitive piety) conceives "objectivizing" mythology to be of the essence of religious thought, it is odd indeed to find so sensitive a thinker as Hillis Miller contending that literary motifs take on "a properly religious meaning" *only* "if some supernatural reality . . . [is] present"[60] in the world of the literary work. For, in his book of 1965, *Poets of Reality*, he brilliantly demonstrated that the progressing history of literature in our period—as it moves from the time of Conrad through the time of Yeats and Eliot and on into the period of Stevens and Carlos Williams—records a great shift in religious consciousness, from transcendentalist spatialization of the Holy in some *terra incognita* to a profound recovery of the divine in the dimension of *immanence*.[61] Yet, as one can only conclude, so influential is the prevailing

[57] Thomas L. Hanna, "A Question: What Does One Mean by 'Religious Literature'," in *Mansions of the Spirit: Essays on Literature and Religion*, George A. Panichas, ed. (New York: Hawthorn Books, Inc., 1967), p. 80.
[58] Dietrich Bonhoeffer, *Letters and Papers from Prison*, Reginald Fuller, trans., Eberhard Bethge, ed. (London: Collins, "Fontana Books," 1959), p. 93.
[59] Hanna, p. 81.
[60] J. Hillis Miller, "Literature and Religion," in *Relations of Literary Study: Essays on Interdisciplinary Contributions*, James Thorpe, ed. (New York: Modern Language Association, 1967), p. 125.
[61] *Vide* J. Hillis Miller, *Poets of Reality: Six Twentieth-Century Writers* (Cambridge: Harvard University Press, 1965)—especially Chapter I, where he says: "There can be for many writers no return to the traditional conception of God as the highest existence, creator of all other existences, transcending his creation as well as dwelling within it. If there is to be a God in the new world it must be a presence within things

academic tradition of regarding the religious dimension as a discrete and separable "element" in literary designs that, when he begins to speak theoretically, Professor Miller forgets the lessons he has learned in his own practical encounters with modern literature, and forgets also his own basic interest as a critic in "forms of consciousness" (which, in its focus on those "ultimate concerns" that stabilize a work of art, is an essentially theological interest).

To suppose that the literary situation is given religious import only when the mythical and symbolic machinery of a particular tradition of faith is brought into play or only when the work of art exhibits some supernatural agency as operative in the human order is, of course, to make very nicely manageable the whole issue regarding the relation between religious and literary value. For it is in effect to deny that there is any intrinsic relation at all. Poiesis is assumed to proceed in accordance with its own internal necessities, and the religious issue—which is conceived to be merely an affair of certain types of iconology that may or may not happen to figure in a given literary design—is thus presumed to be inessential to the interiority of the literary process itself. But if the religious dimension pertains most fundamentally not to special systems of rite and doctrine and symbol but to that order of valuation involving the intuition of what is ultimately the ground of all meaning and value and of what deserves therefore to concern us ultimately, then it must be considered to be immanently and essentially a part of the literary situation. For not only is the shape or form that the writer gives his material uninterpretable without reference to the ultimate concerns which that form reflects; but so too is it impossible also for us to win anything resembling what Paul Ricoeur calls "la compréhension herméneutique,"[62] except by way of our consenting to be ourselves interpreted by the work of art—which involves at once our submitting our own sense of ultimacy to interrogation by the work and our attempting in turn, with all the tact and delicacy of which we are capable, to test its deliverance about what is finally our human condition.

So the order of thought within which literary criticism moves is ineluctably religious. Yet to say this is not, of course, to say that literary criticism requires in any way to be regarded as a department of theology.

---

and not beyond them. The new poets have at the farthest limit of their experience caught a glimpse of a fugitive presence, something shared by all things in the fact that they are. This presence flows everywhere, like the light which makes things visible, and yet can never be seen as a thing in itself. It is the presence of things present, what Stevens calls 'the swarthy water/That flows round the earth and through the skies,/Twisting among the universal spaces'. In the same poem he gives this power its simplest name: 'It is being'. . . . The new poetry is therefore 'the outlines of being and its expressings, the syllables of its law'." (p. 10)

[62] *Vide* Paul Ricoeur, "Structure et herméneutique," *Esprit*, 31ᵉ année, no. 322 (Novembre 1963), pp. 596–627.

For certainly the actual movement or process of thought for the working critic does not involve his own ultimate structure of value promptly handing down what his response shall be to a story of Colette's or a Canto of Ezra Pound's. Sensibility—except in the case of a madman—is never devoured in this way by "ideology," and precisely in the measure to which the critic possesses vivaciousness of intelligence and suppleness of imagination it will be impossible for him not to be responsive, or at least not to be responsive *also*, to many visions of the world which are incompatible with his own settled perspectives. The proper business of the critic, as F. R. Leavis has well declared, "is to attain a peculiar completeness of response and to observe a peculiarly strict relevance in developing his response into commentary"—and relevance of response is guaranteed only by his having as his first concern the achievement of genuine "possession of the given poem . . . in its concrete fulness. . . ."[63] His aim is to be "the complete reader": so he does not purpose, as it were, to keep one eye on some yardstick and only one eye on the work of art. On the contrary, says Dr. Leavis:

> The critic—the reader of poetry—is indeed concerned with evaluation, but to figure him as measuring with a norm which he brings up to the object and applies from the outside is to misrepresent the process. The critic's aim is, first, to realize as sensitively and completely as possible this or that which claims his attention; and a certain valuing is implicit in the realizing. As he matures in experience of the new thing he asks, explicitly and implicitly: "Where does this come? How does it stand in relation to. . . . ? How relatively important does it seem?" And the organization into which it settles as a constituent in becoming "placed" is an organization of similarly "placed" things, things that have found their bearings with regard to one another, and not a theoretical system or a system determined by abstract considerations.[64]

But, now, though Dr. Leavis makes a fine statement in behalf of the critic's seeking a proper humility before the work of art, it is to be noticed how obedient he is to what, earlier on, we were calling the Catholic Faith of modern criticism, the notion that the only final context in which a work of literary art stands is a literary context, that, as Northrop Frye says, "works of literature . . . are created out of literature itself"[65] and that the literary universe is, therefore, essentially a universe not open but closed. This is, however, far more a matter of faith than of established fact, and it is by no means altogether certain that the process of literary judgment is

[63] F. R. Leavis, *The Common Pursuit* (London: Chatto and Windus, 1952), p. 213.
[64] *Ibid.*
[65] Northrop Frye, "Literary Criticism," in *The Aims and Methods of Scholarship in Modern Languages and Literatures*, James Thorpe, ed. (New York: Modern Language Association, 1963), p. 67.

simply a matter, as Dr. Leavis asserts, of "things" finding "their bearings with regard to one another"—within the literary universe itself. For literature as an institution is a part of the generality of culture, and though, like everything else, it clearly has its own identity and can therefore be relevantly talked about only on the basis of distinctively literary experience, it is equally clear that its appropriation, like that of any other cultural reality, must always be in relation to one's central human interests. And thus "the organization into which" Milton's Nativity Ode or *The Ancient Mariner* or *The Catcher in the Rye* "settles as a constituent in becoming 'placed' " is not merely, as Dr. Leavis supposes, "an organization of similarly 'placed' things . . . that have found their bearings with regard to one another": it is, far more, that total "organization" of value wherewith the literary critic as a man ultimately makes sense of his world and of his own humanity. So when, for example, the encounter with a work of art discloses a certain outrageous proposition—say, that the affections of Jews are like "some communal life of the pancreas . . . sensitivity/without direction" (Pound's *Canto 35*)—to be of its very poetic essence, one's advocacy of or embarrassment by the given poem will find its sanction in something larger and very much more complicated than any purely literary calendar of value. Literary criticism, in short, as Leslie Fiedler reminded us many years ago, "is always becoming 'something else,' for the simple reason that literature is always 'something else.' "[66]

It would seem, then, that those particular forms of consciousness that find human experience most richly and most adequately "thematized" by the doctrinal protocol of a specific theological tradition are no more likely (*pace* Mrs. Leavis!) than any other "pre-understanding" to have "a disabling effect" on the critic, or to require "to be struggled against." Indeed, to say nothing at all of the kind of deeply formative influence that the Christian faith has exerted throughout large ranges of our received literary tradition and of the quickened access to this tradition that training in Christian theology is likely to afford the literary critic—to say nothing at all of this, it would seem, on the face of it, that, given the large role which is played in literary interpretation by what the German hermeneutical theorists call "pre-understanding" (*Vorverständnis*[67]), the more self-conscious the critic is about the truly ultimate concerns governing his thought the less likely at least it will be that he shall bootleg his own dimly perceived

---

[66] Leslie Fielder, "Toward an Amateur Criticism," *The Kenyon Review*, 12, No. 4 (Autumn 1950), p. 564.

[67] *Vide*, for example, Rudolf Bultmann, *Glauben und Verstehen*, Vol. 1 (Tübingen: J. C. B. Mohr, 2d ed., 1954), p. 227. *Vide* also his famous essay "Is Exegesis without Presuppositions Possible?" in the collection of his shorter writings, *Existence and Faith*, Schubert M. Ogden, trans. and ed. (New York: Meridian Books, Inc., 1960), pp. 289–296.

and unconfessed convictions into his descriptive accounts of literary texts. And, of course, the discipline of theology—which Mrs. Leavis conceives to be so positively disadvantageous for criticism—is nothing other than systematic reflection on what is felt to be *ultimately* real and valuable.

Literary criticism, it need hardly be said, is never, though, an affair of the critic's hawking his own beliefs in the manner of a sectarian zealot. Indeed, in so far as he truly submits himself to the exigencies of the hermeneutical situation his own beliefs will not be any sort of "mental starch"[68] that simply stiffens automatically prescribed responses—for those beliefs, whatever they are, will bear upon themselves the pressure of that new word being spoken by the work of art, and under that pressure they will be defined and undefined and redefined as the dialectic of the hermeneutical experience proceeds.

Keeping the frontiers open between the interpreter and his text requires, of course, one of the most difficult labors of sympathy and self-transcendence that the imagination can ever be asked to perform. And it is a venture in which estimable men who are otherwise competent and impressively learned sometimes fail—not by virtue of any "theological training" such as that which Mrs. Leavis fancies to be an inevitably disabling encumbrance for the critic but simply by virtue of some inadequateness of sensibility, some default in patience or some excess of commitment to a familiar horizon. The literary situation in its most profoundly engaging forms tends to be heavily freighted with religious import, and thus the temptation to bully the work of art into reproducing or confirming one's own conceptual universe does on occasion prove to be irresistible—as when, for example, the Russian Orthodox thinker Nicolas Berdyaev produces a rendering of the Dostoevskian literature which, for all of its fascination, makes those great fictions appear to be little more than marginalia on Berdyaev's own philosophy.[69] Or, again, the literary encounter is sometimes converted into a polemical occasion when, the vision incarnate in a work of art appearing unconformable to the critic's own perspectives, it is then simply contested and quarreled with and disputed. Which is, of course, to substitute forensic maneuver for criticism. Hoxie Neale Fairchild, for example, has devoted the better part of a long and distinguished career to the study of "religious trends in English poetry," and this massive inquiry which was only recently completed is one of the adornments of American

---

[68] The term is E. M. Forster's: *vide* his essay "What I Believe" in his book *Two Cheers for Democracy* (New York: Harcourt Brace Jovanovich, Inc., 1951), p. 68: "I do not believe in Belief. . . . Faith, to my mind, is a stiffening process, a sort of mental starch, which ought to be applied as sparingly as possible."

[69] *Vide* Nicolas Berdyaev, *Dostoievsky*, Donald Attwater, trans. (New York: Sheed and Ward, Inc., 1934).

scholarship in our time.[70] But, given his very strict kind of Anglo-Catholicism, despite the many incidental felicities of historical reconstruction and critical synopsis, his major purpose is too often that of assessing the danger for the Christian faith in the relatively greater or lesser degree of heresy presented by the religiosity of this or that English poet, from the time of the Augustans to the time of Auden and Lowell. Very nearly everywhere, he sees declension from the pure Gospel in the romanticism and subjectivism and aestheticism and scientism that have been so unfortunately epidemic since the eighteenth century. And thus discourse about literary texts becomes largely an affair, however sophisticated, of assigning plus- and minus-marks.

Now from these and other similar failures in tact the earnest young people in our graduate schools are constantly seeking a "methodology" that will offer a guaranteed and certified protection. But the one answer to be given to these troubled searchings is that the best method is simply that of trying to be as intelligent as possible, of trying to be as fully aware of one's own fundamental faith-position as one can be, of trying to know as much as one can possibly learn about the various political-cultural-religious contexts to which the literature belongs with which one has dealings. And, of course, finally and most importantly, one's method must involve an intention to submit one's affections to a certain kind of discipline, for, as Hillis Miller has so finely said,

> . . . the proper model for the relation of the critic to the work he studies is not that of scientist to physical objects but that of one man to another in charity. I may love another person and know him as only love can know without in the least abnegating my own beliefs. Love wants the other person to be as he is, in all his recalcitrant particularity. As St. Augustine puts it, the lover says to the loved one, "Volo ut sis!"—"I wish you to be." If the critic approaches the poem with this kind of reverence for its integrity, it will respond to his questioning and take its part in that dialogue between reader and work which is the life of literary study.[71]

Which may be the last word that needs to be pronounced on that old and once much-vexed "problem of poetry and belief."

[70] Vide Hoxie Neale Fairchild, *Religious Trends in English Poetry*, Vol. 1: 1700–1740, *Protestantism and the Cult of Sentiment* (1939); Vol. 2: 1740–1780, *Religious Sentimentalism in the Age of Johnson* (1942); Vol. 3: 1780–1830, *Romantic Faith* (1949); Vol 4: 1830–1880, *Christianity and Romanticism in the Victorian Era* (1957); Vol. 5: 1880–1920, *Gods of a Changing Poetry* (1962); Vol. 6: 1920–1965, *Valley of Dry Bones* (1968)—all published in New York by the Columbia University Press.
[71] J. Hillis Miller, "Literature and Religion," p. 126.

4

Literature
and Religion

When Is a Literary Work
a Religious Interpretation?

Charles W. Kegley

It is attested on all sides that an unusual situation has developed in the twentieth century concerning the relation between literature and religion. Unlike previous times, many of the contemporary works universally considered among the best, are by authors who are non- or antireligious yet who appear to be wrestling with religious themes and employing undeniably religious symbols.[1] Instances come readily to mind: Sartre's *No Exit,* Camus's *The Fall* and *The Stranger,* Beckett's *Waiting For Godot.*

Although I shall later comment on these works sufficiently to document the above mentioned situation, I shall first scrutinize the assessments of this situation by religionists. In my judgment these assessments involve ambiguities and hidden assumptions the implications of which lead to confusion and error. The point of view from which I shall approach the problem is that of philosophy, more especially of esthetics, and I write in the spirit of linguistic and conceptual analysis.[2]

The first section of my paper, then, is primarily analytical and critical; the second section contains my proposal of new criteria for determining the conditions under which one may properly speak of literature as "religious interpretation" of man and his place in the universe. Through-

---

[1] I have explored some of these relationships in another connection: "Literature and Religion: A Study of Three Types of Relation in American and Western History," Proceedings VI International Congress of Aesthetics. Uppsala, Sweden, 1968.

[2] Readers who operate with religious commitments will not, it is hoped, prejudge the task as unsympathetic, negative, and/or trivial because of this approach. For, although the remarks do aim chiefly at clarification, they eventuate in questions of substance and content both for literature and for religion.

out this paper I shall be trying to clarify and evaluate three notions, a work of art as (1) an "interpretation of religion,"—the case in which a work of art actually takes religion as its subject matter; (2) as a religious interpretation of life—man and his destiny, and; (3) the notion of religious interpretation. I shall reject the first and the third, and indicate the criteria for the meaningful employment of the second.

I

What first arouses the philosopher's suspicion that there are some ambiguities and confusions in contemporary writing about literature vis-a-vis religion in this century is the readiness, often eagerness, with which religionists hail this literature as religious interpretation or as interpretations of religion in life.[3] To be sure, it is a radically new form of religious expression, and its treatment of religious themes and symbols is a far cry from the traditional literature, for example, from Dante's or Bunyan's, to T. S. Eliot's, or W. H. Auden's, as one easily imagines. But it is, we are assured, religious in spirit and capable of exciting theologians to fresh and creative inquiry. Thus, one acute and productive theological critic writes that this literature has a "negatively theological character"; another no less eloquent spokesman says that Eugene O'Neill, for instance, "was antireligious only insofar as the object of the quest is concerned; he was always extremely religious in terms of the quest itself."[4]

These, and a score of statements like them, invite scrutiny.

First, the terminology "religious interpretation," like the expressions "economic interpretation" and "political interpretation," is likely to confuse rather than inform. The adjective either swallows up the noun or distorts the ordinary and accepted meaning which it has in esthetics. The root notion of interpretation, as applied to literature, involves explication and elucidation, but it goes beyond these. Thus, whereas explication seeks to determine, as Beardsley well states it, "the contextual meaning of a group of words, such as metaphor . . . ," and elucidation tries to fix upon the world in which the work operates, such as the character and motives which are not therein stated, *interpretation* proper goes beyond these.[5] It asks:

---

[3] American novelist and critic, Herbert Krause, commenting on this paper said, "I wish you would study the question, *why* theologians-turned-critics embrace so enthusiastically the implications of the religious in nonreligious writers." I agree that this question merits a studied reply, but it would carry one too far away from the main purposes of this essay to undertake it here, even if one were competent to do so, which I doubt I am.

[4] See Nathan A. Scott, Jr., *The Broken Center* (New Haven and London: Yale University Press, 1965), p. ix, and Tom Driver in *Man in the Modern Theatre* (Richmond: John Knox Press, 1965), p. 51.

[5] Monroe C. Beardsley, *Aesthetics* (New York: Harcourt Brace Jovanovich, Inc., 1958), p. 407. Another excellent discussion is John Hospers, *Meaning and Truth in the Arts* (Chapel Hill: University of North Carolina Press, 1947).

What are the themes of this poem, novel, drama? What "statements" or theses, if any, does it affirm or deny, implicitly or explicitly? (I shall later have more to say about themes and theses in contemporary literature.) Now, once we are clear and in general agreement about what interpretation is, it is awkward and misleading to speak of *interpretation* as being "religious" any more than its being esthetic or economic. For each of these studies has its methods and aims and stands on its own. They are independent of, and dare never be prostituted by, any particular stance or a set of assumptions. For this reason I do not think it proper to speak of *religious* interpretation, of *religious* or *Christian* ethics, and the like. Interpretation, like philosophy, aims to be neutral methodologically. As Amos Wilder succinctly states it: ". . . we may speak informally of a Christian discrimination or criticism in the sense that theological and biblical insights are invoked. But there is, properly speaking, no such thing as a Christian aesthetic."[6] In his latest work, *The New Voice,* he is equally emphatic: ". . . I reject the idea of a specifically Christian criticism whether in terms of the experience of the believer or of theological categories."[7]

We shall be told, of course, that we are flying in the face of ordinary usage, for it is as common a practice to speak of a religious interpretation as it is of an economic interpretation of history. What this usually is taken to mean is simply that a literary work is examined, is seen through the eyes of religion. In the case of so-called religious interpretation, this seemingly harmless choice of glasses through which to view something is dangerously ambiguous. What constitutes a religious interpretation? *Which* historic or extant religion? What *set* of assumptions? The presuppositions and affirmations of Buddhism and of Hinduism, for example, are quite different from those of Christianity, even as are the contrary assumptions of various forms of Christianity. If we have no criteria for deciding which set of affirmations is to be employed, how can we talk about so general a thing as "religious interpretation"? Furthermore, how does one decide when such an interpretation is imposed upon or read into the literary work in question rather than discovered in it? Because "religion" is generally agreed to be an existential affair—a phenomenon which involves commitment and deep feeling—how does this feature function in interpretation? One hopes that we are not required once again to deal with the hoary error that only a committed religionist really is capable of interpreting a given work—even to know whether it is or is not religious.

What these reflections and statements such as critic Driver's regarding O'Neill's "extremely religious" quest are based upon, I believe, is the widely held view of Paul Tillich that religion is that which concerns

---

[6] *Theology and Modern Literature* (Cambridge: Harvard University Press, 1958), p. 77. Paul Tillich has equally blunt statements; *see*: *The Theology of Paul Tillich,* Charles W. Kegley, ed. (New York: The Macmillan Co., 1957).
[7] New York: Herder and Herder, 1969, p. 211.

us ultimately. Hence it is not the answers O'Neill, Sartre, or Beckett expound —if they offer any answers at all—but the seriousness and persistence of their quest, which is what makes their work religious. I shall return to the notion of "ultimate concern" shortly, but first a few words of clarification. It is quite correct that whether or not or to what extent a given work of literature is religious or not is *not* to be decided on the ground of its being pro- or antireligious—however this may be defined. For surely a novel or a play is no less concerned with religious issues if it consists, in whole or in its parts, of a rejection, burlesque, or condemnation of traditional or widely accepted religious beliefs and practices. (This may help to explain the allegedly "negatively theological character" of O'Neill, that is, that he is more antitraditional and antiestablishment than antireligious.) The violent opponent of religion is obviously discussing religion as truly as is the fanatical advocate. Are certain works of Marx or Nietzsche, for example, any less interpretations of religion because they condemn religion and religiously inspired morality?

What about the subjective, psychological side—are they religious interpretations by virtue of the deep concern of the author and the effective way in which this is exhibited in and conveyed through the literary work?

There are two reasons why this stress on "deeply religious quest" leads to error. In the first place, this bases one's judgment on the intentions and motives of the writer. In the second place, this and similar expressions are ambiguous.

As to the first, apparently critic Driver does not find the religious elements demonstrably present in the literary and dramatic work of art and so he locates them in the impulses and intentions of the writer. This option, however, is burdened with all the liabilities of the intentionalist fallacy. Familiar as these are to most estheticians, it is worth summarily recalling them as follows.

First, speech about an artist's intention frequently confuses (a) the end or goal for which an artist undertakes his work with, (b) what the artist intends to say in some part or parts of his work. An interpretation must be concerned with the work of art as a whole. The latter—what the artist intends to say in his work—concerns meaning, which is quite different from aim. My intention in shouting "Look out!" may be quite different from the meaning of the phrase, the latter depending, as it does, on context.

Second, much writing about intention is not about either of the above concepts but concerns, rather, the attitudes, conscious or otherwise, which lead the artist to select his themes, or the attitudes which "condition" both that choice and the materials and ways in which he treats them.

Third, and still more serious, it is usually difficult, often impossible, to know what an artist's intention is. It is little help to say, "Ask him" or, "See, here he explicitly told us his intention." As to the former, the artist's not infrequent reply is, "I don't really know." As to the latter, his answer may be inflicted with deception, conscious or unconscious. Painters are notorious for admitting that they often had no clear notion of what they were after.

Fourth, artists often have several and mixed intentions, and these frequently change as they proceed.

Finally, even if all these ambiguities and possible confusions could be removed, and if the artist himself were to say, "This work interprets (or does not interpret) certain religious themes or theses," we should still have to ask whether he is competent to judge the truth or accuracy of his statement. He may be a very incompetent judge as to what his work actually did in this respect. For, one of the problems which occasion this inquiry is precisely the fact that ambiguity and confusions surround the concept of literary and artistic "interpretation of religion."

We spoke above of a second danger concerning judgments about a writer's intentions or motives, and this is the ambiguity of such phrases as "sincerely questing," "strenuously seeking," when these are identified with religion and the so-called religious quest. Again an important element of truth must be separated from what is likely to be an erroneously drawn conclusion. The truth is that, as the poet put it, "there is more faith in honest doubt" than there is in gullible, uncritical, noninvolved assent to religious creeds and dogmas. Applied to the authors we have cited, no extended documentation is necessary to show that they are wrestling with doubts and quests for meaning. But *when is* doubting and questing *religious*? Surely it is not religious per se, though it may have implications for religious thought. As Esslin puts it, we must make a clear distinction between a religious interpretation of life, on the one hand, and the stimulus to think about religious issues which any artist or work of art may afford.[8] In the history and literature of the world's religions, doubt is almost always seen in juxtaposition to faith, and faith, in turn, has at its center trust and commitment. Here, one suspects, is the suppressed premise which leads to a false conclusion, that is, the assumption that honest doubt and sincere questing lead to or imply some kind of faith, and hence are religious in character. But they need not be. Nathan Scott repeatedly assures us that for Beckett, Dürrenmatt, O'Neill, surely for Joyce and Kafka, ". . . what we face is Silence, an Absence, a Threatening Emptiness at the center. . . . Our dominant metaphors," he continues, "are still metaphors of death and privation."[9] The world of Camus's *The Rebel* is the world of rebellion against meaninglessness, it is not one of rapport with the sacred. So, if the

---

[8] Martin Esslin, *The Theatre of the Absurd* (New York: Doubleday & Co., 1961), p. 22. I shall argue, in Part II of this paper, that the crux of this distinction is the "thesis" of the artist, as thesis is there described.

[9] Scott, pp. 78–79.

answer to the quest is flatly in terms of agnosticism and atheism, it is likely to be confusing to speak of the religious character of the contemporary writings we have cited.

Similarly, what are we to say of the characterization of modern literature as being "negatively theological"? In view of what was said just above, there is a superficial sense in which this sounds correct; at least it is clearly negative, that is, denying rather than affirming, rebelling rather than "*accepting* the fact that we are accepted" by the Ground of Being, to recall another of Tillich's favorite themes. But there is an elemental confusion here in language and in the concepts involved. Theology—not St. Thomas's nor Luther's, not Tillich's nor Bultmann's, but theology as an academic discipline—is defined in the Oxford dictionary as the study which treats of God, His nature and attributes, and His relation with man and the universe. What, pray tell, is "negative theology"? It is difficult to imagine how a literature which is agnostic can be described as negatively theological, and it is impossible to see, in the absence of some clear definition and citing of instances, how a literature which is atheistic is negatively theological. Its nonexistence or sterility is foreordained by virtue of its denial that there *is* any God to study.[10]

If, as critic Amos Wilder expressed it, one were to say that ". . . God is using the essentially *pagan* reality of art . . . to provoke the church, to needle it, to introduce ferment into it," the theological critic would, by this distinction and caution, escape the confusion we are elucidating.[11] For we should distinguish carefully between talking about a work of art as being religious or theological on the one hand, and as constituting a stimulus to religious and theological reflection on the other hand.

One more critical comment is required on this matter of quest and of negative answers as these are associated with "ultimate concern." It is by now a standard criticism of Tillich's famous definition that it is too broad, and so allows one to include under "religion" and "religious" phenomena which might as properly be called psychological, philosophical, or simply descriptive of man's basic interests and needs. This observation is relevant to one of our main questions, that is, are the works, for example, of Sartre, Camus, Beckett, Ionesco, O'Neill religious interpretations of life? If, to be sure, religion *is* that which concerns man ultimately, and if the authors of these works are therein voicing their ultimate concerns, the question appears to be answered by definition. What's wrong with this

---

[10] The apparent or surface meaning of the statement we are studying probably is that in contemporary literature we encounter works which do not go beyond the point of the delineation and analysis of man's condition, that is, his alienation, despair, sense of meaninglessness, of futility, and the like. This, however, scarcely makes a work "religious" or theological, or if it does, then so many works are religious or theological that the term becomes uselessly vague.

[11] *The New Voice*, p. 246.

proposal? Two things. First, the definition is open to rejection, as are all definitions of general terms such as "art," "beauty," and the like. The fact is that no formal, genus-species, definition of religion is possible, any more than is a definition of such general terms as "art" and "law."[12] Second, it is so broad that one has no way of knowing where to draw the line between specifically religious literature and that in which any generally human and serious concerns are voiced. What we need, but do not yet have, are precise criteria for determining the conditions under which a literary work may be said to constitute a religious interpretation of life.

The preceding considerations, especially the question of definitions and the quest for clear and workable criteria, lead us to make one more point before we offer a fresh proposal. This is the view that religion always and everywhere concerns not merely man's condition but his destiny—his "redemption," to use the standard theological term, or his reconciliation with the ground of his being, to use Tillichian terminology. There is a long and powerful tradition in philosophy of religion, and a shorter one in phenomenology and the scientific study of religion, which supports this claim. Two philosophers in particular, William James and Henry Nelson Wieman, have argued that a universal and identifying feature of "the religious hypothesis" is a belief that ultimately goodness and creativity are in control, not evil or destructiveness, nor an ambiguous and indeterminable mixture of both. Wieman argues that this is an essential factor in religion and that it is foggy headed to talk about a certain work of art as being religious or an interpretation of religion when it is merely descriptive, diagnostic, and axiologically agnostic or neutral. Thus he writes:

> I do not curtly dismiss art which reflects "the despair in the human predicament." I deeply appreciate some art which does that. I have been disgusted with the kind of art which seeks "to hide any of the human situation in its depths of estrangement and despair."
>
> On the other hand, I think only confusion results from saying that Picasso's "Guernica" "is the best present-day Protestant religious picture." One is spreading religion far too thin if one identifies it with art which articulates doom, despair, and the torn world. This articulation of despair has its own great value. By bringing our despair clearly up into consciousness, we are, in a sense, liberated from it. We can then deal intelligently *with* our own despair. This is the function of art—to make us conscious of the deeper levels of experience. Art which exposes the depth of man's despair may lead on to art which points the way of redemption. But the latter only is religious. Mere despair and the portrayal of it is not in itself religious, even though such art may be of great value. Despair should be portrayed in art as well as in other experiences which profoundly shape the life of man. That is precisely what I meant in my statement

[12] The latter and I have argued in another context. "Observations on Legal Vis-a-Vis Moral Thought and Life," *The Personalist*, 51, no. 1 (Winter 1970), pp. 58–84.

quoted above. But I cannot see that art which portrays despair is religious until it begins to indicate the way of salvation.[13]

If this judgment is correct, then many of the alleged works of interpretation of religion, especially those marked by nihilism and despair, should not be so categorized.

This issue calls for considerable discrimination, and I suggest the following as a beginning. First, the present question is to be distinguished from one discussed earlier, namely, whether a work is an interpretation of religion depending on the positive or negative judgment it pronounces. For here it is questioned whether in many works *any* judgment about "what casts the final throw" is involved. Second, those who build the axiological claim into the definition of religion have every logical right to do so. But they then appear to contradict universal linguistic practice and much empirical evidence. Thus, it is no doubt correct that theism, deism, Hartshorne's Whiteheadian pan-entheism, and all similar versions of a basic theistic outlook *do* involve this affirmative thesis or "faith." But do all "religions" do this? Do Buddhism and Hinduism? Is the Manichaen tradition in Christianity thereby excluded, and if so, on what grounds? It would require an extended study to answer that question; the answer is far from clear but probably is "No." Finally, considerations of this sort render questionable, or mistaken, the judgment previously examined, namely concerning "this negatively theological character of modern literature." What precisely does this phrase mean? One suspects that it means, at least in part, that the authors in question stop short of affirmation of any of the traditionally expressed statements of confidence in the ontological status of goodness. But "negative" is not a neutral, a "stopping short of" term. It implies rejection, a vote of "No," as William James would probably have expressed it, and, as we shall see, much of the literature is of this sort. But then one is at a loss to know what "negative theology" is.

II

The proposal we are finally ready to make may be tentatively stated as follows: A literary work of art may be called a religious interpretation of life of its discernible (a) themes, (b) theses, and (c) symbols, are characteristically those of historic or extant world religions; if they are not, it probably should not be so called. So stated, these elements may be said to constitute the sufficient and necessary conditions for determining what is a religious interpretation in literature and drama. After making clear what I mean by

[13] *The Empirical Theology of Henry Nelson Wieman*, Robert W. Bretall, ed. (Carbondale and Edwardsville: Southern Illinois University Press, 1963), pp. 236–237.

each of these three terms, I shall employ them or test them out, so to speak, with reference to three prime candidates among literary works.[14]

A theme is described by an abstract noun or phrase, such as the joys of reading, the viciousness of deliberate cruelty, courage, the law of compensation in life; the theme of Job, for instance, is the suffering of the righteous man. Now it is a neat move, which the esthetic critic may find it difficult to make at times, to draw a distinction between a theme and the subject matter. Professor Beardsley holds that the "subject" is denoted by a concrete rather than an abstract noun, for example, *a* civil war, the Taming of *the* Shrew. We need not press the point here, but I suspect that this distinction is difficult to maintain consistently, as in the case of an essay by Emerson which I deliberately cited above. For surely this is a literary work whose theme *and* subject appear to be the law of compensation—or tolerance, and so on—in life.

A thesis, unlike a theme, always involves an affirmation or a denial. Thus it can, again unlike a theme, be judged true or false. The theme of Plato's *symposium* is love; the thesis Socrates espouses therein concern the nature, forms, stages, and comparative values of these forms of love. We ponder—or practice—"love," but we agree or disagree with what Plato or Paul or Freud say *about* love.

With symbol we are less likely to achieve a clear, satisfactory, and workable criterion. We are dealing in this study exclusively with literary symbols and this field itself is plagued with ambiguity and disagreement. Yet we can and must say some things about symbols in literature, about their relation to themes, and about their occurrence in religion, because the connection here is very important and interesting, though frustratingly difficult to explicate. Symbols connote, they point to a meaning or set of meanings, and their power to "move" the reader depends in part on the reader's degree of awareness of these meanings. They may be dynamic—actions, gestures, and so on—or static—objects, markings—and, unlike signs, they are abstract, that is, they represent, remind, or refer, as Suzanne Langer so well puts it.[15] They are *vehicles* for the conception of objects, events, conditions. As Paul Tillich always stressed, the *religious* symbol is material taken out of the world of finite things, to point beyond itself to the ground of being and of meaning. Tillich's statement reads: ". . . the symbol actually participates in the power of that which it symbolizes." Again: "The religious symbol has special character in that it points to the ultimate level of being, to ultimate reality, to being itself. That which is

[14] No one, I believe, has more clearly stated the case for theme and theses than Monroe C. Beardsley, and I acknowledge gladly my debt to him at this point. *See Aesthetics, Toward a Philosophy of Criticism* (New York: Harcourt Brace Jovanovich, Inc., 1958), pp. 403 and *passim*.

[15] *Feeling and Form* (New York: Charles Scribner's Sons, 1953) and *Reflections on Art* (Baltimore: Johns Hopkins University Press, 1958).

the ground of being is the object to which the religious symbol points."[16] By no means are all philosophers willing to go that far, and most stop short of Tillich's famous claim that a religious symbol "participates in the power of the ultimate to which it points. . . ." This is so partly because he never made clear what this phrase means.

We now have enough with which to work with symbols in literature, and need to add only that theme and symbol often have a confusing relationship, indeed are often indistinguishable. For example, a theme of Hawthorne's *The Scarlet Letter* is adultery, but this is also a central symbol. In Albee's *Tiny Alice* we encounter the intermixture of theme and symbol; in fact there are so many symbols here that we become dizzy trying to fix upon their meanings with any assurance. So symbols may be taken as a "soft," not as a "hard," a sure and certain criterion. They furnish a supporting criterion for determining whether a literary work is an interpretation of religion. But they may play the determining role.

With this too brief discussion of theme, thesis, and symbol, what might be said about certain prime candidates for literary works which are religious interpretations or interpretations of religion? Consider three: Sartre's *No Exit,* Camus's *The Fall,* and Samuel Beckett's *Waiting for Godot.*

In the case of Sartre, as, indeed, of other contemporary artists, the art form chosen becomes for the artist a way of working out his philosophy of life. In this respect, as Focillion and others have said about painting, the art(s) perform a function which formerly was performed by religious thought and experience.[17] Illustrative of this is the deep feeling of involvement one experiences in the works of Sartre, Camus, and Beckett and this involvement is both on the part of the artist *qua* creator and on the part of the contemplator of their works of art. Commitment and involvement, it hardly needs be said, are characteristics of religious phenomena. Their presence, however, is no guarantee that the work of art expressing that involvement is a religious interpretation.

It is not, however, on this feature of Sartre, or on the effects *No Exit* proves capable of eliciting that I wish to dwell, nor to allow to hang the answer to the question concerning literary interpretations as religious. It is rather on the work itself, because *No Exit* is probably a

---

[16] *Religious Symbolism,* F. E. Johnson, ed. (New York: Harper & Brothers, 1955), pp. 109–10. In a parallel discussion, Tillich writes: "A real symbol points to an object which never can become an object. Religious symbols represent the transcendent but do not make the transcendent immanent. They do not make God a part of the empirical world." In *Symbolism in Religious Literature,* Rollo May, ed. (New York: George Braziller, 1961), pp. 77–78.

[17] It is worth mentioning, but it would carry us far afield were we to follow up another revealing aspect of the work of Genet and Artaud, that is, their fascination with myth and ritual, both prominent features of the religions of the world.

paradigm of a "nonreligious artist," indeed, an atheist, dealing centrally and specifically with religious themes and symbols.[18] Among these themes and symbols are: (1) estrangement and alienation versus the possibility of communication and rapport; (2) the quest for self-identity; (3) possible objects of ultimate commitment, with insistence upon the ambiguity of the ethical, all expressed in terms of freedom and responsibility, and, finally; (4) the "root category," as Anders Nygren would call it, of religion, that is, the eternal. There is neither the space nor the necessity here to engage in an extended exegesis of *No Exit*. Fortunately, this has been done, indeed several times, with great competence, as, for example, in Howard Parsons's "Existential Hell."[19] I wish to amplify briefly the four points made above.

Just as rapport between man and God and between man and man has been a steady theme of all religions—indeed this traditionally has been one definition of religion—so in *No Exit,* communication, rapport, the sharing of life, or, more accurately in this case, the apparent impossibility of this, is a central theme. All three characters in hell voice and strive for the trust and communication which they sense is necessary for human, that is, authentic existence. They find themselves, on the contrary, condemned to torture each other, hence Sartre's now classic sentence, "Hell is other people." Hell is the tie which binds, to use the phrase from the old hymn, but which, instead of being blessed, is the tie that never kills because it never releases. So isolation and alienation in the ever-living eyes—none of them has eyelids!—of others is their permanent relationship. Each person, in his relationship to the others, is incapable of creative interchange because each is dependent, dominant, and detached. These are three concepts which have a prominent place both in theology and in the psychological work of Karen Horney, and the philosophical work of Charles Morris, among many others.

Second, as "the nature and destiny of man," to use Reinhold Neibuhr's phrase, is central to religion, so Sartre makes central the quest for self-identity on the part of Garcin the coward, Inez the introvert, Estelle the sensual-sadist. Garcin concludes, "I'm dead. Dead and done with." Estelle concludes that she is a shattered crystal and "a hollow dummy," Inez that she is ". . . a dead twig, ready for the burning." The fact that these judgments are acidly negative is irrelevant. What is relevant is that the question, "What am I?" is one of Sartre's central preoccupations.

Third, all three characters are in hell *because* of their "bad faith"; as in Garcin's case, because of his failure even to use *or* to abuse his freedom, and in the cases of Inez and Estelle, because they possess neither a

---

[18] Sartre identifies "Heidegger and myself" as atheists, even saying that he (Sartre) is "a representative of atheistic existentialism." *Jean Paul Sartre Existentialism and Humanism,* Philip Mailet, trans. (London: Methuen & Co., Ltd., 1946), pp. 26, 27.

[19] *The Journal of Religious Thought,* 31, no. 1 (1964–1965), pp. 25–42.

capacity for social responsibility nor for acting as free persons. They are incapable of achieving self-identity through courageous choice. Part of the power of *No Exit* is in the fact that Sartre's analysis is cast in the contemporary psychological terms (appropriate to present-day religious thought) rather than in the medieval terminology of out-dated metaphysics and morals.

Fourth, the category, and in a sense, the symbol of the eternal is central in *No Exit*. So Inez observes, "We've lots of time in hand. *All Time* . . . So here we are, forever."[20] In Sartre's hell time *has* a stop—there is no "break," no meaning to anticipation, because what goes on goes on indefinitely. Past and future are both fixed, not merely the past, as in finite existence. Again, hell never releases, as we saw in another context; just as, presumably, heaven, if there be such a condition, always relates. Finally, Sartre's entire analysis is premised on the view that hell is not a consequent event in time, but is an unending present.

The step from Sartre to Camus is a short one, and the terminology and even more the symbols and metaphors congenial to the interpretation of religious themes are just as emphatic in Camus. His very titles seem to say indirectly, "The problems I am treating are of such depth that only the essential metaphors of biblical religion are rich and big enough to carry my meaning." For example, *The Fall, The Descent of the Dove, The Plague, The Stranger*. Indeed, the parallel with Sartre in *No Exit* is explicit, because Jean Baptiste Clemance, the narrator in *The Fall*, comes upon the realization that from the heights of Eden where he was the Patron and Protector of Justice to the widows and orphans of Paris,—note the symbols—he has fallen into hell. Camus's hell is the condition in which Clemance is forced to realize, and to be known, for what he really is, a creature whose predominant feature is self-love. So with enormous skill and perceptivity, Camus probes the motivations of his central character, delineates their passion to dominate and use (shades of Kant) other people, their capacity for self-deception and duplicity, all through the abuse of freedom. There are important differences between the causes, nature, and consequences of Clemance's fall, that of Adam and Eve, and in Paul's description in the biblical accounts. But again, as in the case of Sartre, this is a matter of interpretation: *what* is interpreted are the motivations and conditions of man.

An examination of Beckett's *Waiting for Godot* would afford further documentation, now from a Dublin-born author, of the same kind of themes. There is a psychological, axiological, and ontological significance to the phenomenon and symbol of "waiting," as Beckett portrays it. The parallel with the basic Judeo-Christian formula of grace and response is

---

[20] *No Exit and The Flies*, Stuart Gilbert, Eng. version (New York: Knopf, 1949), pp. 57–61.

too striking to miss, too clear to require extended exegesis. The theme is persistent from Abraham and Isaac to Paul and Luther. The symbol is so tantalizing that readers and critics have written extensively concerning its meaning—or its ambiguity.

Judged in the light of the criteria proposed, it is clear that the three works cited satisfy these requirements as regards themes and symbols, this irrespective of the fact that they were written by non- or antireligious authors. One of the main results of this paper is to raise questions about the nature and validity, or perhaps we should use the softer term, propriety, of the criterion of thesis. What are we to conclude if no thesis is stated in the work under consideration, or if it is contained only implicitly and not explicitly? The case of Beckett's *Waiting for Godot* was selected because the thesis appears to be that the waiting is fruitless, indeed pointless. What if the thesis, as most critics seem to agree in this instance, is ambiguous? Or, to take a different case, what if Sartre's summary thesis is, or is agreed to be, that life is ultimately hopeless and is hell? What are we to say if it is Camus's thesis that the Fall is inevitable and meaningless? The answer to all these questions hinges, in the context of our analysis, upon whether we agree that religion is inherently affirmative and redemptive in character. If we do, then we must conclude that these works are not religious interpretations.

5

The Twilight of Drama: from Ego to Myth*

Tom F. Driver

Try as I will, I cannot see that the Age of Aquarius, whatever its virtues, will be an age of theater. *A fortiori* it will not be an age of drama.

I have been asked to write about the future of drama under the title "Emerging Images in Arts of the Word." Yet I have great trouble envisioning the future of the drama and even greater trouble imagining it as an art of the word. Such it has been throughout most of its history, certainly in the periods we regard as those of its greatest glory. But the contemporary theater has, to all intents and purposes, forsaken the word. It is not clear that it will regain it in the time we can see ahead.

Take, by way of departure, that theatrical offering which has been no less bold than to announce the dawning of the Age of Aquarius. *Hair* is a wild success. It has kept the box office of the Biltmore Theater active for four years with little sign of slackening. In addition, as everyone knows, it has been exported through the length and breadth of the land and throughout the world. How dare one say that even as it announces the beginning of the new age under the sign of peace and joy it does not also augur a renaissance of theatrical art?

However much pleasure *Hair* has given to me, to my children, and to the populace at large, its virtues lie almost wholly in its music and not in its use of resources that can be specifically named theatrical, let alone dramatic. It is a common experience of those seeing the show to be disappointed if they have previously listened to the record album. On disk, *Hair* has more vitality than on stage, and this is no accident. It is not simply the result of a superior studio performance. Every production of *Hair*, in fact

* Reprinted by permission of the Author and his agent, James Brown Associates, Inc. Copyright © 1972 by Tom F. Driver.

almost every performance, contains novel elements; but nowhere has it achieved the power that it has on the recording.

This is the more amazing when we consider that on stage the show is full of much playing around, an abundance of that jest and gesture which it is the function of actors always to provide, and when we further consider that the staging of this work catapulted its director, Tom O'Horgan, into fame, establishing his reputation as a kind of theatrical genius. A genius Mr. O'Horgan may be, but his talent does not run to what, by any traditional yardstick may be called theatrical.

For one thing, and this is perhaps basic, O'Horgan has only the most obvious sense of how to employ stage space. He uses a good deal of spillover from the stage proper to the house; he introduces a lot of running up and down the aisles; the actors are likely to be found at any moment making hoopla in the balcony as well as on the stage; they will swing on ropes from forward boxes over free air into proscenium territory and back again; they will stand on ledges or improvised balconies high at the rear of the stage area, and they will enter and leave the stage space through the wings or whatever with the greatest *élan* and abandonment. All these antics belong to the general repertoire of your young director who has been "liberated" from the restrictions of the fixed stage, but none of them results in a *theatrical* realization unless it happens by some exercise of taste and judgment that we finally sense ourselves, while being in the theater, to be the occupants of a particular finite space in which the parts are subordinated to the whole, in which every minute gesture succeeds at last in defining the parameters of the available space and laying hold of it with significant movement.

Such articulation one will find in the best examples of dance, whether ancient, modern, or contemporary. One may find it fully exemplified in the work of Martha Graham and in that of her better progeny. One found it also, to take a famous example from recent theater, in the Royal Shakespeare Company's production of *The Homecoming* by Harold Pinter. Yet while this quality is not infrequently to be met with in the dance it is, for better or worse, increasingly rare in the theater. One is most apt to find it if he searches out some of the old troupers, of whom Miss Graham is herself one, and of whom another, to take a contrasting example, is Ethel Merman. An important question to ask is why the contemporary theater has been unwilling or unable to avail itself of dance, which is conspicuously absent from those avant-garde productions that would seem most to require it.

The O'Horgan technique, if that's what it is (perhaps it would be better to call it a style), is almost the opposite of the dance-like and the theatrical. It is as if he and a number of other directors who are his contemporaries have set out to destroy theatrical space rather than to use it to full potential. Space, we might say, is not their medium. Their forte is of an utterly different order and many be called improvisation.

There exists a kind of improvisation which fulfills itself in the creative use of space, but in and of itself improvisation does not necessarily require this bent, and in the contemporary theater it has forsaken it. Instead, improvisation here means the coming together of certain events, gestures, games, and playful innovations in a particular moment of time. It is time which rules, not space. To aim toward the filling of space would be to aim for the creation of something which was, in and of itself, memorable. That is to say, a form in some sense or other ideal.

The formation and fulfillment of finite space belongs to the order of a society which knows what it is about. This activity has the character of maintaining an established sense of proportion, even if one refines and enlarges that sense as one goes along. It will be associated, therefore, with a certain social tradition, with a sense of the difficulty, craft, labor, discipline, and artfulness of achieving that which is formally correct. And while I describe this in vocabulary which perhaps seems a little academic and stuffy, it is of great vitality and freshness whenever we see it happening.

The aim of *Hair* and O'Horgan (which I take here as emblematic of the thrust of the contemporary theater, choosing an example which, while not the most pure, is surely the best known) is not in any sense to achieve an ideal form. It strives not for that which seems "right" in space but for that which is fortuitous in the moment. It coincides with that emphasis on the *now* which is so thoroughly characteristic of contemporary culture.

The virtues and pleasures of *Hair* have almost nothing to do with anything we could name by the term proportion, let alone anything to do with narrative line, establishment and development of character, or definition of the limits of human experience. On the contrary, the virtues of *Hair* lie in its rhythm. Its excellence is, as I said, a function of its music, and what is particularly right about the music is its rhythmic drive. In short, we have here an art which cares not a fig for anything that Nietzsche or anyone else might call Apollonian. It is utterly devoted to Dionysus and his ecstasy. Wherever it approaches this, it fills the spectator with mirthful joy, even at times a joy touched with sadness, as in the threnody which is the penultimate moment in the show.

The ending of *Hair* is astonishing in its rapid shifts of mood. The finale begins with the surrealistic antiwar song, "Three-Five-Zero-Zero," its lyrics at once biting and mysterious. The driving rhythm of this song and its raucous intonation by the cast yields, by a rapid modulation, to a recitative of Hamlet's soliloquy, "What a piece of work is man." Here again, rhythm takes precedence over meaning, though I do not mean to say that the latter is insignificant. Yet the meaning tends to escape us because of its appearance in this particular context. Nothing previous in the show prepares for it, and it leads clearly to nothing thereafter. Perhaps the passage was chosen because of its references to contagion and pestilence.

From this piece of high art so unexpectedly thrown into the insolent musical we move almost directly to a song notable for its banality, yet this also seems to "work." "Good Morning, Starshine" is nothing more than a ditty. If its rhythm is nevertheless suitable at this point, it is precisely because of its simplicity, even its naïveté, after the more sophisticated beat of the Hamlet recitative. Finally we move to the popular rhythmic song which I am inclined to think is, in context, a lament—"Let the Sunshine In."

The succession of these apparently disjointed moods makes a very striking effect and gives to the musical an almost dizzying ending. The audience is expected to, and frequently does, move into a state of delirium. Thereafter, it is customary for the cast to invite the audience to join in the dancing on stage. By the time I saw the production, this had become routinized and no genuine Dionysiac release was allowed to happen, but I have no doubt that the potential for it existed in the audience. Only the fatigue of the cast and the stage manager, who have to do eight shows a week, prevented a kind of orgy on the stage. The show's one occasion for dancing was aborted.

My affection for this show helps me, I think, to discern those things about it which are, in their context, exactly right and perhaps right also in the social context in which it was written and in which we all see it. At the same time, I have no hesitation in saying that it marks not the renaissance of theater but its demise. It is as if the theater were yearning to be something that it has not recently been and indeed never has been; or if it was, that was at a time when no "institution" of theater existed and when society was of a very different order from what it is now.

My remarks about the antitheatrical tendencies of contemporary theater are not meant to suggest that the theater is merely undergoing one of its periodic changes. I do not mean to say theater of the type represented by *Hair*, by The Living Theater, by the Theater Performance Group, by most of the work of The Open Theater, by the majority of what is produced at the Cafe La Mama, by experiments going on constantly in university and college theaters, and so on—that all this represents a departure from the theater with which those of us over thirty were familiar in the days of our youth. Changes in style and form, even severe and radical changes, have marked the course of the modern theater ever since the beginning of the nineteenth century. Nor is it as if the theater were an unchanging form before that time. One who is conversant with the history of theater will recognize how relative a phenomenon it is, judged by its forms and styles. All that being true, I am suggesting something much more radical at the present time—a fundamental change in spirit, beside which the mutations in theater and drama from the days of Aeschylus until a decade ago seem pale. What we are watching now is not simply a change in theatrical style but a shift away from the theatrical sensibility entirely. It may be discerned from two points of view.

First consider the sensibilities of our theater practitioners who have been the most aggressive, indeed the most creative, over the past decade.

Almost anywhere you look you can discern the tendency I have already noted in *Hair*, which is to make of the theater something that it has never been in all of modern history. This tendency is to be observed not only in the directors and the performers but also in the writers. It is present as much in Sam Shepard as it is in Tom O'Horgan. It is noticeably present even in the work of the more "literary" of the contemporary playwrights, in the style of Israel Horowitz, Terrence McNally, Lanford Wilson, LeRoi Jones, and many, many others. Anticipations of it reach far back into the history of the modern theater and are noticeably present in that strange figure, Antonin Artaud, who has become posthumously a kind of guru of contemporary theater. Artaud dreamed of an impossible theater, which could not exist, and to which he gave himself utterly in a strange cascade of writings that lambasted the existing theater and promulgated one which, for all its fascination with concrete, gestural reality, can only exist in the head of its dreamer. In the modern theater, which is now passé, this supra- (hence anti-) theatrical tendency was coupled with a deeply ironic view of man and his world. I have described it at length in a chapter entitled, "Irony and the Destructive Fulfillment of Theater" in my history of the modern theater.[1] Since about 1960 we have passed into a new cultural period, not only in theater but in all other arts as well, and the destructive fulfill- ment of the theater seems now virtually complete. This does not mean that people are not writing and producing plays. It means that a certain theatri- cal instinct, if I may call it that, has vanished, and creativity strains to find a new vehicle for expression. To the extent that this straining is tied to the theater as we have known it, it seems increasingly pitiful, like a fledgling bird that attempts to fly without leaving the nest. Watching this theater, one dreams not of a larger and more adequate nest but of a departure into another dimension, of which as yet the fledgling has no knowledge but toward which it is driven by a kind of instinct, an innate and inarticulate sense that one stage is past and another yet to come.

We may see all this from yet a second point of view that is more sociological. An unprejudiced observer of our society would not conclude that the theater is important to us. Certainly he could not reach such a conclusion from any statistical data. Whereas in times past the theater stood near the center of culture and represented a focal point for the telling of stories that were enlightening to the informed members of society and at least entertaining to the rest, today the theater is on the periphery and by no means extends around it. The audience for theater, whether we are speak- ing of the avant-garde or of Broadway or of both together, is numbered at about four percent of the upper middle class. The numerical decline of the theater audience began, one is not surprised to learn, with the advent of

---

[1] Tom F. Driver, *Romantic Quest and Modern Query: a History of the Modern Theater* (New York: Delacorte Press, 1970).

the mass distribution of movies. It further declined, by comparison with the total population, during the great depression, when the building of theaters virtually ceased in this country for a long period. It rose again during World War II, though not in any vast degree, and since then it has declined steadily. For the first time in modern history there is an entire younger generation which does not consider the theater to hold for it any important expectations, and this phenomenon occurs, significantly, even more clearly in the urban centers than elsewhere. Moreover, that generation which is now, let us say, between the age of forty and retirement, and which was at one time devoted to the theater, has turned its attention elsewhere. In addition, let it be noted that I speak not only of your "average" working adult but also of your leaders of taste and cultivation. Whereas at one time they would have felt themselves unpardonably ignorant not to have seen the most recent and most talked-about stage productions, now they no longer feel any such obligation. They sense correctly that the visions which are necessary to the aesthetic and spiritual life are not apt to be found in the theater, and so they have defected from its audience and left it to those who are content to fan old flames.

In this respect, the situation of the theater is parallel to that of the church, from whose ranks have departed not only the young (in such number that one scarcely expects anymore to see them around, particularly in the urban centers) but also their parents and mentors, particularly the most spiritually sensitive. These have left the church, returning to it only on rare occasions. And as your younger theologian hardly assumes that the church, in continuity with its earlier self, will be the place where spiritual renewal occurs, so also your devotees of the theater, its principal critics and theoreticians, no longer quite expect that this institution will renew itself to become once again a center for aesthetic and spiritual vision. Instead, they look for this to come in other dimensions of our culture.

Technology is inimical to theater. The fundamental aesthetic reason for this is that technology erodes one's sense of the importance and meaningfulness of finite space. It breaks the shell of earth, propelling us toward the moon and no doubt into vaster regions beyond. It suddenly disrupts, and seems at times even to obliterate, local topography, the better to create rapid means of transportation and facilities for the production of power, which shall be transported instantaneously over long wires strung across the land to facilitate the comfort and the computing of people in distant cities. Technology emphasizes function over form. It knows of no resting place. It is concerned only with function and energy.

The tie between technology and a new spiritual vision will come, no doubt, in the concept of energy—energy which is ceaseless, which is constantly pulsating, which is restless, which knows much about change and little, if anything, about substance. For technology, space and substance are both fictions. Energy is all. The occupation of space is a mere necessity, some kind of atavistic obstacle which has at most to be put up with and in some way has to be overcome. Thus in all the contemporary arts there is a dissolution of forms, not merely a rapid change in them but a striving to surpass them, to move into another dimension which is characterized by preoccupation with energy and time.

From the point of view of a generation which has imbibed the "wisdom" of Marshall McLuhan, the drama is an insufferably linear form. I do not know that McLuhan has said so, but the drama is even more linear than is the printed word. Aristotle characterized tragedy as having beginning, middle, and end. That has long since seemed rather simplistic, but it remains the case that the drama, insofar as it is wedded to narrative in performance, retains the character of a process which, once initiated, undergoes certain complications and comes out eventually at a stage we can recognize as terminal. This sense of linear progression, so closely wedded to an ancient sense of the linear progression of a human life in its one-way passage through time, is now strongly resisted by almost all creative work in playwriting. Not only resisted; it is mocked and parodied. All manner of strategies are used to overcome it and, as it were, get beyond its inherent limitation. One strategy most often used to this end, which goes back to very early work in the twentieth century to the early work of Paul Claudel, much of the work of Bertolt Brecht, and can be seen in such a recent play as *Operation Sidewinder* by Sam Shepard, is to treat the linearity of a story in the manner of a comic strip. Human situations are rendered as cartoons and are then tied together one after another with the same flat strung-out sequence as may be found in the Sunday comics. Human linear time is thus burlesqued. It is made to seem brutally comic and absurd.

Meanwhile, another sense of time begins to gather into itself the aesthetic importance. One might call this punctual time, a concentration upon the moment. In work which treats of human time as a comic strip, there will occur certain moments which do not come as if prepared by what went before and as if leading to what will come after but which emerge somehow suddenly and fairly unexpectedly as concatenations of energy—a song or some kind of dance or some brief moment of highly charged rhetorical dialogue, in which a number of energies which did not find their expression in the linear pattern are suddenly released to create a moment valid in itself, which then disappears, never to return, in most cases to have no consequence.

In the war between technology and theater, contemporary society sides almost wholly with technology. It is difficult to see how it might do anything else, for modern society in its historical development has become so saturated not only with technology but also with the spirit thereof that to oppose it in any consistent way is to suggest that society and civilization are to be abandoned. If that were done, one would find himself upon chaotic seas in a new wave of barbarism almost impossible to contemplate. Not the most politically radical, not even the most spiritually radical, of the younger generation seems eager to take that route. They may oppose the political game, the system, the establishment, the whole way in which technology is understood and employed, but they are wise enough to know that in the long evolution of the human species technology as such is an irreversible fact as long as there is any value whatever to civilization. Therefore, what they aim at is not the overthrow of technology but the fulfillment of it according to its human and spiritual potentiality.

Theodore Roszak, in his *The Making of a Counter Culture*, has made it quite clear that the foe of the counter culture is technocracy; but he makes it equally clear that there is a distinction to be made between technology and technocracy, however closely associated they may have been until now. The opposition to technocracy, which the counter culture displays and which it may possibly be able to put into effect through some kind of transformation of society in the years to come, does not mean that technology itself will be forsaken; and it does not mean that the dramatic sensibility will be able soon to flourish again, because that which is inimical to drama is not technocracy but technology and the aesthetic sensibilities which technology fosters.

We may be able to get rid of Herman Kahn and his Hudson Institute, which is a prime symbol of technocracy. We might be able to get rid of the computerized Pentagon and the whole mentality of crisis management. We might be able to dismantle the military-industrial complex and devote our energies to more rational and loving ends. But we shall not get rid of the electronic circuit—not unless civilization entire shall collapse. Yet the electronic circuit knows nothing, and will ever know nothing, of the theater. It has no knowledge of, and no use for, the home and the womb of theater, which is a finite and organic space—the threshing floor of Greece, the altar area of the temple, the inner courts of the inns of Elizabeth's England, the house to hear and be seen in, and the house of human spectacle (the Renaissance opera house). Nor does the electronic circuit know anything of a street and a neighborhood. It knows nothing of cabarets, nothing of a circus tent. It does not know and cannot learn of the mysteries of a mask and an unveiling. It has no sense of the difference between a symbol and what is symbolized. It cannot learn to be aware of the expanding value of a symbol and its intimate connection with the life of feeling and organic responsiveness. The electronic circuit knows only of function, energy, forward thrust, and cyclic return. The electronic circuit is pure energy. It exists all in the dimension of spirit. It has no appreciation of the value of dirty finger nails. Beside it, the theater is dense and lethargic, and I do not believe that one can devote himself to both at the same time.

Let the reader not think that I hold the theater to be human and the electronic circuit inhuman. That is not the point. Rather, I speak about two different understandings of the human, two different notions of the spiritual locus of man. They are so different, indeed so antithetical, in their spirit that the ascendancy of one marks the twilight of the other.

II

> Drama is the art of ego. "What a piece of work is man. . . ."

The birth of drama coincides with the detachment of the ego from its communal ground, and drama celebrates the ego as a center of action and value transcending that sea of nature from which humanity by slow stages arises. There is a parable of this in the story of 'Thespis. It is told that he was a member of a chorus. We may assume it was a chorus that danced and sang, recited poetry, and emblemized the audience which sat around it at the edge of the threshing floor. It occurred to Thespis, so we are told, to detach himself from the body of the chorus. As a separate individual he addressed it, engaged it in dialogue. In that moment the One arrogated to itself a value no less than that of the Many. The One was no longer the whole, but the part, which asserted itself in willed independence. It defended the powers of its own reflection in dialectical opposition to the larger body which had given it birth.

Wherever in the history of mankind we find the drama to flourish (which has not been terribly frequent yet has been repeated often enough for us to understand the reality here implied) we find the hero in defiant posture. His is the song, the action, and the destiny of ego turning against nature and the crowd. In such posture Prometheus occupies his rock midway between awe-struck mankind and jealous Zeus. So also does Oedipus assert his own mind and will against the instinctual wisdom of Teiresias, Jocasta, and the Theban elders. Heracles resists murky Death himself in order to rescue Alkmene. So Hamlet, a single, lonely man, is born to set right the time out of joint in a Denmark devoid of other heroes. Ibsen, like one of his own characters, sets himself against the mediocrities and the normal life-flow of Norwegian society. He beats his fists, perhaps even his head, against the recalcitrance of mankind and against the death-destiny of us all. Even Shaw, who has no such metaphysical rebellion in him, and who is at one, or so he hopes, with the life-force itself, nevertheless sings the praises of a hero who is the avatar of that which is yet to come and which life struggles to form and to release.

Only those societies can appreciate and cultivate the drama who appreciate and cultivate the ego. I have wanted almost to say the rampant ego—the ego that is convinced that in its own individual story there lies a value which the whole of society taken together cannot equal because the values and the energies of the social body rise to their glory not in the mass but in that crown and flower which is the ego magnificent in its own eyes, even in its own defeat.

The age of ego is passing away. For long or for short one cannot tell. For a time, at any rate, it seems to have run its course. Its last great spokesman was Sigmund Freud. "Where Id was there shall Ego be." Few things in recent history are as striking as the sudden rise and equally sudden fall of the attraction of Freudianism. If it has not yet departed the scene, surely its grip upon the imagination has lessened, and in a way that would have been very difficult to foresee as recently as twenty years ago.

Freudianism is Romantic and Victorian. It understands its business to be the release of ego from irrational compulsion grounded in the past. More recent psychology turns more to the group, comparatively less to the individual. It touches base now with ancient "psychologies" in which reside the stored wisdom of ages of human experience and in which the ego is not of prime value. Astrology becomes popular, largely, I think, because it is, as Carl Jung recognized, the most ancient system of human typology. Jung himself found the clue to the understanding of man not in that which separated and individuated him from the species but in the collective unconscious. Eastern mysticism and Eastern disciplines of meditation that lead to an ethic centered upon the sacrality of all now infiltrate our culture, gradually changing our ego-sense of how we are located in this world. R. D. Laing, who is probably an avatar of the age into which we are coming, advocates

> the dissolution of the normal ego, that false self competently adjusted to our alienated social reality: the emergence of the "inner" archetypal mediators of divine power, and through this death a rebirth, and the eventual re-establishment of a new kind of ego functioning, the ego now being the servant of the divine, no longer its betrayer.[2]

That new kind of ego function does not yet appear. It seems that a necessary stage in the transition toward it is the loss of ego and the submergence of the self in a kind of experience that is neither fully controlled nor well understood by the governing self. The counsel we meet in almost every hall leads to the abandonment of self, letting go, freaking out, giving oneself to sensations the ego has long suppressed in the interest of achieving or retaining its magisterial function. It is not insignificant, as it certainly is no accident, that one of our more intelligent contemporary theologians, Thomas Altizer, writes now a book, *The Descent into Hell*, in which he describes the enormous contribution to eschatological Christianity which is to be made by Buddhism.[3]

The central insight of Altizer's book is that the Western ego wants

---

[2] *The Politics of Experience and the Bird of Paradise* (London: Penguin Books, 1967), p. 119. Quoted in Theodore Roszak: *The Making of a Counter Culture* (New York: Doubleday & Co., 1969), p. 50.

[3] Thomas J. J. Altizer, *The Descent into Hell* (New York: J. B. Lippincott Co., 1970).

now to be submerged or perhaps dissolved in an awareness, long known in the East, of the participation we all have in the totality of being. The statement here is much more radical than the earlier one of Paul Tillich, which sounds almost the same. Here the ego is a positive enemy, a powerful illusion, and its being dispelled is a cardinal step toward the reception of that grace which Altizer sees in the radical eschatology of the Christ. This was betrayed by the church, he thinks, from very early days, starting with Paul.

The rise of eschatological thought and its attendant apocalyptic imagery in our day is quite remarkable. It is to be found not only among theologians and in various sects where it has always maintained an existence but also in many more "secular" quarters. Apocalypticism presupposes the evacuation of meaning from ego. It presupposes the submergence of ego-values into values of an utterly different sort that can be spoken of only in terms of a new age, a new creation.

There is a deep connection between the apocalyptic imagery of our time and the contemporary rhetoric of revolution. (I speak of rhetoric though I mean nothing negative by the term.) The contemporary pervasiveness of the rhetoric of revolution indicates that in our day "revolution" is a mystique. What is meant by the word is perhaps nothing very specific, at least on the part of most of those who use it. It suggests primarily the turning of a wheel such that all previous values are changed—transvalued, as Nietzsche put it—for the sake of a new social reality, a new "creation." It is all highly Romantic, but not in the Freudian way. It has very little use for ego theory, and it does not aim at the cultivation of any heroes. On the contrary, in the name of that new age which is to come, it adopts a very suspicious attitude toward any heroic posture whatever. This is in fact the way with most revolutions in their early stages. It is only later, when the revolution has come about and stability becomes the order of the day, that a society will look backward and make of some men heroes to celebrate, thereby to consolidate the new. Christianity, in order to keep hold of the new age in Christ, made of him a hero; but the role has never quite fit, and the more we learn of his eschatology the less heroic can he seem.

Our age, however, is prerevolutionary, or at least imagines that it is, which for the moment is enough. We should recognize that this stance is alien to drama. As the art of the drama is the art of ego, so also there is no great prerevolutionary drama. There have been great dramatists who thought ahead of their time and who helped to bring about change. Ibsen and Shaw were such in recent times, and perhaps, further back, we could think of Marlowe and Euripides. But on the whole, drama is reflexive rather than innovative. The changes it effects have to do with gradual shifts in awareness and reasoning, not with sudden revolutions in values. As a dramatist, Brecht is a bad revolutionary; and as a revolutionary, he is a bad dramatist. (But the tension between these qualities in him is fascinating and adds a kind of drama to his drama.) The greatest of dramatists, Shakespeare and Sophocles, are the best of conservatives: they preserve the past and make it viable for the future by revealing its moral essence. That is exactly what Arthur Miller tried to do. But the age of Miller has passed. It was past before he began. The waters rush now to spill themselves in cascade.

III

What is the response that may be proper to the new cultural age on the part of Christian theology and Christian faith? The question has been with us for quite a long time, ever since the Enlightenment, when many of the crises of Christian faith in the light of modern consciousness began to be recognized. If the question becomes more urgent as time goes by, it is because an acceleration of forces proceeds apace, and leads us to that point where now, in the middle of the twentieth century, observers on every hand are wont to tell us that we are turning a corner in history.

It may be that the turn has come, as McLuhan says, because of a communications revolution. I doubt that his thesis is sufficient, but what he discerns is no doubt taking place; and when we find a mind as different from his as that of Margaret Mead telling us that we have passed through a frontier of time and that our children are native to a world where we are merely immigrants, although we have not changed the place where we live, but only the time in which we live, then surely we cannot ignore the prophecies.

For my own part, I must testify that I was reluctant to engage in what I regarded as popular, exaggerated descriptions of the cultural changes until I was forced to acknowledge their validity by meditating on the fortunes of theatrical art throughout all its history and especially during the last 150 years. The time that I have spent researching and attempting to understand the peregrinations of the theater in modern times has convinced me that it has indeed entered upon alien territory. If this is true, it is of signal importance for the self-understanding of man, certainly for Western society.

Many of my colleagues in theology have been brought to a similar point by their reflections upon the history of Christian faith. It is important to note the deep restiveness manifest among them, especially those who learned their theological lessons in the halls of neo-orthodoxy at the very end of the modern period and have had since to perform their professional labors in a climate which that training did not foresee.

One cannot prove, and should not try, that terms such as new age, new cultural period, and so on, are adequate. We are too close to the phenomena we describe to have a sufficient historical perspective upon them. It may be that by the day after tomorrow they will have taken their place within an historical stream unbroken by cataracts. However, this is a matter about which one has to make a decision. If someone yells "Fire!" you don't have to stampede, but neither can you wait for all the evidence. I come more and more to the conclusion that we are better advised to think of ourselves as at an historical turning point than to think of ourselves as merely undergoing a kind of turbulence from which the ship of culture as we have known it will, after a few years, emerge.

If this be granted, then the proper response of Christian theology to this age is not the "translation" of ancient theological terms and symbols into their contemporary equivalents. The name in theology with which such enterprise is most closely associated is that of Paul Tillich. The terms had to be translated, he maintained; and he spent his life trying to make a correlation between traditional theological terms and modern experience. He was a keen interpreter of both.

To translate or not to translate was the great issue that lay between Tillich and Reinhold Niebuhr. When Niebuhr heard the biblical and theological language undergo a transformation in the mouth of Tillich, he drew back. He had his reasons, for Niebuhr knew how to use the ancient theological terms to puncture complacent assumptions. He challenged American policy with the realism of Augustinian theology.

Tillich foresaw that this strategy, however effective it might be in the short run, was insufficient in the long. With unerring instinct he felt that the experiences to which moderns are exposed, and the interpretations of experience they consequently make, increasingly alienate them from the language of classical theology. He therefore fought what I will, in an uncomplimentary phrase, call a rearguard action, and did so in the name of change. That is to say, Tillich's aim was to defend the tradition by translating it. In this respect he was at one with the giants of the modern age in all fields, excepting only natural science, where the Einsteinian revolution proceeded in heady disregard of the extent to which it departed from the axioms of Newton.

In painting, in sculpture, in architecture, in literature, in the theater as well, the giants of the modern age attempted to preserve the tradition by accommodating it to the stresses of modern experience. That is the way in which we should see Freud also. He wished to preserve the tradition of ego-value. He knew that in order to do it he had to accommodate evidence and stresses that were forcing him to acknowledge, as they forced the unwitting to obey, the reality of the unconscious. Id is antithetical to Ego. Therefore, the ego must be informed about it and provided with the means of remaining master of its own ship, even though it would be acknowledged that the vessel, the currents, and the winds were not of the ego's own making.

Think also of T. S. Eliot—in technique a radical, in substance a conservative, by the account of some of his critics a reactionary. "These fragments I have shored against my ruin." That is the strategy. The tradition might be fragmented. It might, to change the metaphor, be going through seas exceptionally heavy. But if the waves were taken into account, and if strategies not for resisting them but for becoming aware of them and dealing with them were discovered, then the ship of tradition might, by the aid of grace, pass through.

How ancient now it seems. I do not wish to put it down. Valid in its own time, it retains that validity for any who have the slightest degree of vicarious imagination. But it is not our game. And it is not in that enterprise that we sense that our energies will be the best expended. So, in theology the task cannot now be to save the tradition by translating it into terms that seem to have their equivalent in the modern vocabulary. A few years ago that is exactly what we would have expected. Then it seemed a liberating thing, to air out the stuffiness of the churches and the literature. Not now. Now such an enterprise seems a bit—shoddy. It lies too near the surface. I do not mean that Tillich is shoddy, only those who would do now what he did then, in the period of the two world wars. His project is inadequate to this present moment, which has arrived upon us with such force only a few years after his demise.

As the task is not to translate the tradition, neither is it to discover and enunciate a transcendent theoretical understanding. Of course, the intellect will ever seek theoretical knowledge. It will ever attempt to embrace within concepts and categories the totality of what it encounters. I am aware that this very essay of mine may be read, and must be read, as an attempt to enunciate a theoretical understanding of our situation. But I do not believe that this is the most important thing to be done. And so I write, not a theory of our culture and its transition, but only an essay which would attempt to make us partially aware, in order that we may be able to move with the less encumbrance in the direction in which I believe we are being led by a migration of spirit.

It is not a more inclusive view of any kind that is at the moment required. Rather, we need the insight voiced by R. D. Laing when he says that what is needed at the moment is not theory but that experience which is the source of theory.

The crisis through which we are passing is manifest not merely in the changed environment (cultural and natural, and in both cases threatening) but is manifest also in a faltering of the intellect. There exists a very widespread feeling that the intellect is not capable of coping with all the new quantities and kinds of information with which it is being fed. Confronted with this feeling, our first temptation is to say that the intellect itself is failing, that what it needs is a more comprehensive understanding for all its rich input of data. We tend to think of the intellect as a constant, as some kind of glorified machine, which, if it is sufficiently acute and sufficiently revved up, will in the nature of things come to an understanding that will enable it to put all in order. Thus, if the human intellect is not sufficient for its task it can be extended or amplified through the use of a computer, which is an extension of the brain in certain of its capacities, just as a jack-hammer is an extension of arm muscle in certain of its capacities. I call this a temptation because I believe it is a misguided reaction.

The computer itself may alert us. The suggestion that our intellect can be significantly enhanced by the computer is on the one hand attractive and on the other, alarming. We realize by reflection that a computer serves not only to solve problems but equally, and perhaps even more, to compound them. For every solution to a problem at which a computer arrives by virtue of its vastness and rapidity, it yields at least an equal number of problems, and for a simple reason: The processing of data breeds as many questions as answers because every answer is also a question, yet not a question identical to the one that was first fed in. Even a library, which is a cumbersome instrument for storing and processing data, shows this. Ecclesiastes knew long ago that "of making many books there is no end." He may have been thinking of those produced by man's imaginative and disputatious nature, but we know also those that are generated in geometric proportion by the logic of research.

The computer, which is a vast library combined with a very rapid and specialized brain, is a great help but at the same time a great danger. It is, in fact, a huge leap forward in evolutionary specialization, and we are aware that if a species overspecializes in any one direction it places itself in peril.

The crisis in which we stand is not to be resolved or overcome by an increase in theoretical understanding or in the solution of problems that our present input of data have generated. That is only apparently the case. The more nearly real case is as follows.

Our crisis of intellect arises not because the intellect is overfed but because it is undernourished. We have not too many data but too few. Or rather, to be slightly more accurate, we have an insufficient awareness of the data input. The information we need is inaccessible to us at the proper points and impinges upon us merely as a kind of disturbance, a vague irritation of the skin. We know we are being tickled, but only God knows by what.

In order to solve our problems we must have a greater awareness of what they are. This awareness is not going to come to us through the intellect itself. It is going to come only as we are made more responsive, more resilient when we are touched by what occurs in life.

I would like now to turn to one thing I think is occurring and try to describe it in such a way as will point toward the way we must follow if we are going to reach an awareness sufficient for our understanding.

I do not think it is sufficiently appreciated how deeply alienated we have become from our past. I do not mean only the young, who are famous for their lack of interest in history. I mean almost everybody. And by the past I mean especially our "formative past"—that is to say, that portion of what has happened to us and our forebears which has served to provide a meaningful shape for cultural experience and which gave our forebears their general orientation in the world. It is precisely from such a formative past that we are increasingly alienated.

Our alienation is deepest from that classical and Judeo-Christian past (frequently called tradition) which we have believed and hoped would serve to provide our orientation. One might note, for instance, an observation of Alberto Moravia made on the occasion of his review of Federico Fellini's *Satyricon*. Moravia observed that the period of classical Rome is one of the most fully researched periods in the human past. It has left a plethora of monuments both verbal and nonverbal and these have been pored over by generations of scholars to the point where it seems that no further research could tell us more about what happened through the course of the Roman Republic and Empire. Moravia then went on to observe that in spite of (I would say because of) this enormous amount of research we are becoming ever more separated from that classical past. He said that it would soon begin to appear as remote to us as the earlier dynasties of Egypt, perhaps as remote as the prehistoric past. Because of this, he said, Fellini felt himself free, in a sense even obligated, to treat that Roman antiquity in the form of a dream. Moravia proceeded to review the film as if it were Fellini's dream of a remote period about which we knew almost nothing and therefore about which we had to dream if we wished to say anything at all.

It is a peculiar transformation, the metamorphosis of history into dream though it occurs often enough. I shall have more to say about things related to that later. For the moment, let us observe that the task confronting Christian theology is not that of attempting to restore a lively relation to the Judeo-Christian past. On the contrary, it is to enhance our awareness of how deeply alienated from it we are. A better historical understanding of that past cannot now be of any help. That formative past is already over-researched, and in the process of its being researched it has progressively lost its mythic power. If it is to return at all, it must do so as a dream. It cannot come back by the historical method, no matter how sophisticated.

I do not quite wish to say that those colleagues of mine who are engaged in historical research on the ancient periods should cease their labors. I suggest only that they be willing to recognize that they are going more and more to assume the role of archivists. The immediate and existential relevance of their researches will be less and less obvious and will have less and less impact on contemporary society. That will be true no matter how sophisticated and no matter how novel their interpretations of their researches turn out to be. As long as they do their work in a stance predicated upon the validity of the historical method of investigation, they shall find themselves contributing, whatever their intentions, to the evacuation of the mythic power of the formative past.

This trend, it seems to me, is quite irreversible at present. The counsel of wisdom is not to try to reverse it but instead to seek to accelerate the prevalent tendency by recognizing and bringing evermore to the fullest awareness the alienation from the formative past that has now overtaken us and from which we cannot be delivered by any form of retrogressive movement.

Perhaps we shall one day recover that past. I do not know. I do not believe that any man now knows. I feel certain that if we do recover it, it will be when we meet it in the future, meet it, as it were, circling round to confront us once again in our forward motion through time and not because we have made any kind of deliberate attempt to recover and reconstruct that from which our spiritual ties have now been severed. A lost past can meet the future only as dream.

This is perhaps one of the more radical things that a person belonging to an historical religion such as Christianity might say, and yet I believe it must be said. Perhaps if one were to look far enough he would find reasons, even within the tradition, for saying it. But at the moment those reasons are not the ones for which we should seek. Rather we should seek the reasons which come from our understanding of the way in which we ourselves are progressing because of contemporary movements that are forcing themselves upon us and which we are helping to create though we may not know it.

All spiritual movements evolve in a certain way. They begin with a mythic consciousness and proceed toward an historical one. They move from the transcendent to the immanent. We find this whether we look at the criticism of religion made by the prophets of the Old Testament, or whether we look at that rational and dialectical criticism made by Socrates, or whether we look at the iconoclasm which belongs to certain periods of Judaic, Islamic, and Christian history, or whether again we look at the trend toward secularization which has been characteristic of Christianity for the last five hundred years. We notice ever the same impulse, which is to move the religious conscience from its preoccupation with the mythic realm toward the historical and the concrete. It seems that religions and the various spiritual movements that arise within and around them all proceed through a cycle of that sort.

Once such a cycle is complete, a new one must start. It is possible to view this cyclic process as one in which the religious life from time to time exhausts itself and is replaced by a mundane concern, but I myself think that we do not need to view the progression I have mentioned in such negative terms. Perhaps it would be better to take a larger view and suggest that to cycle between the mythic and the historical is endemic to the religious consciousness itself and therefore we ought not be surprised when we find the process repeated over and over again, nor dismayed that we find ourselves at the end of a cycle at the present time.

Many of our more prominent and visionary figures have, since the latter part of the nineteenth century, believed that we were at the end of one cycle and possibly the beginning of another. One thinks of Matthew Arnold's vision at Dover Beach about being between two worlds, or of Yeats's theory of the cycles of two thousand years, one of which he felt to be ending in his own time. One remembers Paul Tillich's raising the question whether the Protestant era had come to an end.

My own suggestion, and it is not a novel one, is that Christianity, at least in the form in which we have known it until now, has come to the end of its age. It began with the faith of the early Christians, according to which Jesus was seen in mythic context as the Man from Heaven, the Son of God descended to earth and ascended again in order to bear and to be the salvation of mankind. This mythic awareness, perpetuated through the better part of two millennia, has gradually and in recent times with accelerating pace given way to an emphasis upon the humanity of Christ, researches into his historical existence, and the bending of the Christian ethic ever more earthward rather than its being determined primarily by the economy of salvation to eternal life.

As the process of secularization has broadened and deepened in modern times so that it has come to saturate the consciousness of almost everyone, the priestly ministries of the church have become less important, at least for most people, so that now what is in question is not only the mythic awareness itself but the entire priestly nature of the church in the world, including the priesthood of all believers. One gets a very clear description of this situation, set forth from a theological point of view, in Thomas Altizer's deeply heretical book, *The Descent into Hell*, to which I have already referred. I regard it as the great strength of Altizer that he has discerned this pattern and that he puts it forward not with apology or lament but as a necessary operation of spirit. Another strength manifest in that book, as well as in earlier ones, is that Altizer immediately turns from the acknowledgment of the exhaustion of mythic Christianity to a new concern with the sacred. In this respect he is surely in tune with much that is happening in our culture, for this is a period in which the formal religions are in low regard while at the same time the period manifests in countless ways its deep hunger for spiritual grace and expression.

The drive toward the realm of the historical, the actual, and the concrete has seldom been manifest in any religion as clearly as in the Christian. I am thinking particularly of its doctrine of incarnation. At the heart of this religion from its inception, and in spite of its highly mythic character at that time, there was imbedded the notion that the full realization of the Word of God could come only by its manifestation as flesh.

The whole history of Christianity in its movement from the transcendent to the immanent, from the mythic to the historical, is thus present encapsulated in the earliest doctrines of the Church in the form of the Man from Heaven made flesh and dwelling among us. This tendency, in time and according to the general law of movement of all religion from the transcendent to the immanent, will produce in the modern period the phenomenon known as secularization, and it will drive such a radical thinker as Thomas Altizer to suggest that the real mission of Christ is the "emptying of heaven," the radical turn of the religious consciousness from the mythic to the historical. It is in this context that Mr. Altizer places the phenomenon known as the death of God, which he himself has helped so much to popularize and which here he surely understands correctly. But we must note that the "death of God" is itself a mythical apprehension even though it arises exactly at that point in the dialectic of religion where we find the ascendency of the secular over the sacred. Seeing this, we can appreciate the value that a mythic understanding can lend to that very movement toward the historical which characterizes the development of religious consciousness. Mythic understanding helps prepare us to imagine that the cycle will probably begin again.

I am tempted to say the cycle must begin again and that what we shall enter upon in the new age is a new mythic consciousness. We may look forward to a new spiritual movement, born from the ashes of a previous one which is manifest at the present time as a kind of religious appreciation of the secular. The scientific age will give rise to a new and lively appreciation of the mythic sphere.

This is not news. The only surprising thing is that we don't believe it. Ego fights hard. Even when it has lost its stage.

Northrop Frye suggested in the *Anatomy of Criticism*, without many takers, a cyclic patterning of literary periods. He apportioned literary development into five modes, the first of which is mythic, the second archetypal. Then follow the periods he calls high mimetic and low mimetic, the one reaching its excellence in tragedy, the other in the realistic novel and in ancient romances. Finally, there comes the ironic mode which he regards as characteristic of early twentieth-century literature. In the ironic he notes the gradual return of the mythical, as if in periods pervaded by the ironic sensibility it were necessary somehow to recover the apprehensions in which literary creativity had found its original inspiration. Professor Frye looks forward to the recurrence of the cycle and a new period of literature which will be dominated by mythic consciousness. His book is itself rather mythical and thus exemplifies something of what it predicts.

Myth proper is the articulation in narrative or story form of a symbolic and anthropomorphic apprehension of reality. The personnae of myths are gods or other supernatural beings who stand for forces and principles discerned to underlie the phenomenal world. A myth, W. H. Auden once said, is a story that is designed to tell me why it is that a certain type of thing occurs and will recur time and time again. In this respect, a myth is a general theory. But it is not represented in the form of an abstract rational theory, in which the effective agents are certain principles under-stood under the guidance of conceptual thinking. Rather, a myth accounts for experience by personalizing it, by representing forces as masks that have salient human features. A myth is a generalization, but it is of such a kind as that human reality and nature are of the same piece. The human being feels that he belongs deeply to existence, even if he may also feel threatened by it and stand under the jeopardy of being destroyed or cast out. In which case, nature has turned against herself. The gods are at war.

Myth is based on experience. It is based on a lively rapport between the experiencing self (usually a self in community) and the natural world. In fact, no dichotomy between these exists, only the trace of a crack if one chooses sides in the war of the gods. The fissure occurs later, under the impact of what we call rational and objectifying thinking, which means that in the war of the gods a side is chosen for keeps. All rational thinking makes alienation. That which is alienated first (and last?) is the rejected god.

Myth arises when the natural world is felt to invade and pervade the human reality. Culture, cult, and tradition, insofar as they are com-patible with mythic consciousness, are subordinated at every point to an awareness of the all-important dynamic of the natural world. Myth, then, is the human appropriation of the natural. It renders the natural meaningful in terms of human existence, human struggle, human awareness, human feeling, and vice versa. Myth therefore spawns, in time, what are generally called "nature religions." Such religions do not require faith. Instead they require an immediate consent to the awareness of that which is spoken of in the myth. It is at later stages, when the religious consciousness becomes aware of the distinction between the transcendent, chosen god (choice *is* transcendence) and the immanent processes of nature that faith will enter the picture. At that stage a radical gap will be created between earth and heaven, between the contingency of all things here and the eternal necessity of that which is their ground and hope. Then faith, which is the substance of things hoped for, will become regulative. The religion of faith will therefore be inimical toward the nature religions because they know nothing of faith and because (same thing) they do not *choose*. Yahweh is not mythical, because he is a chooser and is chosen. If he is not chosen, the covenant is broken. Not mythical, he is not historical either. I do not know what he is. That is my one point of contact with him—*via negativa*.

One of the things that makes a mythic consciousness so attractive at the present time is precisely its naturalizing tendency. In this connection we may refer once again to technology. It has two faces. On the one side, technology embodies and makes gloriously manifest the radical contin-gency of all natural phenomena. That is to say, technology is possible, and we know this, because of the triumph of the rational intellect over the contingent operations of the natural world. Thus technology is the result of a continual and highly successful series of problems solved, and these are problems which could not have been solved without the prior assumption that nature is capable, in its contingency, of being subjected to the ordering capacities of the transcendent theoretical intelligence. Technology is our invention and we have control of it.

On the other side, technology seems quite different. Far from being in control of it, we often feel ourselves to be its victim. Which of us feels himself to be like Samson, endowed with power to embrace and pull down the pillars of the technological construct? There seems no way out of the miseries technology has produced except by the employment of further technology. All of a sudden it seems as if the radical contingency which is basic to technology has been transformed into a radical fate. The contingent reveals that it is also inexorable.

The mythic consciousness which is growing in the latter part of the twentieth century understands technology to be, at least to have become, a part of the "natural" environment. Under the tutelage of thinkers as different as Teilhard de Chardin and Norbert Wiener we come to see technology as a product not only of man's transcendent engineering capacities but as a phenomenon belonging to the long and mysterious process of evolution. The electronic vacuum tube and the transistor are no less a product of evolutionary capacities than is the cone of the pine tree or the phosphorescent glow of the lightning bug. Once this is perceived, mythic consciousness allows that the phenomenon of technology may be radically naturalized.

The new mythology which no doubt lies ahead of us will be one in which no sharp distinction is made between nature and such human products as technology. ("Over that art which you say adds to nature/Is an art that nature makes.") It will no doubt have fairly little of high esteem to say about the more strictly cultural products of civilization which occupy the shelves of our libraries and hang upon the walls of our museums. All this, together with the way in which that material is most frequently brought into education and thus transmitted from one generation to the next, can be grouped under the heading of tradition. With respect to tradition the mythic consciousness is likely to be very skeptical, or perhaps to bypass it altogether. Tradition belongs to the realm of the specific, the historical, whereas mythic consciousness addresses itself to the universal, to the general. And while myth may be able to make very good use of a developmental hypothesis such as the one we call "evolution," that is because evolution is not so much a tradition as a process and not so much an invention or a contrivance as a capacity of life. Here we encounter mysteries which the mythic consciousness will find itself attracted to as bees to the flower. For although we may speak about evolution, and although we may describe its processes with the aid of painstaking and scientific research, the closest we can come to an "explanation" of it is to resort to narrative.

We do not know, as Loren Eisley has reminded us, how it came about, or could have come about, that green plants appeared on the face of the earth and began to supply oxygen to the atmosphere by a trick that they learned of utilizing the energy of light from the sun. We have a name for it (photosynthesis) but, like most names, it is the name of an ignorance.

Without that oxygen, no animal life. Without animal life, no human life. Also, as Mr. Eisley has made dramatically clear in his essays, the development of the human brain appears like a miracle in the story of evolution, a sudden entrance, as it were, upon the evolutionary stage.

If these and other parts of the story have simply to be told with no general way to account for them, so much more the rise of the entire process from some original explosion or whatever to create what is as of now an expanding universe, or the subsequent appearance of life processes on this planet whether parallelled elsewhere or not we do not know. All this is shot through with mystery, and the mystery pertains not only to the questions *why* and *how* but also to the question *what* is the nature of this process. What is its meaning? What is it about? What does it have to do with the psychic and emotional economies of its most complicated product —man and his consciousness.

The Christian religion, it seems, is of no help in addressing this mystery. It has not passed beyond the enlightenment, which is really a darkening, that is spoken of in the Book of Job through the questions God addresses to Job that remind him that he is not privy to such secrets. As far as Job, indeed the whole Judeo-Christian tradition, is concerned man simply was not present at the creation. No answers to its riddles are to be expected by him. The book of Job turns from such preoccupations to questions of justice and salvation, and the Christian religion has done so as well.

Whatever the virtues and values, perhaps even the providential causes, for this may have been, the result in our time is that the human being has come into a situation in which his entire existence appears to him as absurd. At the very least we have to say that he is continually threatened by the possibility that absurdity may overwhelm his consciousness of who he is and where he is. Such a threat is not conducive to survival. In spite of the grandeur of the myth of Sisyphus, there are not many people who can engage themselves in the furtherance of even the minimal, let alone the maximal, aims of existence if they know or think themselves to be in the situation of Sisyphus. At the same time a purely transcendent address to the human situation, according to which the contingency and possible absurdity of life in this world is of no account compared to the glories of eternal life or the radiance of the eschatological age which is promised now or in the future, are not sufficient for a people who have been radically cut off from participation in the natural world which has given them birth. Therefore the tendency on many fronts is in the direction of a new mythic consciousness which would be based on an immediate and profound engagement with experience.

It is helpful to think of a "return to experience" in the contemporary period. It can be seen in numerous phenomena:

1. It is present in that acceptance and affirmation of the human body which is to be discerned throughout contemporary culture. At its worst and most superficial level this is of course nothing but sybaritic indulgence, but the deep social reasons for it are also to be discerned. They have been set forth most cogently, I suppose, in the writings of Norman O. Brown, in particular *Love's Body*.

2. We may note also a resurgence in recent years of "primitive" rhythm in music and in poetry. It is as if the arts, having passed through a phase in which they felt themselves primarily indebted to the understanding intelligence, have now begun to reverse themselves and to discover their primary rootage in the pulsating rhythms of energy upon which life depends. Here is a new shamanism and a new sacrality of the "given," understood as basic to all the constructs of the aesthetic drive. The rootage of poetry in the human organism's response to its total surround has been argued recently at great length by Stanley Burnshaw in *The Seamless Web*.

3. In all the arts we see at present a strong emphasis upon the use of what, borrowing a term from photography, we may call "available light." In photography the use of available light, rather than light artificially arranged, expresses a sense of deep rapport between the technical apparatus, the camera, and that which is "given" in nature. There may be art and artifice in such photography (surely there is) but it is an art which sees itself as fulfilling and complementing the potentialities which nature herself creates. So also the graphic artist returns at present to a preoccupation with "found objects." In music John Cage and others have treated as "music" natural sounds picked up by the tape recorder. We should point out also the strong motif in virtually all the contemporary arts to use without significant transformation all the detritus of the consumer society—its comic strips, its commercials, its junk packaging, its banal constructions on the neon strips of our cities. As Wallace Stevens put it, the stuff of our poetry shall be "the actual bread, the actual stone."

4. The "drug scene" also belongs here. Whatever else they may be, and however dangerous their use to society, drugs offer themselves as ways of intensifying experience. All spiritual movements have discovered such ways, frequently by the use of artificial stimulants, sometimes by the use of more natural methods such as dance and meditation, sometimes by retreat into the vast and disorienting heat of the desert. It is with a sure semantic instinct that the users of drugs speak of "taking a trip." Journeys are undertaken by man for the sake of cultivating experience, and this motif is prevalent to an extraordinary degree in our time.

5. The phenomenon known as "dropping out" is also a part of the return to experience. Perhaps here we can see the tendency manifest in a

very clear form. What is forsaken when one drops out is adherence to tradition. It is an old motif known to students of literature as that of the pastoral idyll. Let us forsake the courts of the city and place ourselves for a time in the Forest of Arden. If that forest is now equipped with hamburger stands, motorcycles, and some of the costume of the cowboy, nevertheless it retains its essential character; and the aim is now, as it ever has been, to bracket the tradition for a time, if not for always, in order that experience may flow without the constraints of the authority represented by culture.

6. We must speak also of sexual liberation. In part this was alluded to earlier when we mentioned the affirmation of the body, but not all affirmation of the body takes the form of sexual activity or sexual imagination. In our time sexuality has been released from cultural constraints in a manner without parallel in modern history. In few areas is the conflict between nature and culture so obvious as in that of sexuality, for it belongs to the task of culture to restrict sexuality and to bend its energies into tasks that are culturally creative and economically fructifying. To discard or break loose from the cultural restraints on sexuality is to declare that the forbidden realms of experience must once more be made accessible. It is to say that the experience of sexuality will in itself be a better guide to the proper expression of that drive than is the collected wisdom of generations of mankind. Whether that expectation is well grounded or not is not a subject I wish now to discuss. I point out only that sexual liberation forms a part of the motif of the return to experience.

7. Finally we should mention the discovery which the West in our time is making of the East. Especially pertinent here is the discovery of Eastern religion, which, from the point of view of the West, is viewed as "natural Wisdom" unfallen into history. That is, to be sure, a terribly romantic view of the matter, but I speak not of what the most mature judgment would have to say but of what the attraction of Eastern religion is for the Western mentality now. Most Westerners are in large degree ignorant of the amount of tradition which is bound up in Eastern religious ways. What the Westerner perceives in Eastern mysticism, Eastern meditation, and Eastern rapture over the participation of the individual in the whole, is something antithetical to his own tradition, something from which his own tradition has alienated him. Therefore what attracts him in the East is a means of getting past the inherited cultural forms on his own side of the water and finding techniques and a few rationales for his own immersion in the sea of existence. For the Westerner, what is involved here is not a new theory, certainly not the transfer of his allegiance to a new religious cult, but an avenue for the influx of a type of experience long denied him.

These are some, though certainly not all, of the signs to which we might point that indicate the deep longing for a return to experience on the part of Western man. Many of these phenomena are taken for granted by the younger generation, who participate in them virtually wholeheartedly. Such participation will either prove disastrous or, as I am inclined to think, it will provide the basis for a new mythic consciousness.

IV

Two questions now arise for the Christian, especially for the Christian who is or has been particularly devoted to the drama:

1. Will the "return to experience" enable us to discover once more the reality of the Christ? Will the new mythic consciousness lead us toward the One who bears myth into history?
2. Will the "return to experience" lead to a regeneration of the dramatic form? Will drama arise once again out of a new mythic soil as has happened more than once in the past?

We must be careful lest in the very asking of these questions we find ourselves to be holding on to an old "law." We must be wary lest in the very posing of our questions we attach ourselves once again to symbolic forms that have now lived their lives and are ready to perish. We should keep in mind and take to heart the admonition of Paul Tillich that symbols, including religious symbols, and not excluding the religious symbols of Christianity, are born in certain historical contexts, flourish so long as they are capable of expressing the ultimate concerns of those who participate in them and, when other times bring forth other concerns, die, on the analogy of all organisms and all life forms. Perhaps then it is best not even to ask the questions which I have put forward above. They may be the questions of a people who have come into a new territory and insist upon bringing with them some of the furniture and bric-a-brac of the land in which they formerly lived.

Yet we do bring them, some of us, nevertheless. Perhaps there would be something inhuman, something merely contrived, if we burned all of the mementos and orienting objects of our previous existence. So the questions are there, and they will not go away. But perhaps they will not get answers. Perhaps the best way in which we can regard them is as if they were objects to remind us where we have been rather than objects which are instrumental in the place we now live.

Instead of worrying these questions, therefore, may one suggest that the proper thing is to turn with full pressure to the experience of that which is given us in the present situation and which seems to be emerging for the future? Thus, we shall not castigate John Cage because he is anarchistic with respect to the tradition of Western music. We shall not castigate the young playwrights because they show so little interest in the maintenance of narrative control, in the development of deep characterization, in the shaping of clear contests between protagonist and antagonist, in all of that shaping function which we have learned long ago to associate with the exercise of the dramatic craft. We shall instead say that the artists now at work could learn these things if they chose (indeed, many of them *have* learned them and turned away) but that they are the harbingers of a new style reflective of a new awareness and are no more to be judged by traditional expectations than are the perspectival paintings of the Renaissance to be measured by the objectives of Byzantine art.

Let experience be what experience is. Let us bracket for the time being, because in any case we do not know how to deal with it, the question of knowing what in our experience and in our present creativity is good, true, and beautiful. What we shall bend ourselves toward is the searching out of our experience for that in it which leads to ecstasy, to the sense of the presence of the absolute.

The modern age came to a close some ten years ago in virtual slavery to the contingent. Its great creative thinkers and artists fought against the purely contingent nobly and heroically. The record of their struggle will perhaps never be forgotten, but they did not succeed. And so the modern age passed into history and has been succeeded by that which, for want of a better name, we call the contemporary.

For the modern age it finally came down to this: there was nothing awesome to make one catch one's breath. There was much confusion, there were many stresses, there was what E. M. Forster called "the gigantic horror," and there were occasionally heroic gestures made and titanic madnesses endured upon what seemed so much of the time to be the heath of Lear. But the horror of that horror was that it was the work of nothing but contingency; and for that reason, while it could wring from man great cries, it could not induce him to catch his breath in awe.

The modern age lost all touch with Spirit, save only that which it retained in memory. "These fragments I have shored against my ruin." The posture is defensive, the expectation, such as it is, transcendental. To kill or to evacuate the transcendent was the intention of Wallace Stevens: "A tune beyond us, yet ourselves/It could be nothing else."

Wallace Stevens brought the modern age of poetry to a close, just as Samuel Beckett brings the modern age of drama to a close. Neither ends with a bang. There are some who hear in Beckett's works a whimper. I myself am not among them. His use of the English language is too beautiful, too magnificent in its achieved simplicity ever to be called a whimper. And certainly the cadences and the elegant vocabulary of Wallace Stevens are not those of a whimperer. But in both cases the modern age seems to end with authors who have concluded in a spirit of resignation that there is less and less to say.

What is there to say when he who is so articulate as Wallace Stevens reminds us more than once that we dare not use "the rotted names"?

It is not a time for ultimate or even penultimate words. Our words have become too transcendental, too far removed from our deepest non-verbal apprehensions, our rootage in that nature to which we owe our existence and the beat of our hearts.

The Word which we spell with a capital W is at the moment breathless. Not, I suppose, because it is dead. It is difficult to think of death as ultimate except in a chronological sense. Only that which is alive may hold its breath. The Word of creation, knowledge, and joy is at the moment holding its breath in wonder and in awe, awaiting that time when the natural shall revive and the Word may find a stage, a *skene,* a tent in which to reverberate.

The modern age had nothing at which to catch its breath. Also, and this is not a paradox, it forgot how to breathe. One of the things we are learning from Eastern yogi is the importance of breathing. The disciplined yet relaxed control of the movement of air in and out of the body so that it fills the inner cavity is, it seems, a key to meditation and to the participation of the self in its surround. Western man is discovering that he needs to know how to breathe just at the time when he is discovering that his technology-polluted air is not worth breathing. He will have to discover the technical means to prevent the air from being fouled, and he will be able to do this only as he rediscovers the importance of breath to the physical and psychical economy. With luck, his attention to the ecological problems will reinvigorate in him a sense of how he belongs to the entire natural world, conceived on the analogy of his own being as an organic and living reality. He may then recover a mythic awareness of that whole of which he is a part. He may then prepare the way for his renewed articulation of transcendence, and he may become able once again to take part in a dialogue with transcendent power. If that happens, he will have rediscovered the basis of dramatic form.

The path leads forward through mythic awareness. It does not lead backward through the o'er-heightened historical consciousness which the last few centuries have seen. The story of man moves through cycles, but it does not move backward. The earth must be holy before heaven can be holy. The chorus must dance before the actor can perform. Our stages must be silent for a time. They are waiting for the fields to sing. These fields are not quite the simple meadows our ancestors knew. They are the manifold fields of our experience. They are pulsations of energy beating from the heart of life, and in their presence it behooves us to be not still but reverentially dumb.

6

Images
of the Life of Man
in a Sample of Poems

Movements, Modes, Long Poems,
Images of the Life of Man, Scheme

Tony Stoneburner

As we prepare to consider poetry which I will be calling Modernist, Transitionalist (Confessional), and New Humanist (Immediate), it will be well to remember that literary movements come into being as correctives to the established mode of their period. They speak in the name of a dimension of human existence which the dominant mode omits. The established mode is dominant usually for two reasons: the literary reason is its ability to speak the special quality of existence for the generation which rules the major institutions; the extraliterary reason is the politics of ingroup publication, reviewing, and prize-awarding. Emergent movements in their corrective reaction against the established mode tend to look both marginal and antisocial.

Although the dominical dictum (new wine, new wineskins) holds in literature (new matter, new manner), the work of the emergent movements may not be literature according to the standard of the established mode. The rulers dismiss it as subliterary (autistic jottings or jumble) or supraliterary (subversive pseudoscripture).

The established mode focuses on one aspect or phase of being as central among several, and says what it sees. Emergent movements have another outlook and insight and utter it. But neither established mode nor emergent movements are all-seeing. Therefore in a pluralistic society the total community of poetry is likely to be superior to both the relatively reiterative, static dominant mode and the relatively exploratory, dynamic corrective movements. No single standpoint has a monopoly in spiritual authenticity or authority, no single viewpoint a monopoly in literary excellence. For the reader (the critic, the theological interpreter of the arts), only an arduous eclecticism that approximates catholicity is adequate. Attending only to the fashionable or most recent movement is a mistake. Modernism as a movement is dead and as the established mode is over and done. But the fragment "From Canto CXIII" by Modernist Ezra Pound (*The New Yorker*, 30. XI. 1968, p. 64) and the poem *The Tribune's Visitation* by Modernist David Jones (Fulcrum Press, 1969) are as fine as all but the finest poetry by each poet and as true voices of their moment and epoch as those of any other poems published those two years, even though their mode no longer reigns or recruits apprentices.

As we look for new images, we will consult the poetry of several schools, Modernist, Transitionalist (Confessional), and New Humanist (Immediate); we will consult them in the chronological order of the rise of the movements to which they belong; we will consult one voice each of the two earlier movements and three voices of the most recent one; but our doing so does not imply that the compositions according to no longer fashionable poetics are obsolete. One can say that the young writer entering upon his apprenticeship to poetry must refuse the invitation of a movement which offers him an outmoded matter-manner. Elections and rejections are part of the discipline by which the poet enables his gift to be true to his sense of things. But one cannot say the same thing for the reader. If he desires to orient himself in the world, he must listen to the colloquy of the community of poetry and not regard one source or sort of utterance as the promulgation of infallible formulae. The newest word of the youngest mode may be the last word in all its freshness, but so may the newest word of the oldest mode. The poetry of Gary Snyder will not have more to say to us than that of David Jones merely because his mode is the more recent to emerge. Let us not permit the model of literary history as a succession of modes developed by movements to lead us to imagine that the sequence is a progression from low to high, simple to complex forms. Let us assume that a single period will have many different voices, each with an equal reason for being heard.

The present essay is not a report on a systematic survey of current poetry, a United States census or a piece either of CIA intelligence or of FBI investigation. It is no more than a personal report. I have chosen poems which both have spoken and speak to me. Although I discover each of the poets to be the member of a movement, I do not claim either that he is the most representative figure of the movement or that the sample of his poetry which I discuss exhibits the distinctive characteristics of his body of work. The individual poem and the individual poet may be peripheral, eccentric, or central to the group to which it and he belong. I claim for each poem only that it is an accomplished poem and a true voice in the ensemble of the poetry of our polyphonous time and place.

I have tended to prefer the long poem, an elastic category which includes, in the present essay, works in several parts from not much over 100 lines to not much under 200 pages.

Although I will soon introduce a scheme that is the soul of simplicity, it is merely a device for focusing. Its employment is not an inadvertent tip-off that I have a favorite typology which I have chosen poems to exemplify. The poems are those about which I am most eager to speak within my circle of acquaintance (poems which are also not encumbered with so much discussion that it muffles its subject). Having first chosen them, I then have attempted to analyze what they say. Some may fall within the simple scheme; some touch it, but only tangentially; and some be altogether beside its point. The testimony of a poem is significant for our moment and epoch whether it fits the scheme or not. What I am assuming is that each of the poems embodies, and thereby bears witness to, an image of the life of man, a vision of human existence, an archetypal story, a myth.

Images therefore does not refer primarily to sensory impressions, such as the marvelous auditory imagery in the poetry of Galway Kinnell.[1] It refers to a larger unit, a sketch of the place or role of man in the dialectic of selves and things. The sketch is the outward expression of an inward disposition, deeper than thought, feeling, sensation. It is the primordial gesture of the self among other selves and things, a tropism modified by experience. Recently I saw tall, clean boles of beech, elm, and oak, elongated before arching and forking into foliage-thick branches by their thrust for light as they grew, first, in the forest shade and, then, in the shadow of high-roofed two-storied Victorian summerhouses; the phototropism is identical but the results different in trees of the same species which grew in an open space and spread their branches closer to the earth. Similarly, the inward disposition is more than the aboriginal drive of the self. It is that drive redirected and condensed or expanded by the reception which world gives self. I am assuming that every poet writes out of, and articulates, some such experience-altered angle of approach to selves and things. His poems express his modified tropism. I will be straining to focus on that entire posture of the poem when I discuss *images*.

The first image of the life of man within the (double) scheme which I propose, does not have, to my knowledge, a paradigmatic literary expression. But it was an existential vocational option in Ireland during the Age of the Saints. If a young man desired to serve God, he would, after a period of monastic training and with the permission of his superior, either alone or with companions, in the spirit of Abraham who went forth not knowing

---

[1] I have in mind not only the sound effects of urban dawn in the opening section of "The Avenue Bearing the Initial of Christ into the New World" but also such phonic notation of natural and artificial noise as *flop, croal, haish, yaw,* and *brong ding plang ching* in *Body Rags* (pp. 3, 15, 22, 29).

whither, go down to the seas, launch a coracle, and, using oars, mast, sail only the time it took to get beyond protective headlands and then throwing overboard all instruments of propulsion and steering, surrender the craft to the elements—currents, tides, winds. The Lord of the Elements would utilize the elements of water and air to direct the hidebound boat to its destination, the place of resurrection, the place of exile for the love of Christ, of service during the rest of life, of death, and of burial.

To cast oneself upon nature is to find it the Creation, not a process indifferent to personhood and sanctity, but a medium of divine guardianship and guidance. To cast oneself upon nature is to throw oneself upon the care of God.

Type one is a throwing of the self into that which supports and fulfills it.

The second image of the life of man within the scheme has a paradigmatic literary expression, one of the most powerful poems of the last decade, "Falling" by James Dickey. Its epigraph, a quotation from *The Times,* offers a synopsis of the action.

> A 29-year-old stewardess fell . . . to her death tonight when she was swept through an emergency door that suddenly sprang open. . . . The body . . . was found . . . three hours after the accident.

The stunning poem is parabolic, for what initially seems melodramatic and most unusual gradually becomes an account of each of us as we rapidly accelerate toward death.

As we remember hearing in the lecture by our first teacher of general science, it isn't the falling that does the damage, it's the impact when we hit. Epic and prophetic poets dramatize falling as divine judgment against the proud self-deifiers. Existentialists say that man is thrown into the world, condemned to be free, and that he lives authentically only if he lives in the awareness of his death. "Falling" excludes the perspectives of the epic and prophetic poets. The airline stewardess is not a rebel like Prometheus, an overreacher like Icarus, a desirer of illimitable experience like Faust. Her fall is not the fall of Eve. She does not defy, disobey, or desire inordinately. She is merely doing her duty of caring for people.

The poem forces the reader to concentrate on the problem of what one is to do with his plunging. Ignore it? Perform time-passing activities? Perfect skills? Dream of rescue? Strive to escape it? Struggle to overcome it? Surrender to it begrudgingly? Relax and enjoy it? Conventional notions about life seem to disregard the deathward plummeting of the self.

Air does not sustain her. She cannot reach water (with its promise that if she enters it properly, she will rise from it unbroken). Earth kills. To fall in nature is to find it lethal. To fall is to have to invent what one does with himself for the brief duration.

Type two is a falling of the self into that which is indifferent and destructive to it.

Bon Voyage: David Jones, the Last Modernist

David Jones belongs to a line of great British artist/authors or painter/poets at the head of which stands William Blake. He is also the last of the Modernists.

By designating David Jones a Modernist, I am placing him with such practitioners of Modernism as T. S. Eliot, James Joyce, Ezra Pound (as Eliot himself does in his Introduction to *In Parenthesis*), and William Carlos Williams.

Modernism can be described generationally and stylistically thematically. It occurred when our culture no longer had the institutions for proportionately transmitting its experience, skill, and purpose because of their disruption or destruction by capitalism, industrialization, and urbanization. Persons of that generation found themselves thrust out into an emerging and alien world without guidance. Although they had a past, they did not know it from growing up in their culture but had to work it up on their own. The result was paradoxical: the homemade, the individually invented, the private tradition.

The practitioners of Modernism are "exiles" (Eliot in London; David Jones in Harrow; Joyce in Trieste; Pound in Rapallo, the cage near Pisa, and St. Elizabeth's in Washington) but they celebrate places, frequently cities (Eliot, London and the sites named by the titles of the *Four Quartets*; David Jones, London, Wales, the British Isles and their waters, the Holy Land; Joyce, Dublin; Pound, Venice; Williams, Paterson, New Jersey). They render the ugly details of life in the twentieth century in their full sordidness and vulgarity, but arrange them against, or within, an ancient or perennial pattern (the four-foldness of elements and seasons in *Four Quartets*, *Finnegans Wake*, and the original quadrilateral design of *Paterson*; the grail quest in *The Waste Land*, *The Odyssey* in *Ulysses*, *The Gododdin* in *In Parenthesis*).

An extension of the dramatic monologue of Browning, the works are either interior monologues (*Ulysses*), voices spoken through masks of imagined historical or invented characters (*The Waste Land*), or both.

The works combine drastically different levels of discourse. The colloquial and the formal, the low and the elevated, are cheek by jowl. The languages of advertising and oratory collide. The works are macaronic, multilingual (Eliot, Sanskrit, German, French; David Jones, Latin and Welsh; Joyce, the Berlitz instructor, babel; Pound, Chinese, Egyptian, Greek, Latin, Italian).

The works are fragmentary (the subtitle of *The Anathemata* is "fragments of an attempted writing"). It is as though no one can hold a whole world in his head. At the most one can clutch a collection of broken pieces. The works juxtapose scrambled periods. They are not continuous stories told in the third person by an omniscient narrator. The reader has to piece together the action and situation (like a clue-gathering detective). The ordering of the works is thematic in a musical sense (statement, repetition, inversion and other variation). Modernist works are indirect and require alert, sustained participation by readers if they are to grasp the composite whole.

The works are prophetic, appealing to the past against the present for the sake of the future. They announce that the technological present is the end of the West unless there is renewal of linguistic, communal, artistic, spiritual tradition.

Interestingly, there is an appeal beyond the dominant tradition of the West in most of the practitioners of Modernism (Eliot, to the high religion of India; David Jones, to Celtic lost causes; Joyce, to Western heretics; Pound, to Confucius; Williams, to the New World Man, whom Williams presents in *In The American Grain* and whom Lewis Mumford analyzes as combining primitivism and pragmatism in a Romantic mix in *The Transformations of Man*).

The works incarnate the renewing moment (for Eliot, a mystical and/or sacramental moment; for David Jones, good work and the myth—for every myth adumbrates the Gospel—and the eucharistic liturgy; for Joyce, an epiphany and an archetypal event; for Pound, the species-perpetuating patterning of seeds and a vision of goddesses).

David Jones is the last Modernist because he is the youngest (he is seventy-five years old on 1 November—or *Calangaeaf*, as he has taught us to say), because Pound and he are the only practitioners of Modernism still living, and because he came to writing only in maturity, toward the end of the twenties, after he had already made some of the most distinguished sculptures, engravings, and paintings of our time (but before he began, a decade later, to make the equally distinguished inscriptions).

An abbreviated biography of David Jones presents a succinct summary of the motifs of *The Anathemata*. He was born in Brockley, Kent (1895). His father, a Welsh master printer and an Evangelical lay reader in the Church of England, and his mother, daughter of a Thames-side master carpenter and of a woman with some Italian blood, met as teachers in a Sunday School. These few prenatal facts already state with two exceptions his major themes: Wales and all things Celtic; London, its tidal river, ships, and the sea; craftsmanship; Rome, as imperial and ecclesiastical capital; and Christianity.

As a quiet maker of things and an erudite autodidact, David Jones has had, with two exceptions, an essentially uneventful life. During World War I he served with the Royal Welsh Fusiliers in France, receiving a leg wound at the Battle of the Somme (July 1916) and, later, almost dying from trench fever, and then served in Ireland with occupying troops.

Perhaps the most important event of his life occurred during the war, probably in 1917. One day gathering firewood just behind the lines, he saw a more or less intact farmbuilding that looked promising. Approaching it, he looked through a wall hole before he entered, expecting to see the moted dusk of an empty interior. He was surprised by glowing candlelight on an improvised altar, disclosing a celebration of the Mass by a group of soldiers which included persons whom he had not connected with Christianity. He could see that the eucharistic action was concerted and unific. Thereafter, although he did not become a Catholic immediately, the Mass has been the heart of his life and art, as we find in *The Anathemata* and other poems (for example, the newest part of the work-in-progress, "The Sleeping Lord") and in his paintings and inscriptions. World War I added one major motif to his repertoire, the soldier (the representative man) and altered another, a Christianity concentric to the Roman Mass.

Both before and after World War I, David Jones attended art schools. In 1921 he joined the Catholic Church and joined a community of craftsmen of which Eric Gill was a leader. David Jones spent much time with Gill, at Ditchling, Capel-y-ffin, and Pigotts, engraving, painting, and writing, until Gill's death in 1940.

The second exception to the evenness of his life has been a series of breakdowns, particularly the middle and apparently most devastating one (as though something detonated long-buried explosive experiences assumed to be duds—experiences of childhood in family or of war or of both —and laid waste the creative life, leaving it a no-man's-land). In 1934 friends arranged a voyage to the Near East and back, a rest-and-sea-cure. Feeling slightly ill, hurried, and fatigued, he seemed to have only the most superficial response to the scenes of the stories about our Lord and other biblical figures. But, typically, in a decade these impressions, enriched by profound immersion in the imagination, began to surface. The trip for recovery added the final major motif to his repertoire, the Holy Land.

In 1937 *In Parenthesis*, a decade in the making, appeared, two decades after the events recounted and transmuted. If *In Parenthesis* is *The Iliad*, the war epic of David Jones, *The Anathemata* is *The Odyssey*, his epic of a homecoming voyage.

The Anathemata, an eight-section, 200-page eucharistic poem in free verse and prose, arranges the already designated motifs around the theme of worship.[2] The whole poem is the interior monologue of a person at a Roman Mass in Great Britain during World War II. The Axis powers, ruling Europe, prepare to invade the British Isles. It is a time of danger,

---

[2] Amos Wilder has been one of the first critics to write extensively about *The Anathemata*. See his *The New Voice* (New York: Herden and Herder, 1969). See also Fr. William T. Noon's *Poetry and Prayer* (New Brunswick: Rutgers University Press, 1967) and various essays in the David Jones special issue of *Agenda* 5, nos. 1–3 (Spring–Summer, 1967).

isolation, loss, and, perhaps, doom for this people. I would guess that the Mass takes place on Christmas Eve (the night of the Nativity is one occasion within the ecclesiastical calendar during which it is normal to recall at one and the same time the Birth and Death of Christ, as the-person-at-Mass does in both sections VII and VIII) and takes place in London or environs (The Pool of London is the navel of the poem: sections IV and V).

The long interior monologue integrates several extensive imagined dramatic monologues by women (pp. 86–88, 125–168, 209–215) and a similar dialogue by men (pp. 118–124) but most of it is the meander of a mind among a number of motifs as the on-going action of the Mass proposes them. The interior monologue is not stream-of-consciousness. David Jones does not attempt to build up the scene by circumstantial detail through a mosaic of sensation, feeling, thought as Joyce did in *Ulysses*. Although the-person-at-Mass surrenders his mind to external suggestions, their single source is liturgical. The stimuli that set off the monologue seem to be restricted to the priest, the place where he acts, and the things which he handles.

At the very beginning of the poem, a poem about worship, we face the problematic character of worship in the present and foreseeable future. Section I opens in a churchbuilding whose architecture and decoration (mass-produced imitations in material and scale other than those of the originals) reminds the-person-at-Mass that there is not only national but also civilizational doom. The nation is in peril because of enemies. But the culture, having coarsened and declined into a civilization, is unable to create a living expression of either secular or sacred society because it has reached, to use the notions of Spengler, its winter phase. If Great Britain dies, it will be because others kill it. If the West dies, it will be because it has used itself up, running through its phases.

The underlying question at the beginning of the poem is, are the dead forms in the midst, and by means, of which we make our offerings (*anathemata* means offerings) the result of the West's being moribund or the result of mankind's undergoing a cultural mutation through the West-centered but earth-covering spread of technocracy? If it is the former, new cultures may be springing to life elsewhere and creating new forms and symbols. If it is the latter, the control of nature and the engineering of society by means of manipulating abstract symbols, man as the being who contemplates, loves, serves concrete symbols as the core of personal and communal individuation and as the depth-disclosing manifestation of mysteries, personal, communal, cosmic, divine, is at an end. Is the West alone suffering a death of imagination and spirit? Or is all mankind submitting to the dehumanizing "overcoming" of its own nature?

The Mass has a heightened significance if Great Britain is falling under foreign tyranny, or if the West is concluding its cycle of life. But if mankind lays aside the concrete symbols by which persons and things become dear, familiar, intimate, moving, vocative of respect and reverence, then the Mass is a nonfunctional holdover which merely mocks us, for the bread and wine cannot become the Body and Blood of Christ. *The Anathemata* returns to these matters to touch on them briefly but sharply (pp. 93, 115, 231–232). Our subsequent concentration on the triumphant affirmation of human destiny in the poem ought not to lead us into accusing it of expressing too luminous and easy an optimism, for the very situation of the fiction of the poem is dark and difficult.

The thought of the-person-at-Mass zigzags back and forth like the rapid woof-bearing shuttle in the dextrous hands of an expert weaver. From the question of the dooms of Great Britain, the West, and mankind as a symbol-nourished being, and of the end of the Mass, the shuttle shoots to the origins of the Mass, mankind, and (geologically) Great Britain, in section I ("Rite and Fore-Time" means the Mass and Prehistory and includes a powerful passage which compares what the cave painters of Lascaux did for their society and what priests at altars do for theirs: "that the kindred may have life" p. 60) and of the West in section II ("Middle-Sea and Lear-Sea" means the Mediterranean Sea and the oceanic waters around the British Isles, the sea routes opened for commercial and industrial purposes along which the ancient cultures and religions of the Near East and Europe reached the British Isles).

In section III, the shuttle reverses to fly, in the opposite direction, toward the present ("Angle-Land" means England and as the repetition of *Sea* in section II emphasizes voyage, so the contrast of *Land* in section III emphasizes settlement, by sea warriors, who themselves set off a section-concluding chain of associations about nation-determining naval engagements, Nelson at Trafalgar and the fratricidal English and German fleets during World War I and World War II).

In sections IV and V, the shuttle again shoots toward the past, first, the mid-nineteenth century and, then the end of the Middle Ages ("Redriff" means Rotherhithe, on the London-facing southside of the Thames, the locale of both sections, and "Lady of the Pool" means not only a woman of the town but also the spirit of the place: in the first, Eb Bradshaw, maternal grandfather of David Jones, in the last period when being a craftsman was still a normal vocation in society, speaks for every craftsman about the autonomy of the mystery which he serves, with adherence to traditional ways and devotion to the job well done, boasting that neither for more money nor for earlier salvation would he hurry or skimp work; in the second, lavender-vending Ellen Monica speaks to her present lover, a sea captain, about her previous ones, a soldier and a priest-scholar, from the three of whom she has gotten a liberal education (!), enacting the close relation of knowledge and love, and reciting the history of the Church under the allegory of a risky voyage by a storm-buffetted and -battered vessel which, in spite of damage and danger, makes harbor, "rejoicing them/ for that she *cannot* be lost"—p. 142).

Section VI demonstrates the associative method of the interior mono- logue as a thinking of several similar things on the basis of one thing. "Keel, Ran, Stauros" means keel of a ship, battering ram, cross. Each is a log worked to a beam by a craftsman. The two horizontal ones express man's historical expansiveness. The perpendicular one expresses simul- taneously man's historical limitations and God's intra historical introduction of instrumentalities for a man-fulfilling transcending of those limitations. The three beams are used by sailor, soldier, and priest (the three lovers of the Lady of the Pool), which triad defines man, the craftsman-venturer- antagonist whom God redeems.

Sections VII and VIII demonstrate the associative method of the interior monologue as a thinking of many widely different, farfetched things which, arranged in a linear order, form a concatenation of accidental connections. "Mabinog's Liturgy" means Christ's Mass (Christmas) and "Sherthursdaye and Venus Day" means Maundy Thursday and Good Friday (the first the form or the manner and the second the content or the matter of each Mass, the first the rite and the second the sacrifice). In section VII, the poem establishes the time of the Nativity. It compares the birth and death of Christ (as section VIII also does). It praises the beauty of Mary as greater than that of the Greek goddesses in the contest which set the Trojan War in motion, greater than that of Gwenhwyfar (Guenevere), wife of King Arthur, in her best churchgoing clothes.

The description of her and her garments (with parenthetical desig- nation of the source of her materials and patterns) takes eight pages. The long passage in all its elaborate detail is Welsh and Celtic not only in matter (Arthur is crucial to the matter of Britain) but also in manner, which assumes that anything mentioned has a story to tell and frequently tells it or, by the compact form of an epithet, tells us that there is one to tell but goes on to the next item. A Welsh argument, description, or narra- tive has both its mainstream strong to drive from beginning to end as directly as possible and its trail-off eddies to arc into curlicues lazing con- trary to the carry-all current the whole length of the course. Or, the bole of the thrust-straight tree is looped with the gadding and knotting vine. For example, the garments of Gwenhwyfar have fasteners made of polar ivory. The poem tells a story of how Manawydan obtained the ivory on an arctic voyage. Then it asks if the story is a lie. Then it considers other pos- sible sources (did he make them himself by magic? did he obtain them by trade?). Every object is a mystery. It has a story. But that does not exhaust the mystery. It evokes infinite speculations. Every object is the proper subject for endless contemplation. A world composed of such things awakens wonder. The associative linking in the Welsh manner reinforces the associative linking in the Modernist manner. By being a Modernist, David Jones is most faithful to his own precious heritage.

The passage about Gwenhwyfar suggests the next passage because the service for which she has dressed in her best clothes is a Mass for Christmas Eve, when creatures neutralize the negativities of their natures in acknowledgment of the ultimate fulfillment of the Creation begun by the Incarnation. Plants blossom; animals, including wolves, kneel; and witches, bluestocking intellectualistic witches, arch and as copious of allusion to the sisterhood of women as women's-liberation propaganda, lay aside their magic (from a sense, they say, of solidarity with Mary). As quaintness moves through quirkiness toward queerness and we begin to ask if the out-workings of the Incarnation are only fanciful or fantastic, the poet introduces a piece of World War I autobiography: English and German soldiers at the Front arranged their own local armistice and met one another in no-man's-land to exchange gifts "BECAUSE OF THE CHILD" (p. 216: the contrast with the English-German fratricide at the end of section III qualifies its evil). The rest of section VII, also linked by the idea of Mass on Christmas Eve, recounts how the city of Rome celebrates the liturgies of the Nativity.

What (besides seeing that it traces unsystematically the natural and cultural contributions which in their intricate individuating integration constitute the uniqueness of Great Britain) are we to make of a meander of mind so erratic and so eruditely at worship? Those who have received standard instruction about worship have been taught that their role in a service is to concentrate, to pay attention, and in every way to pour self (feeling, thought, will) into the clerically led, lay-assisted congregational liturgical moment. They assume that they cease to worship if they permit their thoughts to wander. Yet *The Anathemata* dramatizes that they need not feel sheepish if they woolgather. They are not unfaithful—on the contrary, they are faithful—to the Lamb of God slain from the foundation of the world for the sake of all people and the whole Creation, if they let their mind go back and forth through space-time, for they recollect at random the persons whom the Lamb ransoms and the things which He redeems. Wanting to present all things as their offerings to God, they cannot get off the subject. Their wandering thoughts cannot go astray but only touch on what God already holds in His care and acts to save. In the Canon of the Mass the prayers for the living and the dead are close to the words of institution. As we recall Christ, we also recall all mankind. It is as appropriate for worship to let the mind go through space-time as to concentrate it on the liturgical leader and setting.

The abandonment of one's thoughts to their associations resembles the throwing away of steering gear by the seaborne Irish monks in the Age of the Saints.

So far the account, by stressing the interior monologue and letting the mind go, makes *The Anathemata* sound individual, mental, and passive. Nothing could be more misleading. *The Anathemata* celebrates the active, physical, social dimension of existence.

The zigzagging wool flies athwart (and over or under) the tight-stretched warp. *The Anathemata* sings a series of ship voyages, lavish in sensory details, nautical know-how, psychological penetration, economic, political, religious, social contexts. In sections II through VI, a number of voyages and captains appear. There is voyage after voyage, but it is all the one human voyage, a going beyond the known into the unknown. The first level of meaning is historical. Ships carry the cultures and religions which contribute to the formation of Great Britain. The second, third, and fourth levels of meaning are figurative. Ships bring Christ to Great Britain (sea-crossing witnesses bring him in Word and Sacraments). The churchbuilding, priest, and congregation resemble ship, captain, and crew. The Mass itself is like a voyage (see pp. 53, 106, footnote 2, a crucial footnote). The all-inclusive one human voyage becomes (as it were, at the moment of Transubstantiation) the voyage under the eucharistic Christ as captain. God brings mankind safe to Himself.

Of course, each historical undertaking suffers failure, loss, wreckage, but as we labor at that voyage Christ comes to us in the daily or weekly Mass to pilot us, crew and passengers, gear and cargo (for our God-established works follow us), to harbor. Each Mass participates by anticipating the eschatological total retrieval of the divine gathering of all persons and things into transfiguring Eternity. To call to mind in the Mass persons and things no longer historically present is to know them glorious in the life of God.

The result is that *The Anathemata* has a radiant ultimate universalism. Nothing is permanently lost. All is finally perfected and fulfilled. Great Britain may suffer defeat and the West may collapse in ruins (yet live forever in God). Yet mankind reaches God for God guides mankind to Himself. The proper farewell is *bon voyage*.

If the abandonment of one's thoughts to their association resembles those self-castaways, the Irish monks, the divine guiding of the one human voyage to heaven resembles the bringing of the monks to their place of resurrection by the Lord of the Elements.

In spite of its honoring of the role of craftsmanship in human existence (by it, persons serve their neighbors and express themselves; by it, persons gain communal dignity and self-respect), the underlying image-of-the-life-of-man in *The Anathemata* is close to the God-trusting image of type one.

Necromancy: John Berryman, Transitionalist

The Anathemata appeared in 1952; *Homage to Mistress Bradstreet* by John Berryman—an eighteen-page poem with fifty-seven stanzas—appeared in 1953.

John Berryman, born in McAlester, Oklahoma, 25 October 1914, studied at Columbia University and Clare College, Cambridge, and taught at Wayne, Princeton, Brown, and Minnesota. Although he was chiefly a poet, he also wrote fiction (the famous "The Imaginary Jew") and criticism (especially his study of Stephen Crane).

In 1968 the last of his prize-winning *Dream Songs* came out. The 385 three-stanza poems compose a substantial, difficult, brilliant long work, a poem more confessional and jagged, even split-level, than *Homage to Mistress Bradstreet* (although it has its own confessional and jagged moments: see stanzas 33–34).

It is the lurch toward Confessional poetry and the cracking or irregularizing of verse form that I have in mind when I call John Berryman a Transitionalist. Like Robert Lowell, he started out as an apprentice to the admired practitioners of Modernism. His notion of what poetry is and does derived from their poetry and theory. Yet he belonged to a subsequent generation (he was twenty years younger than David Jones) and had different experiences and faced different problems and terrors. The *Dream Songs* alter the center of gravity (and levity) in his poetry and extend his notion of its being and function. They incorporate more and more of his experience, including, as their title suggests, dream, delirium, fantasy, and other states of consciousness, particularly an awareness of the world of literature and the condition of being a poet. In their incorporation of experience, they resemble the poems of the New Humanism; but in their ingenious contrivance, they resemble the poems of Modernism. In their technical self-advertising, they are themselves, Transitional and Confessional.

Modernism regarded experience as swampingly inchoate, overwhelmingly chaotic, or downright demonic. For Modernism art orders experience by imposing a pattern upon it. Art is sorted-out experience. It distances, frames, selects. It condenses and intensifies by means of indirections. Modernism betrays a distrust or fear of experience. Having been thrust out into life without instruction in how to conduct it, does one dare simply to respond to experience (does one dare to eat a peach?)? Apparently not.

In contrast, the New Humanism trusts experience (it is what we are; it is all we have). For the New Humanism, art does not have to impose a pattern upon experience but has merely to be faithful to the pattern inherent in it. For the New Humanism, poetry does not have to be complex, indirect, and intense. It can be straightforward, simple, relaxed, quiet, meditative as well.

But not the poetry of virtuoso John Berryman! His early set of songs was called "The Nervous Songs." His poetry has to burn with the twentieth-century pyrotechnic equivalent of a hard gemlike flame. It has to be, work by work, a tour de force. Poetry—no matter how much it incorporates his experience—must always be doing something impressive. John

Berryman was a Transitionalist not only generationally but also in the two-directional development of his poetry (the matter more and more experiential, the manner more and more contrived—as though reality were primarily contortion and torture).

Like *The Anathemata, Homage to Mistress Bradstreet* is rich with the self-presentation of a feminine speaker. It, too, includes a voyage of foundation (of New England rather than Great Britain). It, too, shows the influence of the poetry of Gerard Manley Hopkins, who brought over into English devices in line-and-stanza-formation (alliteration, consonance, rime) from the Welsh system of sound patterning (brought it over as a means of giving punch to key works, rather than of homogenizing sound into a smooth, harmonious flow) and who invented sprung rhythm, a system of line formation by stresses, rather than by metrical feet or syllables.

Mistress in the title is an earlier form of our *Mrs.* Yet, as we shall see, there is a pun on the more recent meaning of the word as extramarital lover. *Homage* also has a double meaning. It is an act of respect shown to a person who has authority by rank and/or by accomplishment. Our first thought is that the poem acknowledges the poetic accomplishment of Anne Bradstreet. Later we recognize that it acknowledges her human accomplishment both in undertaking the difficult vocation of poet in an inhospitable country and in living into her death under the double disadvantage of colonial life in the wilderness and of Puritanism with its theocratic repression and its identification of human disasters as corrections from God. Our final thought (which does not exclude the earlier ones) is that the homage is a service of devotion done the beloved according to the code of (adulterous) courtly/romantic love.

The fiction of the poem is as queer as anything in section VII of *The Anathemata*. It is a dialog between a twentieth-century man and a seventeenth-century woman whom he summons from the grave. He makes, as we would say, improper advances and proposals. And she does not refuse them, until the memory of her children gives her fulcrum for the leverage of a "No."

The fiction is grotesque. But as the unlikely witches of *The Anathemata* permit a presentation of the drastic benign change in human and cosmic destiny accomplished by the incarnation, so this unlikely fiction permits the exploration of several important relations in depth.

We ask, what do they see in one another? Who is Anne Bradstreet?

She was a historical person, one of the early settlers in the Massachusetts Bay Colony, daughter of one leader, wife of another. *Homage to Mistress Bradstreet* is a vivid historical reconstruction of her life, the more marvelous in that the woman utters her own self-awareness. Her voice carries to us, conveying her sense of self and world fresh and strong. Historians who want to fault her "self-portrait" for showing a liberal sympathy with Anne Hutchinson, Quakers, redmen without documentary evidence have to praise it for showing, in a few bold strokes, many drawn from the evidence, her domestic world and somatic being in its sensuous immediacy.

She is a religious person, living and understanding her life within the communal and intellectual structures of reformed theology which Puritanism brought to this continent.

She is a woman. A womanizer can relate to her, even if she is not his usual soft touch kind of victim. Perhaps her almost daunting difference makes her even that much more desirable. If the beloved of courtly love is to be inaccessible, she is a perfect candidate for that role.

Most important, she is a poet, a writer of religious and domestic verses and meditative prose. Her first book, *The Tenth Muse Lately Sprung Up in America*, appeared in London in 1650. The lover regrets that her poetry is not distinguished. Even so, she was one of the very first persons to try to be a poet in America. English poetry did not equip her with powers equal to the experience of the New World (nor, Berryman implies, did reformed theology). Much of the time her poetry writing was a back-looking activity: "I phrase/anything past, dead, far,/sacred" (stanza 12).[3] Her lover, 300 years later, is still attempting to be a poet in a country indifferent, superior, or antagonistic to poetry (or a country which, if it honors the poet, idolizes, glamorizes, and destroys him as though he were a movie star). It still lacks a poetic adequate to experience. As he says to her, "Both of our worlds unhanded us" (stanza 2).[4] He proposes that he be her love. She consents but soon her children call her to herself.

What are we to make of such an absurd fiction? Is it simply a bit of arbitrary and gratuitous naughtiness? I think not. First, a general perspective; secondly, a specific interpretation.

Epic poetry often includes an episode that is an interview with the dead. Saul has a demoralizing encounter with Samuel called up by the witch of Endor. Odysseus asks questions of Tiresias. Aeneas takes the golden bough and speaks to his father in the underworld. Jesus has probing colloquy with Moses and Elijah about man-liberating undertakings and outgoings at the Transfiguration. Virgil escorts Dante through regions of pain and instructs him about them. Milton enters the body of Blake. The speaker of *Four Quartets*, on firewatching duty during World War II, meets "a familiar compound ghost." The-person-at-Mass on Christmas Eve in London during World War II summons up his grandfather to speak for the artist in everyman. Only by entering into a dialogue with the past can a man become a member of his culture and an autonomous person. Only by confronting his heritage does he enter into, and go beyond, it. The twen-

---

[3] From *Homage to Mistress Bradstreet* by John Berryman, copyrighted 1956 and published by Farrar, Strauss & Giroux, Inc.

[4] From *Homage to Mistress Bradstreet* by John Berryman, copyrighted 1956 and published by Farrar, Strauss & Giroux, Inc.

tieth-century lover-poet condemns himself to be less a person and poet than Anne Bradstreet until he considers her life and work seriously.

Specifically, the poem dramatizes what writing and reading imply, a laying of the self open to the other. Indeed, either act invites another to enter one's life. Time, even three centuries, does not alter the structure. As we give ourselves imaginatively to a work which a person has made imaginatively, we have the power to call him up from the dead, summon him back to life, command him to speak. Literary experience is necromantic.

The structure of giving the self to the work resembles the structure of giving the self to the beloved. Our attraction to a new work, our fascination with it, is like our falling in love. The poem is the trysting place for the assignation of writer and reader. Literature has its ardors and risks.

The eventual refusal of his advances and proposals by Anne Bradstreet (in the fiction of the poem) as her children come to mind indicates that, for her, being a poet was secondary to being mother and wife.

To the extent that the poem is a ghost story, it conforms to the rule of the ghost story that an emotion of the ghost and an emotion of the haunted person link them. Shall we say that her emotion is some dissatisfaction, frustration, or wistfulness that she did not realize her full poetic gifts and therefore draws near a careful and demanding reader of her poetry? And that his passion is to be a great poet, even in America? Her failure to be great (prefiguring so many other such failures) and her womanhood wrenches from him sympathy and understanding. He gives her words (that fulfill her gifts), and, at the last (stanza 54) calls her, not mistress, but *sister*.

Only what preoccupies her comes to utterance (as with the major character in a Japanese No drama). She recalls her life more or less chronologically, but with gaps and leaps between vivid recollections, both big events and small quotidian commonplace happenings. The poem is a dramatic dialogue but in her speeches inner pressures determine the scenes which rise from the past (scenes linked associationally, as in stream-of-consciousness).

One of the masterful accomplishments of *Homage to Mistress Bradstreet* is the presentation of womanhood in its full circumstantiality. The poem reminds us how much the life of woman is the life of the body, receiving sensations, budding in adolescence, awakening to sexuality, altering in pregnancy, laboring in childbearing, relaxing with a luxuriant sense of wellbeing in nursing, suffering sicknesses, dying (stanzas 3, 21, 26, 27, 45, 57); and how much she has traditionally lived her life and had her important moments within the routine of the household and the circle of children.

Another of its masterful accomplishments is its making clear that a people claims a land less by doings, material culture, or intellectual comprehension (voyage, treaty, treefelling, housebuilding, fieldplanting), than by the dyings of loved ones in a place ("Sticken: 'Oh. Then he takes us one by one' "—stanza 23; "This our land was ghosted with/our dead: I am at home."—stanza 44; "My window gives on the graves, in our great new house/(how many burned) upstairs, among the elms"—stanza 51; also stanzas 7, 23, 41, 52).[5] The place of burial is beachhead for making America ours.

The image-of-the-life-of-man in *Homage to Mistress Bradstreet* is: life is grounded in organism, which, when it is in harmony, brings us the world, and, when it is dissonant, brings us its own cacophony; meanwhile dyings give a stake in the world.

It is closest to type two but it has a social dimension (the dyings of others) which the image of falling lacks.[6]

Three New Humanist Poets

There has been no more steady proponent of meters for poetry in our time than John Crowe Ransom. By example in his own verses, by precept in guiding would-be poets, by analysis of poems and by general theory in his criticism, he has urged and argued their importance as a means of composition and as a dimension of meaning in the poem. An acquaintance who took a course in verse writing with Mr. Ransom has reported that the one piece of critical praise which he received the whole semester was for his employing the permissible substitution of an extra unaccented syllable before a heavy caesura in the last lines of the sestet of a sonnet! It is an event of significance in literary history—an earthquake—that former students of Mr. Ransom like Robert Penn Warren, Robert Lowell, James Wright, Robert Mezey, who had already written a body of mature poems in traditional verse forms, undertook the additional apprenticeship to their craft of learning to write in other than the meters of which they had been such wholehearted admirers, such flashing practitioners. There has been a major shift in sensibility. The hippies parade it; the hypotheses of Marshall McLuhan attempt to explain it; and the change in line formation of poems from metrical composition to free verse (or sprung rhythm or syllabics) is its seismographic confirmation.

Modernism as literary movement and as established mode has performed its task. Transitionalism is still in power. But the New Humanism, an expression of the major shift in sensibility, rises and spreads.

[5] From *Homage to Mistress Bradstreet* by John Berryman, copyrighted 1956 and published by Farrar, Straus & Giroux, Inc.

[6] The same image-of-the-life-of-man is, no doubt with modifications, in the *Dream Songs*: the first one ends, "Hard on the land wears the strong sea/and empty grows every bed." The last one begins, "My daughter's heavier." As the songs accumulate the long poem becomes more and more a collection of elegies for the dyings of contemporary writers. *77 Dream Songs* by John Berryman, copyrighted 1959, 1962, 1963, 1964 and published by Farrar, Straus & Giroux, Inc.

The New Humanism can be a misleading title (I borrow it from a book by Roger Shinn). There has already been one New Humanism in this century, that of Babbitt and More. Like the old humanism of the Renaissance, the old New Humanism of the first half of the twentieth century was literary in the sense that knowing the ideas in the writings of the great human minds and spirits of the past was integral to the formation of the full human being in the present. There was something elitist and leisure class about these humanists. There was time to retire from society to library or study. But adherents were not mere bookworms escaping self and world behind walls of volumes. The ideas gathered from books infused their minds and irradiated their persons. The process did not simply refine them; by increasing their powers it prepared them to be responsible to the public good. The oration was their medium, or, in a period of altered acoustics, the essay. They addressed the educated sector of society in a concern for the common life, stressing education, ethics, politics, and religion. The old New Humanists wrote with dignity and high seriousness.

Roger Shinn has something else in mind: the artistic, economic, political, technological internationalization of experience as promoted by the thaw in the cold war and the expansion of mass media, the discovery that nationalism is a prison that produces paranoia and ideology a piece of apparatus that obscures the world and encumbers its bearer. A new openness toward others and their cultures, in their sweep of differences, develops.

No doubt, the old New Humanism is repeating the tag *Nothing human is alien to me* meant *I can consider any experience so long as it reaches me in a literary form.* It would have assumed that one would encounter the sweep of differences in persons and cultures with the resources of the inner check (with a "No" for some possibilities of our nature) and would be selective, seeking the highest.

Austin Warren reports that Mrs. Babbitt, who grew up in China, used to protest, when her husband, an expert on Confucian and Buddhist thought, spoke with authority about that country, "You have never been there, you don't know how it looks and how it smells." Mr. Warren adds, "The rebuke passed as superficial."[7] The old New Humanism thought so, but not the new New Humanism. For it, another culture is not primarily a subject to read about or a museum to visit but a house to inhabit. Anthropology, with its field work, is the model of the new New Humanism. To understand a culture one enters and participates in it. Contact is the basis of knowledge; practice of customs, the basis of sympathy.

The recent shift in sensibility expresses itself in poetry by more than the means of line formation. Both manner and matter change, and the relation of the life and the work of the poet alters.

---

[7] Austin Warren, *New England Saints* (Ann Arbor: The University of Michigan Press, 1956), p. 156.

The New Humanist poet becomes a wayfarer. He travels—Galway Kinnell in France and Iran (see his novel *Black Light*), Denise Levertov in Europe and Spanish-speaking America, Gary Snyder in India and Japan. The poet travels to teach and to study, not as a tourist (to observe), but as a postulant (to penetrate). A sure sign of that direct participation is that the poet is bi- or multilingual. He savors the speech of other tongues, the salt, spice, and tang of them. Galway Kinnell has translated François Villon and Yves Bonnefoy; Denise Levertov, Guillevic; Gary Snyder, Kanzan or Han-Shan and Miyazawa Kenji.

The poet travels to protest. Galway Kinnell spent a year doing voter-registration work in the South; Denise Levertov, half a decade doing war resistance across the country; Gary Snyder, an even longer time advocating ecological sanity. The poet identifies himself with those whom society exploits and excludes, and with daily life, its ordinariness and ugliness. He is sensitive not only to nature in ways made familiar by Romanticism but also to the city in ways made familiar by Modernism.

The poet is religious, but in individual rather than institutional ways. Eclectic and syncretist, he treats dream, audition, vision, visitation with respect and does not turn away from ecstasy. The New Humanist poet trusts his own experience, including his own religious experience. Galway Kinnell seems to have total ambivalence toward Christianity (his poetry abounds in items from it but uses them equally with acceptance and with repudiation). Jamshid, the protagonist of *Black Light*, a Muslim, speaks, per-haps, not only for himself but also for his creator when he expresses sur-prise and a little disappointment at the flimsiness of religion. Denise Levertov combines Judaism and Christianity, like her father, and other experiences (available through artifact and myth) as well, Apollo, Ishtar, Zochipilli, and the object hymned in "Psalm Concerning the Castle." Gary Snyder pioneered in exploring the relation of primitive religion, Buddhism and drugs.

The poetry of the new (anthropological) New Humanism is an attempt to name, be faithful to, and uphold the experience to which the poet gives himself without fear or holding back. To say it another way, the New Humanist poet feels that life and not simply poems are to be an expression of the imagination. There should not be a dichotomy between existence and utterance, a hiatus between being and saying. The poem should keep close to life. It should not attitudinize or posture but be at least as honest as talk among friends (Jeffers said that he could tell lies in prose).

Galway Kinnell, Wayfarer

Galway Kinnell has written many long poems. The earliest, longest, and perhaps most powerful, "The Avenue Bearing the Initial of Christ into the

New World," catalogs the poverty, pain, wearing out of things, age, for-getfulness, group hostilities, genocide of six million Jews, as well as the orchestra of street sounds at the beginning of each day, the miraculous abundance of fishes at the market every day, and the doggedness and a more nearly liberating aspect of faith—as they are found in urban slum life, especially for Jews along Avenue C in New York City. In spite of the dismal setting, the saddening events, and the terror, people say of their city, "what a kingdom it was!"[8]

Its rival in length and power is his recent "The Last River," a sur-realistic reflection of his experience doing voter registration, a contemporary version of Dante's *Inferno* (with Henry David Thoreau taking the place of Virgil), a hell the more horrible in that it is not a clearly marked and well laid out place of law and order which invited a guided tour. The presentation is fragmentary, hallucinatory, unpredictable. Scene chases scene as when one strains to regain consciousness after fainting. It is not (as Eliot said about Pound's hell) a hell just for other people but one which includes us all.

Also in *Body Rags*, his latest volume, is a trio of poems about the vocation of the poet (as the representative man): in all three—"Testa-ment of the Thief," "The Porcupine," and "The Bear"—there is the motif of self-consumption. In the first, there is the parasitic pewk-worm "whom you can drag forth only by winding up on a matchstick/a quarter turn a day for the rest of your days:/this may of my innards" (p. 55). In the second, the poet compares himself to the porcupine who, falling from a tree, punctured himself on a branch which snagged his intestines and played them out as he landed, running, and "spartle through a hundred feet of golden rod/before/the abrupt emptiness" (p. 58).[9]

Although all of these may be more nearly central to the fundamental disposition which the poetry of Galway Kinnell embodies, I have chosen to discuss my favorite poem of his, even if it has atypical features, and even

---

[8] "The Avenue Bearing the Initial of Christ into the New World" from *What a Kingdom It Was* by Galway Kinnell, published by Houghton Mifflin Company.

[9] "Testament of the Thief" and "The Porcupine" from *Body Rags* by Galway Kinnell, published by Houghton Mifflin Company. Recurrent images of figures of self-consuming fill his poetry, for example, p. 4, *Body Rags*. One is falling, but let him throw the self into the fall to make its arc as intensely conscious, imaginative, responsive, vital as possible. See p. 36, *Flower Herding on Mount Monadnock*; also pp. 4, 15, 18, 38, 41, 45–46, 54.

[10] I possess a typescript copy of version A, called "For the Hundredth Birthday of Robert Frost." Version B, called simply "For Robert Frost," appears in *Flower Herding on Mount Monadnock* (pp. 22–25). Perhaps Kinnell revised version A to version B because he thought that the death of Frost before its publication pulled the rug out from under the fierce, respectful irony in the title and body of the poem—the long persistence in life of someone "essentially dying." I think that it is a greater poem with the birthday

if it is that anomaly, an impressive poem in two versions, neither of which is altogether satisfactory.[10] It considers, not without humor, the most well-known and popular poet of the century, Robert Frost.[11]

It is atypical in its degree of contrivance and explicit literariness.[12] It is, first of all, literary criticism. Secondly, section III is a piece of pastiche, a passage woven of phrases from poems by Frost. Thirdly, it presents a story invented to explore an explanation of the central mystery of the famous poet (and therefore approximates contrived, literary *Homage to Mistress Bradstreet* in considering a historical, New England poet).

There were several impressive Robert Frosts and several demonic ones. Kinnell concentrates on three: the poet of New England landscape, the poet of human darkness, and the ceaseless private talker to visitors (he omits the public performer, the man doing public relations for himself or the nation, the poet who regarded other poets as competitors).

What purpose is served in the outpouring of incessant speech? Is it to prevent others or self from seeing or saying something? Kinnell supplies a story to explain the nonstop talk.

Section I raises the question which the rest of the poem answers. Section II recounts the one time that Robert Frost was silent in public, blinded by light at the inauguration of J. F. Kennedy. Section II describes a trip that Frost once made through snow to the midst of the woods. Section IV recounts his decision to return to persons and things in spite of the fascinating white mystery at the core of the dark woods. Section V relates

---

joke. I admire almost all the other excisions between version A and version B but I judge the aspect of the revision which substitutes one phrasing for another to be uneven. The pruning away of castles and chapels improves the poem. But the replacement of "blessed" by "cursed" (in naming the deep disposition of Whitman, Melville, and Frost, in section V) is mechanical; the replacement of "essentially dying" by "not fully convinced he was dying" (also in section V) sabotages mythological truth for superficial biographical accuracy. The conclusion of version A is superior. It does not speak of "The Great Republic" or imply that the fulfillment of poetry is its memorization.

> On your hundredth birthday I am to say,
> The door stands open, Your old footprints indent
> The old snow, on the dark trees a leaf clings,
> The house and woods make one land for your birthday.

One hopes that version C, synthesis of the strengths of the two earlier versions, will supersede them.

[11] It is instructive to compare the ambivalence in the *Dream Songs* which Berryman devotes to Robert Frost (number 35–39) with that in the poem by Galway Kinnell. Berryman includes the deception, malice, and poetic achievement but omits the incessantly outpouring, often sparkling, talk, behind which Kinnell gropes for the very fountainhead of what Berrymann, punning, calls his "gorgeous sentence."

[12] He has one other work on a poet confronted by American experience: "The Homecoming of Emma Lazarus," *Flower Herding on Mount Monadnock*, pp. 6–8.

this turning back to his making a poetry which assimilates and defines American experience.

According to the invented story, Frost, who is attracted to the woods, sees them as nonhuman, and, at their center, death (cessation from the pain of living, surcease). He would like to lie down there, for his great desire is to have an end of desire (the irony of the original title of the poem, "For the Hundredth Birthday of Robert Frost," is that we should congratulate a man with that desire for living a century).

He does not do what he wants but leaves the soothing woods, returning to the human world, out of a sense of love for, duty towards, persons. Yet, bringing his woods wisdom with him, the whole civilizational enterprise seems unreal in the light of the knowledge of the heart of whiteness in the darkness of the trees. Satisfying secondary desires seems a futile, self-mocking going-through-the-motions of life if one perceives that they cause pain and get nowhere and that there is a way out of the busywork of living. Yet the persons who draw one back are real. One has, and wants, to respond to them. One wants neither to inflict his vision of emptiness on them nor for them to discover it for themselves, so one speaks endlessly to distract their attention. His speaking synthesizes their intimate world (New England farmcountry, for example) and his knowledge of illusion. He presents them with familiar language and landscape which hide within them the darkness with the central whiteness, the kindness of death to those tormented by life. By making the music, accurate notation of scene and speech, wit of his poetry a cover-up of divertissement, he sings our world. He is heroic in his garrulous tomfoolery (he endures the nightmare alienation of a kind of antitransubstantiation when he returns "to the shelter/No longer sheltering him, the house/Where everything real was turning to words," *Flower Herding on Mount Monadnock*, p. 24),[13] and more than heroic (his action of returning is for the sake of others). Frost reverses the story of the Platonic cave. One kindly—out of affection and obligation—keeps to himself what he finds beyond conventional reality for the sake of those still existing in its optical illusion.

The image-of-the-life-of-man (the story which Kinnell made up to find a unity for Robert Frost, poet, public person, private man) is more terrible than that in *Homage to Mistress Bradstreet*. There, death is the destiny to be resisted. Here, life is the destiny to be resisted, except that those with compassion, hesitating to surrender to thanatos, choose to remain in it for the sake of others.

It is not throwing self down and being upheld (type one). It is not falling (type two). Like the image-of-the-life-of-man in *Homage to Mistress Bradstreet*, that in the poem for Robert Frost has a social dimension.

[13] "For Robert Frost" from *Flower Herding on Mount Monadnock* by Galway Kinnell, published by Houghton Mifflin Company.

Denise Levertov, Wayfarer

In "A Personal Approach," Denise Levertov discovers, by a review of her poetry, her underlying image-of-the-life-of-man, or what she calls her myth: a person, on the road, often afoot, moving toward a transforming destination.[14] In her essay, she suggests which childhood and adult experiences (including trudging as a girl down Essex lanes singing *He Who Would Valiant Be* from Bunyan's *Pilgrim's Progress*) contributed to her image-of-the-life-of-man as pilgrim and traces its widely varied but persistent manifestation in her poems.

I would qualify her emphasis on the pilgrim by giving more stress to the picaresque character of the journey of the traveler. A pilgrim concentrates on his goal and lets no obstacle deter him. He is so vigorous in pushing on, he directs his gaze so far ahead, he does not notice what is around him, unless it gets in his way. Then he gives it his attention only to remove, or step by, the barrier or stumbling block. The pilgrim has his mind elsewhere and otherwhen, on the beneficial holy place which he strives to reach and therefore on the future. The picaresque figure is also on the road but demonstrates enormous capacity to be present and respond spontaneously.

> the dog distains on his way,
> nevertheless he
> keeps moving changing
> pace and approach but
> not direction—"every step an arrival."[15]

A brief summary of the life of Denise Levertov (born at Ilford, Essex, England, 1923; married to novelist/war-resister Mitchell Goodman, 1947; came to the United States, 1948; had only child, a son, 1949) permits us to calculate that upon the appearance of *Relearning the Alphabet* in 1970, she was well into her forties, well into middle age, the preoccupation of that book.

Middle age is a problem for her, but neither the common problem of the loss of youth without the compensation of dignity and authority (since our society became rapid changing), nor the special problem of the poet (since the advent of Romanticism) as to whether or not his poetry writing has been only a symptom of late adolescence, a means for resolving his identity crisis, or has heralded a lifelong vocation. Denise Levertov, as what I have been calling a New Humanist, does not refuse anything which, to

[14] *Parable, Myth & Language,* Tony Stoneburner (Cambridge: The Church Society for College Work, 1968), pp. 19–30.

[15] Denise Levertov, *The Jacob's Ladder.* Copyright © 1958 by Denise Levertov Goodman. Reprinted by permission of New Directions Publishing Corporation.

use a favorite word of hers, befalls her, including the experience of middle age, even in its disconcerting and negative aspects (see "What Wild Dawns There Were" and "A Cloak," a poem about how accumulating experience solidifies into characteristic expression and habitual behavior, in the new volume). What happens to her as a person, she accepts and honors, on the one hand; on the other hand, she has been a prolific poet.

Her problem with middle age arises on another front. As a tireless war-resister, Denise Levertov has given herself to solidarity with the young in their vulnerability to our military system and foreign policy. She has identified herself with them in performing acts which make her legally culpable. Consequently, they have included her in their undertaking to create a counter culture. She wants to protect youth where it is open to exploitation by the dominant society and to support the (New Humanist; Immediate) values of the counter culture.

Her identification with youth grew out of her concern for justice and peace and has nothing to do with the idolatry of youthfulness which leaves a number of middle-aged persons looking younger than youth (teeth whiter, skins tanner, waists trimmer, grips firmer).

She wants to give herself to the best part of America, as she sees it, but the very experiences which have formed her, which (so far) are her, particularly the linguistic ones which are central to her vocation as poet, prevent her from simply being one with what the counter culture calls the Revolution). In the act of uniting, she experiences separation. Experientially, she belongs to another world than the one she longs for convictionally.

In part VI of section I of "From a Notebook: October '68–May '69," she probes the problem and discovers her accumulated experience to constitute a speech inpediment. She trips over her own tongue. Her homelife was rooted in the nineteenth century, its fiction and poetry, its range of language. To her, "purge" is a medical term; but to the members of the counter-culture, it is exclusion from party, society, life on ideological grounds. To her, "study" is a fascinated, patient examination of something lovely and/or loved; but to the members of The Revolution, it is the most grime-gritted oppressive surface of the whole academic grind. Language is her home. Can she change it, particularly if changing it means moving into the jargon of the counter culture and losing the spacious range of language which she indwells at present?

She yearns toward the reader "to whom I would give/all that arms can hold, eyes/encompass" (*Relearning the Alphabet*, p. 97) but recoils from remaking her language ("My diction marks me/untrue to my time;/change it, I'd be/untrue to myself"–p. 98).[16]

---

[16] Denise Levertov, *Relearning the Alphabet*. Copyright © 1970 by Denise Levertov Goodman. Reprinted by permission of New Directions Publishing Corporation.

<pre>
        I choose
              revolution but my words
   often already don't reach forward
              into it—
                        (perhaps)
        Whom I would touch
        I may not,
        whom I may
        I would
        but often do not.
</pre>

(pp. 97–98)[17]

She speaks in pain, as in the chilling recognition scene in therapy when the patient discerns the mechanism of his neurosis. He sees that it keeps him from unfolding the fullness of his promise. At the same time, he recognizes that it gives him the greatest and most intimate pleasure and comfort. He would rather be ill with his precious consolation than well without it. Health would be deprivation.

Similarly, the poet does not want to let go of her self-constituting language and the experience which it incodes.

Of course, her response is exaggerated. Whenever we speak to another, we push forward the part of our common language which is closest to him. And to learn a new terminology or language is to enlarge, extend, refine, the self. But, by the same token, to give up a language is to shrink and shrivel. Especially is this so for the poet, whose charge is the cultivation of the language. He is to lose no meanings, to know the etymologies, to distinguish among the synonymns, to refurbish old words and coin new, to foster exactness (that keen edge of the axe) and not to muffle reverberations (that trembling surface of the gong).

Probably the poet protests the learning of a new language because she has a profound personal memory of the exhausting process. When she came to this country and moved from British English to American English, she made a decision to change the character of her poetry, wanting it to reflect her concrete experience no matter how ordinary, no matter how raw. Therefore she served an apprenticeship to the poetic implicit in the practice of William Carlos Williams in his early short poems, and transformed her poetry. No doubt in training herself to stick close to the vernacular, as he did, she gave up reaches of language which previously had been special or useful to her. But a self-elected discipline is not basically a violation of the self, does not fundamentally produce estrangement from the self. Yet its metamorphoses of energy are seldom so complete that they leave no after-image of earlier vision, no hangover of nostalgia, no residue of regret. To have systematically substituted one language for another, once, was worth

[17] Denise Levertov, *Relearning the Alphabet.* Copyright © 1970 by Denise Levertov Goodman. Reprinted by permission of New Directions Publishing Corporation.

it: was the making of her as a poet. But to do it again is once too often, or
that, at least, is her first reaction. Yet the title of the book, *Relearning the
Alphabet*, indicates that her considered response is to do it one more time,
and her practice in this very poem, with its inclusion of prose, both her own
and that of others, indicates that she is deciding to risk drastic change and
to establish herself in the new language, but only after she has embodied
in a poem what a traumatic and wrenching act it is. She makes clear that
although she desires The Revolution, she does not repudiate her past. It is a
part of her experience. She affirms her heritage. One has a self to give only
by drawing on his roots. She has deep roots: she is, through her father, a
descendant of one of the leading Hasidic zaddikim, and, through her mother,
of a Welsh tailor-theologian contemporary with him. They nourish her. She
does not neglect them.

One needs roots to be a self and at the same time wants to be part
of The Revolution. Any move seems to threaten deracination or eradication.
Is there a means of transplantation? Denise Levertov affirms that there is
in "A Tree Telling of Orpheus," the masterpiece of the new book.

She has given her own account of the origin of the poem:

> And in the course of writing this lecture, finding myself about to say, "the
> poet must have as vivid a relation to any myth as if he were a tree that
> had followed Orpheus," I embarked on a long poem in the first person by
> such a tree. . . . . . . it seems as if below the conscious level I have some
> rather persistent symbolism of trees as being, or wanting to be, or having
> once been peripatetic, which in fact is alien and even somewhat repulsive
> to my conscious mind. Possibly the meaning of this recurrence of walking
> tree images is a symbolic representation of the concept that all creation
> strives to return to the primal oneness?[18]

Trees walking continues her pilgrim motif, but with the difference
that stability is a problem. In the fiction of the classical myth, the dynamic
which mobilizes is a music, a music which articulates reality (the trees learn
human language by means of lyre-accompanied song), a music which
attracts, drawing them until they release their ancient grip and drag off
lurching to new nutritive ground, a music which instructs them in dancing.
The music enables them to relinquish lifelong roothold, to transfer their
intricate reticulation of roots intact, and to strike them into growth-invig-
orating dirt.

What is the music? The Christian who reads "A Tree Telling of
Orpheus" will notice a resemblance between the dominical call of men to
discipleship and their direct response and the transplantation of trees by
the music of Orpheus, especially when he also sees that the poem has a
kerygmatic or credal kernel about the hero of the Greek myth that is
approximately Christic and pneumatic (a descent into hell, a death, a

---

[18] *Parable, Myth & Language*, p. 24

continuing word from an ongoing voice). The announcement of the Gospel is a music which accomplishes a transplantation.

I am also reminded of a passage by the Marxist thinker Ernst Bloch (which theologian Jurgen Moltmann quotes):

The real genesis is not at the beginning, but at the end, and it commences to begin only when society and existence become radical, that is, when they take themselves by the roots. The root of history, however, is man as he labors, creates, transforms the given facts and gets beyond them. When he has comprehended himself and grounded his life in real democracy without renunciation and estrangement, then there arises in the world something which appears to all of us in childhood, and in which none of us yet was—home.[19] "A Tree Telling of Orpheus" is a radical poem. The trees "take themselves by the roots." They "comprehend" themselves. They "ground their life" in an environment "without renunciation and estrangement."[20] The result is that they are at "home." If we use this statement (rather than gospel narratives about calls to discipleship) as a model for interpreting the moving music, we formulate that music as the understanding of the development implicit in one's nature and an absolute devotion to whatever process is necessary for its fulfillment. Nothing less than the music of necessity would enable them first to tug and then to shrug free their deepdarting roots from all that is not themselves in disheveling upheaval of the earth.

No doubt the Bloch model is too radical. Their own music does not move the trees but the music of a treelike self-sacrificing salvific hero.

The poet embodies her flinching reluctance to change language not only in "From a Notebook: October '68–May '69" but also in "A Tree Telling of Orpheus." The music initially strikes the trees as antiarboreal. It seems wind off water, place of no trees, wind bearing foliage-browning salt; it seems fire; it seems frost: the onslaught of a series of destructive forces (as the Gospel initially strikes one as judgment and yet ultimately is what moves one to bring him home).

The image-of-the-life-of-man as one who agonistically but totally slips out of previously entangling alliances, keeping safe and sound even unto its extremities, to enter into what the music holds out, giving the self to the future, makes a sharp contrast to both type one and type two, because it contains a response to a situation and a direction of self according to a purpose consonant with its own nature.

Middle age impedes the picaresque figure on the pilgrimage but, knowing what true humanity in society demands, enables Denise Levertov to advance by starting over, relearning the alphabet.

---

[19] Moltmann quotes Bloch in *Religion, Revolution, and the Future* (New York: Charles Scribner's Sons, 1969), p. 160.

[20] Denise Levertov, *Relearning the Alphabet*. Copyright © 1970 by Denise Levertov Goodman. Reprinted by permission of New Directions Publishing Corporation.

Gary Snyder, Wayfarer

Buddhist and ecologist, Snyder has a double significance for American culture. As a poet, he contributes to the ongoing colloquy of poetry by which we (not quite) keep up with our experience; as the prototypal Dharma Bum (as presented under the name Japhy Ryder in *The Dharma Bums* by Jack Kerouac), he and Allen Ginsberg pioneered styles of life that furnished much-copied examples for Beats and Hippies, and not for them only (Harvey Cox reports that an encounter with the two of them and Bishop Pike at Esalen Institute, in which they said to him, "Let's rap," has led him to dismantle the lecture as the centerpiece in his classes).

If in the New Humanism the life of the poet and his poetry are kept close, then knowledge of his life is an avenue which gives access to the poetry in a way that may not have been so true for Modernism with its greater degree of indirection and displacement. Gary Snyder was born in San Francisco in 1930, grew up on a farm in the woods north of Seattle, graduated from Reed College as a major in mythology in 1951, studied linguistics at Indiana University briefly, and then alternated between studying classical Chinese at Berkeley and working for the forestry service or logging companies for five years, studied Zen in Kyoto for a year, worked on a tanker touching Pacific and Mediterranean oilports, returned to San Francisco and then Japan, visited Buddhist holy places in India.

The major impression that one gets from *The Dharma Bums* is that Japhy Ryder is a man of skills and knowledge. He does things with economy and expertise. But he is not the Hemingway-like show-off proving himself against death by code-determined hunting, sport, and war. But he demonstrates that the functional action can be graceful. He lives simply (buying his clothes second-hand at Goodwill stores) but fully. He combines action and sensuous enjoyment and scholarship. He likes the arduous: mountainclimbing and study of Asian poets. He is self-sufficient but responsive to communal occasions. And—we supplement the fiction with other sources of information—he has explored the relation of drugs, revolution (as a northwesterner he imbibed the spirit of the IWW), and sexuality to spiritual disciplines.

Like other poets whose work we have considered, Gary Snyder writes the long poem. With the exception of some poems like "A Berry Feast," most of his long poems are made up of a large number of semiautonomous short poems. I especially admire *Myths & Texts*, his second volume, as a long poem (with three sections: "1: Logging," which has fifteen parts and a recurring reference to the fire-withstanding cone of the lodgepole pine; "2: Hunting," which has sixteen parts, one, a shaman song, three poems for birds, bear, deer, one, a poem for the making of a horn spoon, one, a poem called "songs for a four-crowned dancing hat"; "3: Burning," which has seventeen parts, one, a second shaman song, and a group with titles from the mythology of Asian religions, and a concluding part which offers two versions of the same event, "the text" and "the myth"). Although it clearly rehearses three destinies for one region of earth, it is too complicated to analyze for the present essay (for example, the above parenthetical description omits Coyote who appears in II:16; III:11; III:16). Therefore, after making a general description of one newly emerged (New Humanist; Immediate) kind of long poem which Snyder and others have been writing, we will concentrate chiefly on short poems and one part of a long poem.

The unity and order of the newly emerged long poem are not architectural and closed, like Dante's *Commedia* with its 100 cantos, or musical and rounded-out with a resolving recapitulation of all earlier motifs, like Eliot's *Four Quartets,* but treelike, growing along many lines, open and, as likely as not, unresolved, like Pound's *Cantos,* whose number now exceeds a century, or Williams's *Paterson,* which originally had a neat foursquare scheme but which eventually accrued additional parts and lost its quadrilateral symmetry, or Olson's *Maximum Poems* about Gloucester, or Robert Duncan's *Passages.* A tree with its organically extended roots, trunk, limbs, twigs, foliage is a unity just as much as a geometrically boxed house with its floor, walls with doors and windows, and roof. The tree is an outreaching, multiplying-by-dividing unity which embraces earth, water, air, sun, sheltering and feeding creatures, including man. The house is a unity which excludes and admits on a severely selective principle—let the light in and keep the squirrels out—and does not feed. The contrast is a figure of speech to indicate, not a preference, but a difference (between a long poem which, although it is at loose ends, has the unity of all-inclusiveness and a long poem which has a tight-knit schematic unity).

I think that it is worth indicating that the composition of this kind of poem (and none of the poets writing this kind writes only this kind) resembles the launching forth of the Irish monks of type one: the poet entrusts himself to vocation and process in the confidence that they will carry him along a course that is productive.

Snyder appropriately calls his poem in the recently evolved genre *Mountains and Rivers without End* (six sections of it appeared in 1965). Kerouac has Japhy Ryder, who says that he'll spend 3000 years writing it, describes it (p. 157) and Snyder himself describes it in his "Statement of Poetics" in *The New American Poetry,* edited by Donald M. Allen (p. 421). The model is the Chinese scroll painting. As one unrolls part of it, he rolls up another part. One does not look at the whole spread. He may forget what has gone before. He doesn't know what comes next. Its unity is not in analogy to an instantaneous vision of the total work, a holding of the whole in a single focus or within a single horizon. The poem is encyclopedic, informing not only about the scapes of the title, and the travel necessary to gaze upon them and move across them, and the ecological, geological, astronomical understanding of their situation, and perspectives on them offered by Asian culture, esthetic and religious, but also about the nightmare of history.

For a long time Snyder was polemically anti-Christian. He told Dom Aelred Graham that as a child he had repudiated the Sunday School denial that animals have souls on the basis of his own mystical experience of communion with nature. Snyder feels that the Judeo-Christian break with nature, splitting the human from it as that in charge of the rest and splitting the sacred from it by cleaving being into the divine, the Creator, and the nondivine, the creation, releases the devastation of things which includes finally, the destruction of ourselves.

In recent years, as Gary Snyder has grown in knowledge of, and interest in, primitive religion, his attitude toward Christianity has altered. He no longer simply contrasts it with Hinduism and Buddhism to its disadvantage but now stresses that all higher religions are degenerate forms of primitive religion, compromised and made coarse by civilization, that repressive imposition whose heaviness weighs on us all.

There is one topic important to all the poets at whose work we have looked, which Snyder opens up and which will conduct us to consideration of several poems by him.

The poem rises out of the organic life of the poet and gives expression to his body-received-and-transmitted experience (giving it a linguistic body). The poem is more than the thought, feeling, and sensation of the poet. It includes a deeper level, our basic posture, our fundamental, our primordial tropism. Some statements by Gary Snyder encourage my inclination to find a semaphore of the spirit at the hub of the being of each poet (of each person), from which derives his image-of-the-life-of-man. Snyder's statements do not point as far inward as a core stance but they do touch on the activity of the organism in its psychosomatic unity as intimately related to the form of poems. He says that their rhythms rise from the labor that he is doing at the time: *Riprap,* his first book, derives from rock-handling trail building, in the forest service; *Myths & Texts,* from (quiet) firewatching at lookout cabins in the same service and from (bustling) connecting of logs to caterpillars in logging operations. What-the-body-does-daylong contributes to the poem as much as what-the-senses-take-in or what-consciousness-reflects or what-consciousness-dreams-nightlong.

Let us take a close look at "Above Pate Valley" from *Riprap* (p. 15). At first the spare poem seems only a group of statements, a simple list of notes toward an outline on the basis of which, later, one might reconstruct a description and narrative of relaxation after trail building in mountains. Then, through the plain phrases, one hears a repetition of sounds that becomes rapid-fire in the penultimate sentence, with its *-ack* and *-ick* rimes and its dense *d's, k's,* and *s's:* "Picked up the cold-drill,/Pick, singlejack, and sack/of dynamite." We sense something formal and final, rather than something not yet begun and germinal. Then we gradually grow aware that through a set of statements the poet has given us the location-of-man in space-time and in the realm of the spirit.

The opening of the poem reminds us that man labors to build or rebuild and that he rests from his labors. Then it dramatizes that he inhabits contradictions and polarities. Work-end is at midday. Verdure juxtaposes snow (and, by implication, summer juxtaposes winter). Similarly, there are thermal extremities: sun "blazing" and air "cool"; trout both "cold" and "fried." "Trembling shadows" and "glitter" are close together. The inorganic "Black volcanic glass—obsidian" is next to the organic: it is "By a flower." Yet it is not only inorganic but also artificial, a "flake" worked by an Indian craftsman. A feeling of abundance ("thousands") gives way to a suspicion of industrial spoilage and widespread waste ("Not one good/Head"). Man litters a stretch of the planet with discarded failures. If their number impresses, it is nothing to compare in multitude with the stems of "the Bear grass" which hide, or the snowflakes which cover, them annually.

Of course the arrowheads are pointers to an earlier way of life, that of herds-following, deer-hunting tribes. It stands in sharp contrast to ours: they did not have to build trails but used ones formed by the animals on which they depended.

Snyder's trail is his own, not the Indians' trail, not the one which others employ him to help construct or repair, but the one which is quest, which is hunt, not for meat but for saving truth. Notice, the quest is not a search for identity, for the self. The first person singular pronoun is relatively absent from the poem. The "I" is not a problem for Snyder. In the first instance of "I," the pronoun names the knowing person who can identify the objects of the world. In the second instance, it names the person who knows what he himself is doing, who is in charge of his own search. But in the rest of the poem such a knowing, self-directing person is small in the setting of thousands of feet, thousands of flawed razor flakes, and "Ten thousand years."

A man establishes himself as a self in the world by doing his work. At the same time, he establishes himself as a member of a community (notice the use of "We" for the work-crew, in the first sentence, and "They" and "their" for the migratory venatic tribes, in sentences six and seven). Work offers the occasion for the realization of our possibilities, but that is its only permanent accomplishment. Soon—a century or a millenium from now—the trail that the work-crew so painstakingly cleared, laid, restored, will also be a scatter of stone. Man is small, brief, and yet not quite insignificant.

Two other poems in *Raprap*, "Hay for the Horses" (p. 19) and part three of "The Sappa Creek" (p. 32), also have to do with human labor and how it doesn't advance a person or produce progress, in the sense that it doesn't accrue but must all be done over and over again. The investment of effort in that process draws out the person. In both poems, if with ironic underscoring, Gary Snyder shares David Jones's respect for the job well done. In "Hay for the Horses" the irony that an initially unattractive activity becomes one's regular activity does not obscure or undercut the celebration of the haybucker as a good man who does good work. In part three of "The Sappa Creek," the name of a ship, man is not a lifelong falling (that would be too theatrical for Snyder). "Goofing again," he missteps momentarily. Good work does not demand or insist upon our attention, but accidents do. The poet says that he can "salvage" no more than a poem from the experience but I think that the poem itself suggests that there is another gain, the dignity of self that we establish in the world by the performance of the mystery of our work.

On the one hand, there is the routine of human labor which maintains the world but does not yield a breakthrough beyond the emergence of selves. On the other hand, there is a routine-transcending ascent of the spirit. As David Jones affirms the possibility of reaching God through participation in the Mass even at the most desperate moments of autobiography and history, so Gary Snyder affirms the possibility of a refusal of air-treading falling by seizing upon the interior dimensions of personhood. Selves are archways offering access to ascent. Gary Snyder articulates that possibility of refusal most clearly in "John Muir on Mt. Ritter," part eight of section three in *Myths & Texts* (p. 39), which, either in spite of or because of its alliteration, rime, and vocabulary, bears (bares) all the marks of a "found poem," a text taken from autobiographical writings by Muir. His experience in climbing, the "dead stop" halfway up, with its paralysis and darkening of the self, the mobilization and illuminating of the self from a profounder level resembles neither type of the image-of-the-life-of-man. Ascending is not casting oneself upon the elements. It is comprehending depths of the self not already in play as one engages in an action and finds it obstructed or prevented. Therefore it approximates the image-of-the-life-of-man in "A Tree Speaking of Orpheus" more closely than that in the other poems.

Conclusion

As we have crashed through the underbrush around the fine stand of trees which we have been admiring and discussing, we have seen that there has been a change in the character of poetry in the last half century. For example Modernistic poetry transposed personality. Transitionalist or Confessional poetry kept the devices of transposition but employed them to present personality under high pressure. New Humanist or Immediate poetry accepted the self and included it but attended most carefully to the experiences of which the self was the nexus. Yet as we considered the image-of-the-life-of-man embodied in a sample of poems, we have seen that they are not particularly novel. They are more or less familiar from the literature of the past. Probably in the seventies the New Humanist poetry of Immediacy will increase until the matter-manner of the recent movement becomes the dominant and established mode. But it seems unlikely that the coming decade will produce a new image-of-the-life-of-man. Apparently there are only a few archetypes. If one comes to the fore in altered circumstances, others may retire to the background, but the number of the archetypes is constant. Our present circumstances are special, however, in that none has retired. The whole chorus is at stage front in full voice. All the human options address then beckon us. In the seventies we will not be able to say that any single one is the leading lady.

7

Painting as
Theological Thought

The Issues
in Tuscan Theology

John W. Dixon, Jr.

Introduction

Somewhere I once read an essay by a young philosopher who was explicating an intricate passage from a German philosopher and added admiringly, "German is a language which seems to have been designed for the discussion of philosophy." I wanted to add, less admiringly, "On the contrary, philosophy has become that which is discussable in German."

There is no special insight involved, given the context of modern scholarship, in recognizing that specific languages shape our thought. It is less usual but not any longer uncommon to assert that the structure of language itself determines in advance the shape of things we can think. What is much less commonly asserted is that systematic thought can occur in languages other than the verbal. Elsewhere I have defended this assertion ("The Matter of Theology," in *The Journal of Religion,* April 1969). It is my hope now to pay the first installment on the debt I there willingly incurred by making that assertion.

More is involved than simply extending the language of theology. It is, rather, a matter of determining the structures by which men have defined their relation to the world and responded to their apprehension of the manifestation of the divine. To do theology is not to know God in a particularly modern way, but to respond to God in the weight and structure and movement of a given language. The propositional language of traditional theology is a great imaginative achievement and part of the discipline and the nourishment of the spirit of man. But it shapes thought by the specificities of its location (German as against English) and by the generality of its form (the structured action of Indo-European grammar); neither of these is the whole of human experience. Those things that cannot be embodied in the structures of the verbal language can, at best, be talked about and thus are not actively present to the intelligence. Things which are talked about are things of curiosity, of argumentative interest, but they are not operative in the experience of men. It is only as the experience of the sacred becomes embodied, takes shape in those structures that can in turn shape the nervous system that they work rather than standing as specimens in a logical museum.

The substantiation of these assertions requires an examination of a wide range of evidence; the illustration of them can be more limited. I choose two areas for that illustration: the beginning of painting in Tuscany and the art of the twentieth century. Since my final concern is not the particulars of analytic demonstration but method, presumably any period of significant art would suffice for the demonstration of the way in which the method works and I might choose Tuscan art simply because it is the area of my special competence. It is more to the point, however, that Tuscan painting shaped the imagination and sensibility of Western man for nearly 500 years; an analysis of it, therefore, is not just methodologically useful but it is an analysis of the beginning of what we now are.

It is my hope that the method will be sufficiently clear from this analysis so that my treatment of the twentieth-century revolution can be somewhat briefer and less exemplary. Nevertheless, it is vital to the conclusion I want to reach; if Tuscan painting exemplifies where we were, modern painting exemplifies where we *are* and I will argue, finally, that no artistic or theological language has any validity unless it takes into account where we are, not as definitions of rhetoric ("to speak the language of modern man") but as a constituent element of the language itself.

I

It should not be necessary to validate the Tuscan enterprise. A certain priority in the arts has been generally granted to Tuscany but so long as the arts were peripheral in an enterprise to which propositions were central this was of no great moment. What is less generally recognized is the primacy of the Tuscans, particularly the Florentines, in so many other areas of our life. I am told that the foundations of modern business and finance were laid in Florence. The origins of the modern study of history are found in the Florentines, particularly Machiavelli and Gucciardini. Those same two great men and others generated the modern idea of political science. Even science, with business the other major determinant of the modern imagination, has one of its major springs in the Pisan Galileo who worked in Florence. Such energy of imagination manifested over nearly five centuries not only is virtually unparalleled in history, it points to a decisive act of the human intellect. It was the Florentines who shaped the primary imaginative acts of the western world for half a millennium. Perhaps, in the search for theology's definition, it would be well to turn away for a time from the Germans to those of another race and language.

All things have a history, and creativity is never creation from nothing but a response to all that has been inherited. The enterprise of Tuscan theology, their formal and structural response to their part of God's creation was acted out in a particular landscape, in the shapes of a particular city, within the habits of mind and images of order generated in a particular history. What came to them was, above all, a particular sense of wall surfaces, a particular sense of the function, within the economy of devotion, of sacred objects that defined man's relation to the holy.

All Italians grew up in the consciousness of the Byzantine icon. This is one of their circumstances that worked most constructively on the imagination, for the icon is a singular enactment of the relation between the human and the divine and thus a theological act of the highest importance. It is not an ordinary image. It is the point of agreed encounter between man and God. In function it is not just for contemplation or instruction but it was an instrument of prayer. The sacred is present in the icon, not as the god inhabits the idol but as that to which the Lord comes.

It is altogether natural that the art of the icon should have been codified; the sacred does not bear change or interpretation and its very antiquity becomes a dimension of its sacrality. That Byzantine art is unchanging, has no historical development, is as untrue as such statements usually are. That it is unchanging in comparison to the violent changes in Western art is quite importantly true. The persons portrayed are the heroes of the faith. The events are the great acts of the faith as glorified in the liturgy. The form in which the persons and events are manifested lends to them some variety of emotional tone but the intent is always to make an object that in its radiant splendor is fit as the habitation of the holy.

Thus is man's relation to the physical order defined. In the dialogue of history every intense passion tends to produce its opposite and Byzantine theology works itself out against a background of a mistrust of matter and a violent iconoclasm but in the main and finally official position the sacred could inhabit, if not the generality of matter, then the specifically consecrated object.

This is not the only definition of the function of the sacred image. The canonical definition in the Western church was laid down by Pope Gregory the Great: the image is an aid and direction to devotion. It is a reminder of that to which devotion is rightly given and is, therefore, the occasion but not the instrument of the devotional act.

It goes without saying that neither the Eastern nor the Western church was quite so single minded as this account suggests but this does describe the center of gravity in each church.

Under the pressure of the Byzantine authority Western art, in Italy at least, had small chance to develop its concern with the pedagogical and the narrative that inspires devotion. It is precisely here that the issues that concern me are formulated and a specifically Tuscan theology begins to take shape. And what takes shape here shaped the Western imagination from that time on.

Tuscany was a distinct region of the spirit before it was a political unit and the revival of Western art was an affair of the Pisans Nicolo and Giovanni before it was of the Florentines or the Sienese. But it was in Florence and Siena that the final shaping of the issues took place.

The pressures of selectivity compel me to restrict my attention; I shall deal now largely with Giotto and Duccio. They stand at the beginning of Tuscan theology and they stand together on the definition of the issues, however diverse their fate. Giotto is perhaps a little short of Leonardo and Rembrandt as a household word but is, nonetheless, known in honor and most fervently loved. Duccio is known and honored by the specialists but beyond that known and somewhat patronized by those with a taste for the exotic. They do not divide subsequent history between them. Duccio had a few artistic heirs, the Lorenzetti, Simone Martini, finally the cold frenzy of Giovanni de Paolo and Sassetta. Beyond that even the tradition of his native town belongs to the Florentines. Giotto bestrides the next half millennium of the Western mind as few men ever do. Only Paul and Augustine among the verbal theologians so dominate history as did this man. Five hundred years of Western thought is built around issues in large part laid down by him. I speak not only of artistic thought; that honor is given him in every textbook. I speak rather of the shaping of the imagination, that power in men that defines and forms our experience of the world. The doctrines were shaped in other quarrels but the shape of those quarrels was fixed in the image of order laid down by Giotto.

I am not a determinist or even much concerned with linear causality. It may be that Giotto's work was the consequence of forces external to himself and those bearers might lay claim to the honor I here give Giotto. Be that as it may, what comes to us is Giotto's.

But Duccio faced the same issues and it is by no means fixed in the fate of things that he should lose the allegiance of men nor is it fixed in historical determinism that we cannot turn to him for the merit of his answer now that five hundred years' work have used up what Giotto taught us to do. The comparison between these two great men is instructive as such things always are but out of this might come more than instruction.

The unit of all critical investigation is the individual work of art. The theological reference is the image of order embodied, incarnated in the individual work. It is this image of order that determines the choices the artist makes in his contention with his material; it is the embodied image, the organizing principle of the individual work that shapes the structural imagination of those who see it, including the artist who has had his imagination reshaped in his struggle to bring to life a work of art out of the resistance of living material to the imposition of an ideal order.

It is a cliché of historical criticism that Duccio is, of all the great Italians, the closest to the Byzantine. Clichés become clichés because in some way they satisfy the evidence but as clichés they begin to blind the vision. Certainly the Byzantine derivation is obvious. Elegant and eloquent linear rhythms, figures reduced to two-dimensionality, the iconography of the presentation. Against this cliché—again rightly—Giotto is represented as the revolutionary figure who places his figures in a real if limited space, who created solid, massive, three-dimensional persons, who interlocked them in precisely felt dramatic action.

These things are true and very importantly true. Yet there are things, particularly in Duccio, that go outside the cliché.

Duccio is not the culmination of the Byzantine style in Italy; he is a true Tuscan and his awareness of the issues in Tuscan theology is as profound as Giotto's.

No generalization about art is any more nearly true than generalizations about any other aspect of human experience yet it may be more generally true than most generalizations are to say that, prior to the work of the fourteenth-century Tuscans, the sense of personality was absent from art. Since drama is enacted only by persons, since dramatic action is by definition the interaction of persons with moral weight and the power of choice, then dramatic action does not exist without personality. Even the great Greek dramas are not interaction of dramatic personalities but the working out of general ideas in the lives of specific people.

Personality hardly exists outside Christian art. Individuality is the distinctiveness of appearance that belongs to a particular and specific person. Personality is the individuality of moral act that comprises the integrity of the specific persons. Greek art had the sense of moral force that is of the essence of the person but basically saw it embodied in the human type. Roman art had, in its portraiture, one of the most intensely individualized of all arts but with rare (but important) exceptions did not infuse the individual shapes with the moral gravity of true personality.

The Christian artist could not make his forms fit his faith immediately. He used inherited forms and developed a symbolic speech of remarkable flexibility and authority. Byzantine art built up a symbolic vocabulary that could make manifest a wider range of states of the soul than had been present before. The emotional range did not, however, pass beyond the range of the soul in devotion or sacred act even in the extraordinarily passionate works in Mistrà and the Kharie Camii.

Individuality in Western art was not the work of the Italians but the great anonymous sculptors of the French Gothic cathedrals. But there each individual participates in the peace of God radiating from the Christ figure of the trumeau.

Even so great a work as the *Bamberg Rider* is defined more nearly as a role than a person. He is the embodiment of one of the greatest dreams of the Middle Ages, the Christian king. The great Florentine, Donatello, also showing a warrior, demonstrates by contrast the possibility of complex humanity as identical with role and status. The two heads most vividly show the difference. The *Bamberg Rider* lives in the vision of his purpose, his role not simply on earth but in the final dream of God's order. The *Gattamelata* lives in his own authority and offers, therefore, something more nearly like completeness as a person.

My concern here is not genetics so I will not linger over the origins of artistic personality in the masters of the Isaac and St. Francis stories of Assisi nor the debt owed to Pietro Cavallini, Giovanni Pisano, and Cimabue. What I want to see, rather, is the full development in Giotto and Duccio, for there we find, for the first time in the history of art, the fully developed person acting to some moral purpose toward coherent and understandable ends.

Artistic drama is not the imitation of the externals of an action, which is no more than illustration. It is making manifest, for good or evil, the moral purpose of human acts. To this end several artistic instruments are available to the artist. With both Giotto and Duccio the basic instrument is gesture, the expressive act and attitude that reveals the inner moral purpose. Procedurally this means the most intense, the most precise, observation of human conduct and attitude. True gesture is unattainable as a general idea, a general principle. It depends rather on the most intense immediacies of relation to life as it is experienced.

In both men the sensitivity of gestures is such that they could and, in the order of humanity, should constitute a lifetime of study. Anna, with infinite tenderness, touches the face of Joachim returning. Equally, too, the great arch encloses the figures, the circle wraps their upper bodies together. Gesture is Giotto's principal dramatic instrument but composition serves as well.

Joachim is expelled from the temple with the coarse repelling gesture of the priest's inverted hand, Joachim resentfully looking back while lovingly holding the rejected sacrificial lamb. But he is also thrust into emptiness, an emptiness so unprecedented that historians were convinced for years that there must have been a figure painted there but which undeniably is Giotto's speech for the loneliness of rejected man.

Or one of the finest of all, the "Noli Me Tangere," with Mary's infinite longing of reach, Jesus simultaneously moving away, holding her off, blessing her with infinite compassion and love.

Duccio's gesture is every bit as precise, every bit as revealing. Judas avidly grasps after the money and the whole group huddles conspiratorially, the only such congestion of a group on the whole *Maestà*. Or Joseph braces himself on the ladder while he holds the limp dead body which falls out of the sorrowful emptiness above the cross.

Yet it is perfectly evident that the figures making these gestures are very different and in that difference lies the clue to their differing purpose and the seed of the further development of theological work in Tuscany.

Our normal (and proper) analysis in class as well as professional discussion is to present the difference in terms of the greater density of Giotto's figures, the fuller space, the greater range of the action. These are indeed proper subjects of pedagogy but they do not go far enough for these are means and not ends, language but not what is said by means of the language, forms but not the content that is inherent in, inseparable from, the form. It is not even enough to point out the intense awareness of the human drama in each one for this again is pedagogy and not a complete analysis. For these works function so differently that the same dramatic material, even a concern for the same issues, takes up in very different directions.

Giotto's interest is not in tangibility as such. It is, indeed, a star-tlingly new world he offered for contemplation, a newly imagined world that changed the optics of the Western imagination. But there is no evidence to suggest that such formal matters were at the center of his concern. Rather he seems to have sought to translate the drama into the statics of our body's existence as well as the dynamics of its interrelations. The tangibility of this gesture and action is such that our body responds in kind. The weight is our weight, the action is a disposition of our own flesh. Therefore, since in the painting both weight and action, the proportion and rhythms of the event are manifestations of the moral relation inherent in the event, then our participation in the structure and dynamics trains us to the motivating act. Devotion is not contemplation but participation. It is thus active and not passive, transformative and not simply confirmatory.

Duccio, on the other hand, starts not only with as profound a grasp of the dramatic structure but as great a sensitivity to the physicality of the acts; no man is truly a Tuscan if he does not have these two as fundamental to his imaginative language. But he does not seek the tangibility that compels the worshipper into participation. He seeks a visual form that is the symbolic equivalent of the action. The grasping hand is placed with absolute precision exactly where the hand should be placed but it does not truly grasp. It is an abstract curve that is the visual equivalent, or the symbol, of the grasp. The figures are disposed in positions proper to the participation in the action but the rhythm of their placement makes a counterpoint to the drama. Rhythm in Giotto is always submissive to the drama, an enhancement of it as well as instrumental to it. Rhythm in Duccio is appropriate to the drama but independent of it, thus establishing a personality for the picture that is other than the immediacies of the event. The event is transfigured into something else.

Every visitor to the museum of the cathedral of Siena will testify to a further quality of Duccio's painting. It has one of the richest surfaces to be found anywhere in painting. It would be flattery to jewelry to refer to it as "jewel like" in the ancient cliché. The gold background is the setting, the deep rich colors set into it. The colors are absolutely pure, subdued in saturation to be sure that no color is detached from the integral surface. The enclosing lines are fine and sinuous like the intricate wires of the jeweler.

There is no atmosphere, which is to say in a narrative that there is absolute clarity of atmosphere. Where earlier works occupy only a symbolic space, Duccio's has a real sense of space, so the clarity of forms, the unimpeded and unqualified clarity of color, can only signify an absolute purity of atmosphere. Since each form in this purity of atmosphere has complete clarity, each form becomes a jewel for entranced observation.

Thus, the moral drama, the pure Tuscan element of the work, is not, as in Giotto, reproduced in the body of the observer. It is transfigured into a different realm of being. The coherence and intensity of rhythmic structure, the quality of color and line transfigure the intensely realized moral act. Instead of the transformation of the worshipper's life on this earth, the worshipper is caught up into a new realm. He does not see the vision of the heavenly city. Rather it is his own life that is figured in the sacred drama, the emotions, the motives, the physical response of a life on this earth that is held away from the solidity of the earth and so becomes a true ecstasis that is of the substance of a genuine mysticism.

What Giotto and Duccio share, then, is the concern for the life of man in its moral dimension and the expressive attitude of the body—the gesture—that is revelatory of the quality and character of the moral act. They share, too, the analytical and calculated intelligence that makes them so responsive to the particularities of human acts as well as able to construct a work of art that makes their grasp of the dramatic moral act manifest.

This, with Dante at the headwaters of the Florentine enterprise, is the same intelligence that made possible the other Florentine achievements, precise observation, yet penetration through surface appearances to the forces that give structure to the elements of surface appearances. The Florentines created the study of history and politics, not because they chronicled information but because they understood what held that information together.

Thus they established the context in which Tuscan theology worked out the problem around which later solutions congested. Where they differ is the direction in which they took this moral drama. Duccio moved it into the realm of the mystic vision, Giotto into the dimensions of this earth.

This kind of statement is rhetoric made possible only by the fact that Giotto's spatial vision dominated Western thought till the end of the nineteenth century and the reformation we identify with the name of Cézanne.

Because Giotto so shaped our imagination we take that shape of space as normative just as we take as normative those structures of systematic propositions that have been built in the intellectual framework that Giotto designed.

What most decisively differentiates Giotto from Duccio in the Tuscan enterprise is the designated choice of artistic instrument. Duccio worked in the traditional medium of egg tempera, Giotto primarily in fresco. Tempera made possible the extraordinary richness that is so important to Duccio's vision. Fresco provides something else again.

These differences are not simply two ways of making a painting. They are two fundamental modes of thought, two ways of being-in-the-world. Fresco does not happen to be just a painting on a convenient and relatively permanent support. It is the energizing of a wall which is itself a determinant of the imagination. Even in his tempera panels (made inevitable by the realities of the market) Giotto so ordered his colors that his painting had the breadth of form characteristic of fresco, where his basic thinking was done.

What I have pointed to already is enough for a theological revolution: the transformation of figures from being symbols of pathos, pointers to devotional response in the worshipper, into figures of moral density and muscular control with gestures as revelation of inner feeling and moral relation. Yet this is not specific to fresco. The substance of fresco is the congestion of weight onto the surface of the wall.

A wall is an act of the imagination, not simply when it is enclosure, but when it encloses and gives shape to meaningful space. A wall is the boundary of our private selves and can take the shape of our image of order. It is also the shaping edge of corporate space, giving body to the image of the common self held by the community whose vision, through the agency of the masterbuilder, has shaped the space. When such a wall is fittingly frescoed, its meaning has been translated into human drama and the emotional life which was contained by the walls is caught up onto the sustaining surface of the wall to be transfigured in the sacred story. The wall is two dimensional. The great achievement of Giotto (himself a builder) was the energizing of this two-dimensional plane by affirming it and then extending it back into the represented space. The drama is enacted at the juncture of the real space and the represented space. It was the taking up of the third dimension into thought.

It is not just the third dimension that Giotto uses; it is the third dimension cut to the measure of man. The space is clear and intelligible, movement in it is free and orderly. The pictures are unprecedentedly large thus relating the pictorial space closely to the actual space of the spectator. The mystery and magic of Duccio is wholly absent. The worshipper, his imagination stunned and overwhelmed by Duccio, here feels a different exhilaration. He stands apart from the picture at what can later be called "the point of view." Icons are objects in our world, lacking depth and a spatial existence of their own. Giotto's paintings go back from a fixed surface and create a new world which the worshipper now contemplates from within his own space. Thus is the worshipper's individuality clearly established while it is enhanced by his participation in the dynamics of the picture. The worshipper is over against the world of the picture. With Giotto there is never any separation of the two, since it is the life of the worshipper that is taken up onto the wall and there transformed. But when, as it were, the worshipper took a step or two back from the wall and became the spectator rather than the worshipper then the attitude was secularized. The spectator became detached from the world with the result that science became possible as did the form of theology which finds its work possible in detachment from that which is being accounted for by an uncommitted and uninvolved technique.

If this is the final end of Giotto's work it is by projection along one road only of the spacious area that he created. In Giotto the several movements of the spirit are muted into harmony and for this reason so many who come to the Arena Chapel have the sense of coming home. This is the shape of our corporate lives before the modern revolution. Only a few people have been able to respond deeply to the entranced vision of Duccio. Rather it is the radiance of the moral act in Giotto that shaped the European theological imagination, but the moral act is radiant not just in itself but on the surface of the wall. Attention to the moral act alone eventually produces the novel and then a secular psychology. With Giotto the integrity of the wall is never lost even when it is simply the sustaining context of the moral drama.

At this point one final dimension of the analysis is required. Duccio's space is clearly very unlike Giotto's but it is not sufficient simply to identify this difference. Let us, therefore, look comparatively at Giotto's and at Duccio's representation of the same subject, the "Entry into Jerusalem."

Giotto's handling of the subject is in harmony with his general structural principles. The spatial setting is three dimensional but decisively cut off immediately behind the figures and thus subordinate to the action. The city gate is too large to be merely symbolic but too small to be a true gate; after all, people are more important than gates. Jesus is high to the left of center; the ass's neck and head lead across while the blessing gesture is isolated in the open center. The congested rhythm of the apostles crowds in from the left. The receiving crowd spills out of the gate in a falling rhythm that ends in the prostrate figure spreading his robe, a rhythm characteristically syncopated by the figure drawing back in awe. Nature is present but instrumental only. All is concentrated on the drama, fairly simple in this case but nonetheless profoundly realized. The act of the entry is made manifest and the variety of responses but the dominant element is the majesty of the figure of Jesus.

With some complexities, Duccio's space in some of the panels is relatively straightforward, clear, cubic, concise and adequate without being obtrusive. Where the emotional tone of the subject suggests a different treatment, space is treated in unusual ways. The most remarkable of all is the panel with the Entry.

Unlike Giotto's treatment, space here is not simply instrument but is an actor. The painting is formally flatter than Giotto's but symbolically much deeper. The road zigzags up the surface of the panel rather than back into depth but the symbolic movement begins in a field, goes across a road, another field, an expanse of city to a cathedral dome.

In Giotto's painting the point of view is low, moving toward the actual position of the spectator in the chapel and enhancing the majesty of the central figure. The point of view in Duccio's is manipulated in a shockingly sophisticated manner. Essentially it appears to be high, somewhat above the middle of the panel. We look down on the road and at least partially into the orchard beyond the road, and up to the arches of the gate. But we also look up to the lower surface of the lintel of the doorway in the foreground. Actions of all figures are as intelligible as they would be were we standing immediately in front of them at whatever level they are.

Scale is manipulated to the same purpose; the figures just in front of the gateway are larger than the ones close to Jesus, their heads as large as the head of Jesus himself who is much closer to the spectator's position. Thus in moving from left to right the spectator moves from the foreground into the group at the gate and is prepared to enter.

At this point I become aware that I am no longer dealing with the vagaries of medieval perspective construction or even the emotional manipulation of space in the Byzantine icon. Instead there is a highly sophisticated manipulation of surfaces for a peculiarly devotional purpose. Objects and persons equally are defined into faceted surfaces that are angled against each other in a complex pattern that can remind the modern observer of the structured facets of cubism. But instead of the profound structural purpose of cubism, ordering is here a trap for devotional meditation. The glance of the spectator slides from plane to plane, back into the symbolic space to the temple, out again to the figure of Jesus who is crowned by the temple, yet reaches it only through the life of the city.

Since the picture is full of allusions to the experienced world, the circumstance of our common life, the origin of the response is the awareness of this world. But appearances are embedded into the intensity of color structure and the complexity of spatial organization so the common life is transfigured into the uncommon life of a spiritual event. There is no weight to figures or tangibility to stone so the holy event floats like a mystical vision; yet the entrapment of vision is so complete that the serious spectator cannot extricate himself from his participation in the event. Thus the icon to which Duccio is so closely linked is carried still further away from its appointed task and into a distinctly Western vision. This is no longer the occasion for prayer or the instrument of prayer. It is itself an act of devotion trapping not only the conscience but the optical conscious- ness of the spectator into a singular act of involvement with the deepest structures of the faith. From this the worshipper returns into his own cir- cumstances not so much better informed about the nature of the common life as prepared to see the ordinariness of things radiant with the faith.

It is, perhaps, symptomatic of the special nature of this work that it appears on the back of the great altarpiece and ordinarily was seen only by the priests. Giotto's is on the walls of a chapel, accessible to all who came. Here there is no entrapment but complete openness. Space is struc- tured without ambiguity. Movement is measured and weighty, determined by the mechanisms of the body so the worshipper participates in both adoration and blessing and learns in his own flesh, not in his argumentative mind, what it means to bend in adoration of the holy. As he slowly moves through the chapel he experiences in his own bodily dynamics a full range of human acts incarnating the holy history. The event is distant from him and independent of him, resting serenely in the shallow space carved by the paint on the clear and integral wall. Simultaneously it is working in his flesh and the rhythm of his movement. Those who take Giotto seriously do not go back into their world like the disciples blinking on their return from the Mount of the Transfiguration or from the Museo del Duomo of Siena. They go back into a clarified world, a world of weight and sub- stance, of intelligible relations among things, where people move in the integrity of intelligible moral purpose, whether good or evil. The response to Duccio is ecstasy. The response to Giotto is joy.

It is perhaps not surprising that Duccio's work was so unfruitful. A few visionaries could follow him and Siena was a city of visionaries rather than intellectual solidity. The occasion was not Duccio's but Giotto's. There was a formal range to Giotto that created problems still alive in the early years of the twentieth century. There was a moral complexity and depth hardly yet available to intellects formed on philosophy and literature rather than art.

Yet, even so, the world since Cézanne has moved away from him. Space is no longer so clearly rational nor morality so intelligible. The spec- tator must participate in the art work, trapped into its ambiguities, making parts of it in his own entranced response. Thus surprisingly, Duccio, ineffective historically since the sixteenth century, becomes again a leader by making manifest the process of involvement of optics with devotion. There is enough debased Byzantinism in contemporary "sacred" art not to urge a Duccio revival. He remains a Sienese of the fourteenth century. But he outlines the process whereby intelligence is itself transformed into prayer.

II

I concluded the previous section with certain statements that must not be left to rhetorical assertion but supported by such argument and evidence as might be brought to bear on the problem. But, before turning to that task, I want to review some of the implications of what I have tried to do.

The second of these implications will have to do with the critical job that I undertook to do. But prior to that I will have to examine some of the enforced limitations of that job.

While the mode of analysis is not entirely unprecedented in contemporary historical criticisms, it is sufficiently new to require conscious attention. But in one respect at least it is in a perfectly traditional mode of intellectual work. I have operated (so far) on the unexamined assumption that it is possible for a twentieth-century critic to discern and define what is going on in a fourteenth-century art work.

I do not intend here to append the whole debate on the problems of writing history. "Exactly as it happened" is an ideal that historians once held but few are naive enough to hold it any more and much scholarly attention is given to the problems of history. While acknowledging that debate, what I prefer doing is to come at the problem from a different direction for it seems to me that the various treatments of it share one basic fallacy.

That fallacy may, indeed, be a consistent outgrowth from Giotto's achievement. I have tried to describe the way in which he works on the sensibility of the spectator; he does so by making the work of art something other than the spectator, although related to him in a distinctive way. In doing so he created a pictorial world that impinges uniquely on the world of the spectator but is nonetheless a different world which the spectator observes. The history of Western art (what I referred to as "the optics of Western imagination") is in part a history of the various modes of that relation and observation. It is an extraordinarily complex subject, and the study of it has hardly yet begun so I will keep close to my account of Giotto's style.

Giotto's figures have weight and density, they move according to both anatomical and psychological logic, and they act in the context of discernible moral purpose. Whatever Giotto's intention, whatever the experience of the original participants in his work, it was inevitable that the work of art develop an increasing distance from the spectator and, finally, even from the artist. It is one of the clichés of modern criticism that the art work must be understood in its own right apart from both the spectator and the artist (Roland Barthes speaks of "The Death of the Author," *Aspen Magazine*, no. 5–6).

Clearly this separation is essential to the writing of true history as true history has been defined since the time of the great Florentine historians. Clearly, too, it is false to the world. There is no sense in which "I" can be defined as over against my world; I am a part of it, shaped by culture and environment.

This detachment of the "I" from the world, the subject from the object, was the indispensable first step in the Western intellectual enterprise and because of it all sorts of things have been accomplished that could not have been accomplished otherwise. But the price had to be paid and we are beginning to pay it now.

The price was the reifying of process. All human experience is ebb and flow. In the moment we are involved in it by an intricate network of relations, in time we are involved in it as change, flow, process. To objectify any part of it is to excise it from the web and from the flow. Where, "exactly as it happens," everything is an inextricable part of its act and relations, in the reifying of process, things or events are cut loose from relations, fixed permanently in the amber (or plastic) of scholarly language. This *works* in the Arena Chapel; part of the extraordinary power of the paintings is to be located precisely in the suspension of the moment, compelling the entranced attention to absorb somatically the moral structure that is the supporting skeleton of the painted forms. It no longer works.

So far as Giotto is concerned (or any artist) this is both liberation and limitation. Giotto did not paint for me. He painted for men of the fourteenth century. This either has nothing to do with cultural relativism or it is the only true meaning of cultural relativism. The besetting sin of the modern intellect and, as a result, modern pedagogy is the conviction that the thing divorced from this relation and suspended in scholarly plastic is "in fact" the thing itself. Where pedagogy should be set on putting the student into the process it concentrates on the presentations of these mythical things.

Again, this should not be read as polemic (although polemic it must be if it is permitted to continue to rule our pedagogical procedures). It is the inevitable result of the assumptions established early in the enterprise.

Giotto was a particular man, shaped by a particular culture and working within it. Those who participated in his work were trained to the same cultural speech as Giotto. They were not twentieth-century men; they knew nothing of Rembrandt or Picasso or, for that matter, Niels Bohr.

Consequently, and I want to emphasize that "consequently," what they saw in the Arena Chapel and what I see are two very different things.

Historiography takes into account the physical changes in the paint, the cultural differences illustrated in the meaning of symbolic and narrative vocabulary and so on. What it does not take into account is the fact that, "consequently," we are different people. The art work is not a thing working in a certain way on equally objectified persons so that, once we have corrected the aim by the degree of paint damage, shifts in the understanding of symbols and so on, we can come to a conclusion about the nature of the work with the calm, if somewhat presumptuous assumption, that we are defining the work as it was and is and ever more shall be. The art work is a term in a relation that involves the artist and the participant. Change the participants and, while the physical substance of the work is not changed, it is not just a manipulation of language to say it is a different work. In a cultural speech still dominated by positivism that way of speaking is an offense but it is the only way I know to establish in the argument that the work of art is not a thing but a function and a relation. The relation originates in the physicality of the work and is shaped by the material structure of the work and is inseparable from it (I would not care to be thought an idealist) but the physical separability of the material should not suggest that it can be separated in our understanding.

Thus I can never be sure that the work of art worked as I have described it. Equally I am liberated from the obligation to assume that the way it worked then is authoritative now. It certainly works for me as I have described it and my description, placed in the public domain, can be checked by the experience of others. Once I am freed to experience the work as though it had been done for me, for our time, I can then experience it in the knowledge that fourteenth century men were not only profoundly different from me but profoundly the same; they are men with bodies shaped as mine, responding to the world as mine does. Thus my dialogue is not only with Giotto but with them. I cannot know that they responded according to my analysis, neither can I know they did not.

Thus the paintings are not a function and relation simply in one dimension. Rather it is a three-way relation: Giotto and his spectators (or, as I prefer to call them, participants); Giotto and us; the fourteenth-century participants and us. The error, the false step, in traditional criticism is the presumption that somehow the work can be isolated from this functional relation and presented in itself. It *is* these relations, it is not simply a thing that functions differently in different situations.

Therefore, I can now reflect on my own procedure as a preliminary to addressing myself to the modern enterprise. No man is competent to define his achievement but he can at least speak to his own intentions and my intention is to make a real shift in the mode of criticism. "Shift" is not a complete transformation; I undertook a reasonably straightforward formal analysis in a reasonably traditional mode. It was, rather, that the context of this analysis was changed. In traditional formal analysis the unstated assumption is that the analysis is directed toward the "being" of the art work, that this is what the art work "is." What I have tried to define is how the paintings "work." Participation in a painting is not a mystical, visionary, undefinable experience. A painting works in a certain way because it is made in a certain way. My response to the way it is made is in good part a consequence of my history and nature so I can never extract myself—or better, my self—from the analysis. Analysis is not laboratory work but reciprocation, dialogue, discourse, intercourse where the self, or all the participant selves, and the work of art are mutually defined.

A history of Western art (or any art, for that matter) would be and must be an intricate, careful thing and a most consequential thing, for it would be a history of consciousness. Art does not simply reflect consciousness but shapes it. Such a history is the task of several careers, not one paper. What is needed here is the sense of the continuous line of Giotto's heritage: whatever the several modes, a painting from Giotto to Cézanne is an illusory world over against the spectator (at some point in the development, no longer a participant). Such pictures functioned very differently at different times (which is the work of the history of art) but they shared the character of being on the other side of the painting surface, a created world that was other than the spectator and—vital point—in various ways subservient to him.

The objectivity of nature was vital to the growth of science. Now science itself comes to know that the resulting scientific knowledge is not simply part of the truth but a misshapen truth. Not only art but mystic communion gives another part of the truth but also a different modality of truth, which is not different from science to be added to it but, in ways we do not yet know, inseparable from scientific truth. The question really is, whether the Western scientific enterprise is to be denied and reversed or whether it can be restored into wholeness. This is a metaphysical question but also a methodological one and therefore political and social.

This is only in part a digression. At some point along the way science became the determinant of men's consciousness and it is important to the argument to know what took place. But, risky as it is to make such an analysis, I think science grew out of the consciousness shaped by art and, as science falters in face of its own destructive products, art may be the only resource for putting the divided consciousness together again (I am tempted to say "art informed by religion" but I do not want to be held responsible at the moment for demonstrating that assertion so I will exile it to a parenthesis).

All this is the background against which "modern art" (which I define as including everything from Cézanne to our own day) must be understood. As is true with all developmental artistic styles, the whole development is implicit from the beginning and what artists successfully do is two-fold: they develop the implications of the original stylistic idea and they translate the original form into the new vocabulary in order to maintain the purity of the original effect. The first of these tasks is no concern of the present paper but the second is. Every act shapes the consciousness of those who participate in it. They become, therefore, different persons no longer able to receive the originating work in the same way. Preservation of the canonical effect requires a new form that does for the new consciousness what the originating form did for the old. This process can be truncated by the appearance of an overpowering new idea, or it can be exhausted in the failure of the rejuvenating imagination or the changing forms can modulate into a distinctively new effect.

Cézanne stands, as all such men including Giotto do, as the fulfillment of the old tradition as well as the initiator of the new. The pictured world is still palpably three dimensional and solid. Yet it is no longer beyond the picture plane but translated into it. Nothing is permitted to disrupt the surface of the painting; the wall that Giotto energized into drama returns as the controlling plane of painting. Suddenly the painting is no longer subservient to the spectator but is an object in his presence. Much, if not most, of the intensely emotional protest against modern art arises from offended pride at loss of this subservience and from a sense of being crowded. A modern work of art is not over there beyond the frame but obtrudes into the room.

The drama that was the substance of Renaissance painting and a constant presence in post-Renaissance art has been ruthlessly excised from the painting. But it has not been excised from the painting act, the painting relation. This is where most criticism of modern art goes wrong, for the drama is very much present but quite transformed. The painting is so clearly the product of a high intellectual act that to experience a Cézanne is not simply to experience an encounter with Provence or an encounter with a painting. It is to experience the creative intelligence of the artist. It is perfectly obvious to anyone who knows art that there is a creative intelligence behind every work of art but usually that intelligence is absorbed into the work. It is very nearly only in Western art that the intelligence of the artist is so publicly present and so clearly at work solving an artistic problem. With Cézanne this extraordinary presence of the artist in his dramatic interaction with his material becomes one of the factors participating in the extraordinary complex of relations that make up a Cézanne painting.

The surrealistic-expressionistic tradition owes little to Cézanne but the rest of modern art is a working out of the themes he designated. The relative emphasis on the participating factors varies widely. The cubist tradition pursued the problem of interaction between represented space and the integral picture plane. Nonrepresentational art pursued the same problem while sacrificing the assistance or freeing itself of the burden of association with the world of our common life. That world appears, vio-

lently and obtrusively, in the badly labelled "pop" art style. The presence
of the artist is variously established, from the cool remoteness of Mondrian
to the passion of the action painters, who make of their own creative art
both the subject and the occasion for the painting. But constantly the
painting is an object established in the intimate presence of the spectator,
carrying intensely the dramatic presence of the artist (even when, as often
happens, that presence is trivial, frivolous or indulgent).

Within this development, one of the more remarkable stages has
been reached in our own day. One of the major movements of the sixties
(I am reluctant to speak, as some do, of "the art of the sixties" as though the
most original movement is so automatically dominant), comprises a series
of works that go apparently to the other extreme. All signs of the artist's
personality are effaced. As nearly as possible all action and all hierarchy
within the work are abolished. Sculpture becomes pure geometric forms,
color is brought to the same value level to prevent any effect of space
or modelling, space and drama are expelled. The work of art is reduced to
pure objecthood, often without any inherent interest at all. Indeed, the
artist works hard to cancel out "interest," that is any sensuous quality or
any complex of internal relations that can give pleasure or direct attention
in time. The work is totally manifest in the instant of first viewing, it
deliberately eschews anything that can hold the attention of the spectator.

At the same time, the work functions in the attention of the spectator for it is very difficult to ignore it. These artists are given to big
works that cannot be evaded, or things like cascades of felt, or various
materials scattered on the floor that are so bizarrely out of tune with their
setting that they intrude inescapably into the consciousness of the spectator.

This is so unlike anything that has gone before that some critics
(notably Sheldon Nodleman) have interpreted it as the beginning of a new
style and therefore a new consciousness. This is a serious and responsible
position and it is hard to be confident of any interpretation while in the
midst of a volatile situation. Nevertheless, I do not hold to this interpretation; a style (or any human attitude) is human through its negations as
much as through its affirmations. These new works do not appear at some
generalized period of the history of man; they appear in the context of
a culture in which men are surfeited with moral or structural exhortation.
They appear precisely in a culture that has worn out the work of Giotto.
They so exactly reverse everything that Giotto and his successors have
tried to do.

They deny inherent interest and involvement. They are ostentatiously
anonymous. They avoid all drama, all development, space and three dimen-
sionality, everything in short that has concerned Western artists. And by
the denial, they affirm the absence of what they are denying.

It is the artistic statement of the death of God.

I do not much like making parallels of this kind. As every reader of

Spengler knows they are not difficult to do and, if they are false, they can be painfully misleading. Even so I think this one may help.

"The death of God" is more serious than its faddishness and slogan-like quality would suggest (significantly, the art movements have the same inclination toward faddishness and slogans). As theological statement it has grievous weaknesses; in any usable definition of "God" it is as blasphemous to say "God is dead" as to say "God is alive." Either is a statement of undemonstrable faith quite irrelevant to the "being" of God or any other such meaningless statement.

I should think the "death of God" theologians, who are not incompetent or silly men, must weary of reading condescending statements that God is not dead, it is only our concept of God that is dead, particularly when this statement is invariably followed by a reformulation of some outmoded concept. It is, obviously, quite true that our concept of God is dead but these theologians are much too serious to attempt to exploit so unexceptional a statement as that. Something much more important is going on.

I can say with any certainty only this much: it is not "a" concept of God that has died, it is the very concept of having a concept of God that has died. There is no point in trying ingeniously to reformulate a concept of God; there is no language left to do more than make an idol in memory of the lost God. "The death of God" is as good an idol as any other but it is no more than that. Despite the dogmatism of some of the theologians (but not all) the statement has no status as history or description. It is no more than a working instrument to contend with the particularities of a situation. It does, however, have a use that, say, Billy Graham's idolatry of a social order does not have: it does make us conscious that something, call it what you will, has died and that "something" has been essential to the sustenance of the human spirit.

The minimal art of the sixties, the color painting of Stella, Louis, Olitski, the art of many others, makes this same affirmation. They are not affirming vacuity or meaninglessness. To do that would be to stop altogether making art (as, indeed, Marcel Duchamp very nearly did). They are affirming that something once alive is now dead. In so doing they are working very precisely in the methodological tradition of Western art.

It should be clear that there has been a fundamental shift in the manner of my treatment of this material. The whole point of the first part of the paper was to elucidate the way in which two great artists controlled the consciousness of worshippers to particular, if different, devotional ends. In the minds of Duccio and Giotto this appears to have been a conscious (if probably not verbalized) purpose. There was no question of whether God did or did not exist. It was a matter of shaping consciousness to the proper (orthodox?) reception of God. It is possible, even necessary, to speak of this body of material as "Tuscan theology," with the full intention of making clear that both the language and the issues are those of painting, not propositional systems.

No such "theological" interpretations can be offered of the modern material for its use is very different. Yet its procedures are not all that different for its explicit (now at least partially verbalized) intention is to have an effect on the consciousness of the spectator. "Have an effect" rather than "shape" because to shape something is to be in a moral or dramatic relation to it, a relation and a responsibility which these artists have rejected. Rather consciousness is thrown back on its own resources, undetermined by the work of art. This art is (as, of course, all art is) unintelligible outside its own history. It is the affirmation of the death of that history or (if we avoid prophecy) the present exhaustion of that history.

What it can mean to a man of another culture, unaffected by the malaise of our culture, I cannot say. It is often useful to remember that when cultural analysts speak of "modern man" they are speaking only of the educated classes of Western Europe and the United States with their cultural provinces. But I speak with some confidence of this group, at least for this moment. And for this moment the history of Western art is exhausted and some of the most creative artists are giving themselves over to the task of doing more than denying that tradition or affirming its death. They are compelling consciousness to be aware of itself in a way that man has never achieved before. I have always felt that "the world come of age" was a singularly arrogant phrase as though even the greatest of our predecessors was a child as against our maturity. Many of our predecessors have been a good deal more self-aware than that. What is, however, granted to us or imposed on us is, so far as I know, unprecedented—the consciousness of consciousness itself; the awareness of the instruments of our awareness, even the instruments of that self-aware awareness; the symbolic means men have used for the construction of their own integrity.

The history of man has been a history of his generation of symbolic structure for coping with experience and his eventual defeat in the failure of his structures. We are involved now in the common and traditional process of the collapse of inherited structures. Yet, history is not cyclical; there is something to be salvaged from that process and the first thing to salvage is the understanding of the process itself. Understanding is more than description. It remains, therefore, essential to grasp the human reality within the process.

Conclusion

Hovering behind everything I have said, and occasionally emerging into summary statement is a position in historical analysis that cannot be demonstrated but only asserted here. Our criticism (including art history, which is simply criticism in a particular mode) is fundamentally positivistic: the art work is an object which is accessible to the appropriate technique. This is not a pejorative description. The techniques and their application obviously vary widely in quality but good art history has proven itself as a flexible and human instrument, going a long way toward reconstructing the reality of the life work of many hundreds of men. Nothing I can propose, here or elsewhere, is conceivable except as an outgrowth of what these men have done.

Nevertheless, I would make the general analytical statement: the art work is thought of as over there and it can in its essentials be encapsulated in our techniques. The inescapable corollary of this (and all positivism) is that my "self" is encapsulated in me. "I" exist as a distinct entity, detached from all the other selves and objects of the world.

Against this I have proposed that the art work is a functional *relation*. It is, indeed, a structured object; the inherited techniques of criticism need not be superseded for they are the means for defining the structure and it is the structure that determines the character of the relation. The art work is not instrumental only; it is a participant in a complex of relations.

Hence, what I have had to say is both incomplete and distorted if it is isolated from the "human reality" or, to use the divisive academic jargon, psychology. If the art work *functions* in a peculiarly complex web of *relations* among persons and things, then the person is no longer the isolated and inevitably alienated individual but the kind of person who is defined within, literally exists only within, such relations. If so, the art work is not peripheral or incidental to the human enterprise. It is one of the means, perhaps the central and generative means, for the creation of the human personality.

Thus it remains, finally, to move back from the particular to the general and try to define where this introduction, necessarily schematic, moves to. The major enterprise of the modern mind has been set the task of a redefinition of the self and its mode of working and knowing; I want to suggest where I think this investigation belongs.

I take my text, not from the canonical Germans, but from a Spaniard and then an Englishman.

I have several times used the word "circumstances." Without acknowledgement, I was each time quoting Ortega. It is Ortega who made what I judge to be the complete statement of the modern mind, having the merit of unambiguous as well as unhyphenated succinctness and, for whatever it is worth, the further merit of chronological priority: "I am myself plus my circumstances."

The verb "to be" is the most dangerous of all philosophical terms; it is the easiest (because we always think we know what it means) and the most difficult (because we seldom do know what it means). It is both seductive and traitorous. Our thought, even our manhood, founders on this word. We cannot take it as descriptive but as an act of faith.

As such it transforms my relation to my world. I am not "in" or "among" the things of my life. I *am* those things in addition to whatever else "I am." The consequences of this are extraordinary. The world of my circumstances is made up in part of what I am thrown into, but in part it is a world of my choice. It is never a world of final objects which I can describe as fixed and determined. They are part of me, changing as I change just as I change with the changes in them. But they are not just part of me; I do not create my circumstances. They are a part of other people as well and my circumstances interlock with other people's circumstances. I am not just obligated to all these circumstances or responsible for them. I am inalienably, often intolerably, locked into them. Thus those who use that admirable tool, intellectual analysis, to detach me from my circumstances, do not simply impoverish my experience. They alienate me from myself, they divide me into a schizophrenia the therapists so inadequately tinker with. Thus the work of Descartes was not just a *faux pas*. It condemned man to an unfruitful narcissism, an autoeroticism that has brought considerable intellectual pleasure but now little else.

It is not enough to say I am myself plus my circumstances; it is required of us to seek to know *how* we are related to our circumstances. We would be no more than vegetables if we were content to live in our circumstances in the recurrent pattern of the plant that grows in nature. It is rather that our humanness inheres in the tone and rhythm, the range and depth, the insight and interval of our involvement with our circumstances.

More than one hundred years ago, Samuel Taylor Coleridge made the great statement that I pair with the Spaniard's, "...it is the fundamental mistake ... to suppose that words and their syntaxes are the immediate representatives of *things*, or that they correspond to *things*. Words correspond to thought, and the legitimate order and connection of words, to the *laws* of thinking and to the acts and affections of the thinker's mind...."[1]

Thus words are quite immediately deposed from their inherited authority. "Knowing" is not a matter of the right order of words. It is the right ordering of the processes, the acts and affections of our minds. Insofar as words do point to those processes they are surrogates for knowing when we talk, they are agents of knowing. But they are not that knowing, which is an intercourse—a word which, like the biblical "know," has its significant

[1] J. A. Richards, *Coleridge on Imagination* (New York: Harcourt Brace Jovanovich Inc., 1935), p. 122.

sexual reference—an intercourse with circumstances, the self and things in communion.

The force of truth, then, is in that relation, not in the words that haltingly and inadequately describe the relation. Decisive influence belongs to those forces that determine the relation, not to the words that, following, attempt to account for the creativity of those forces.

This is not the occasion to try the full analysis of those forces and the relation between men and their circumstances; my earlier statement must suffice: "Our humanness inheres in the tone and rhythm, the range and depth, the weight and interval of our involvement with our circumstances." But these are the terms of the arts' involvement with our lives. They are the most general terms of the work of the arts, which are nothing if not the working out of our destiny in the pure weightiness of material substance. But, being general, they have the widest reference and thus emphasize the assertion that is the foundation of my case. The words we use, even propositionally rather than artistically, do, in the economy of our brains give access to these relations and help shape them. But the definition of them, the root and origin of being human, is first in geometry, then in the shaping of space, then in the shaping of matter, sound and motion.

I do not propose even a schematic history of this extraordinary process but only a rapid movement from these generalizations to the concreteness of a particular body of material. Thus I do not now go into the question of priority, either in time or value, between the work of the arts and the work of the propositional languages in the discussion of fundamental issues. This is not a very old question. So long as it could be assumed that our words applied to things, then naturally the science of the highest reality—God—could rightly claim to be the highest of the sciences. If, however, our words apply to our ideas about things then the center of gravity shifts to the ability of our nervous systems—the origin of our ideas—to respond to that highest reality. Any language, then, is testable only against the power of the person to respond to reality since it is that response which is the revelation of a reality otherwise entirely inaccessible to our languages.

Further, since this responsive self is made up not only of the conscious self but of the self's circumstances, it is in the intricate, the infinitely complex web of the self's involvement with its circumstances, its entanglement with the specificity and the materiality of the world, that the decisive act of human thought takes place. It is not required of the arts to validate their role in human experience for this network of involvement is the very substance of their work. It is rather for the propositional arts to validate their ancient claim to authority by demonstrating that in their responsible attention to the rhythm and tension, the weight and the spacing of their own structures they are adequate to the treatment of this, the central concern of being human.

The issues as defined here are central to the Tuscan enterprise but they are not the only ones that concerned these two Tuscans much less the great men who came after them. Nor can it be said that the Tuscan theological structure is normative any more than any other—such structure is no more than a partial and tentative answer to the problem of being a man and being a Christian. Rembrandt worked within certain of Giotto's basic assumptions: his figures move coherently in an intelligible space and to the rhythm of moral purpose. But they occupy a space radiant with a light that places personality in the context of infinite purpose and this was no part of what the Florentines did. Thus is Christian destiny worked out in a range of imaginative structures that respond to the range of our entrapment in different circumstances.

Yet what the Tuscans defined has been so dominant, in the economy of history, that it has become very nearly canonical for our culture. It is only partially to the point to affirm that man is thus-and-so unless there are present the structures of the imagination, spatial models of action that can make it possible for men to translate affirmation into action. The Tuscans, specifically in the form generated by Giotto, provided the patterns by which men moved on the earth and in the midst of earth's things for 500 years.

Equally the issues they raise provide in themselves another issue pressing for our time. It is an inclination virtually become a habit to judge that theological structures now outmoded can be discarded in favor of new orderings of life's passions. I have presented the work of Giotto and Duccio as theological systems and I have tried to define the principles that are central to their work and that govern the details that space does not permit me to display here. Comparably it is true that few in our day seem able to order their lives in the patterns of Tuscan theology. Yet only a fanatic few would press the logic of this to the point of indifference to what is there on the walls. While Giotto's vision of human order is increasingly distant from us as a possibility of human action, his paintings are increasingly cherished as imperishable possessions.

The reasons are not, perhaps, difficult to find and they carry the discussion into issues that lie even deeper than the issues that concerned the great Tuscans. Art works are the model of fulfillment, of men working out their destiny within the immediacies of their circumstances. However differently, it has been possible for the intricacies of this relation to be discerned and meaningfully ordered, the experienced world brought within the intelligibilities of human fulfillment. Thus, the museum becomes a demonstration of human hope. The same museum that contains the great Madonnas of Cimabue, Duccio, and Giotto also contains great works by Rembrandt and Rubens, imaginative structures of very different weight and rhythm. They, too, are no longer truly available as guides or models yet again we can respond to them in all the integrity of their contention with the complexities of their experience.

Thus we see continuously the new modes of being "in" the world born in varying debt to the old, in turn giving way to newer modes yet never finally losing their essential integrity or their relevance to us. A complete history uncovers the despairing moments that occur in the intervals between the collapse of older models as living paradigms and the birth of the new. But it also chronicles the constant renewal of images. It has seemed necessary very often in the past that the renewal be made at the expense of the old, even with the active repudiation of the old, as when Renaissance men said that medieval architecture was an architecture of barbarians, the Goths. But this does not seem required of us. That greatest of our modern arts, the sense and the structures of history, make all styles accessible to us. This can obviously nourish the dilettante but it can also nourish constructive hope.

Those things that remain alive to us are then seen not only as affirmations of the human spirit but perpetual possibilities of the human spirit. Our spatial image and our spatial experience are more complex than Giotto's but he who has truly seen Giotto's work not only knows what once was possible in a given circumstance but his own flesh is trained and disciplined to a particular order. Giotto is no longer part of an exhausted order but has become part of our circumstances, one of the means by which we know our own experience. It may be that Duccio's mystical vision is not available to us, but the precise intricacies of his blending of figure and space can bring us to the more technically intended spatial researches of our own day with a deeper sense of their possibilities in the devotional life.

Thus hope is less grounded on abstract argument than it is on the fulfillment of history.

Coda

When I was invited to contribute an essay to this symposium it was under the rubric "Emerging Images in Teaching Religion and the Arts." At this writing I do not know if that title still holds but it represents the general intent of my participation.

Consideration of that subject has at no point been overt in the essay. Having left it implicit, I might do my readers the courtesy of assuming they can grasp the educational consequences of such an argument as this, rather than adding the anticlimax (or, at best, the postclimax) of any formal consideration of the implications of the main body of the essay.

Unfortunately, observation has taught me that the work of greater men than I has been ignored even while used. The work of Freud and Marx, for example, is far from unknown in the academy; their books are read and taught as among the major creations of man's mind. If this work were to be taken seriously, the process of education would be revolutionized. Obviously they have not, in that sense, been taken seriously.

What has happened is exactly what I have described as happening with works of art. The insights of Freud and Marx have been turned into objects. Objects of great interest and elegance but, for all of that, objects to be seen and studied from without.

I do not suggest that the proper conclusion would be to design "Freudian" or "Marxist" universities. In so far as the devotees of these systems have made them into intellectual tools, they too make the systems into objects. Worse, they make them into idols. At least the liberal academy has a lot of these systems—objects to look at whereas a consistent ideological academy would make one of the touchstar of all systems.

Sadly, however, I must say that, for all its claims to liberality the liberal academy is, at base, equally ideological, only its ideology is more of method and attitude than of system. The essential objecthood of all achievements is the unspoken dogma of the academy. Under the only real statement of it—scholarly objectivity—it is rigorously forbidden to enter into profound commitment to the objects of study.

To deplore this is futile but also inhumane. This procedure has given a range and comprehensiveness to the intellectual enterprise that could not have been achievable in any other way.

Nevertheless, the malaise of modern man called so commonly "alienation" is not just a by-product but is built into this system. If, as I have stated, man forms his person, his "self" in his intercourse with his circumstances, to reduce his circumstances to "the other," to make of them an "it," is to leave him naked, a stranger and alone in the world of his habitation.

In so far as it makes any human sense to say "God is dead," education, and theology as a part of education, killed him. They "killed" him by destroying the process, the structured and operative relation by which God can be manifest among men.

It is not that I can say confidently what the new images of teaching ought to be. If they are, in fact, emerging, I am not aware of it. So far as I know none of us is in a position to be sure what these images can be or ought to be. I can offer only a procedure out of which new images might emerge. At the beginning of this paper I assumed an obligation of making a contribution toward this procedure and what I have done is offer a variety of analyses in fulfillment of that responsibility.

If, then, we reappropriate our history in this mode there should emerge a surer sense of what our history has been as changing process rather than as fixed and objectified achievement. If I am right in this mode of analysis, then we should not, at this point, specify a pattern but inaugurate a process. The new work of education should be a total art and no longer an affirmation of the disembodied intellect.

8

Picasso's "Crucifixion"

Jane Dillenberger

With an introduction and concluding remarks by John Dillenberger

Introduction

The essays in this volume deal largely with the future of the arts. What follows in Jane's excursus on Picasso may appear to be a selection of a figure who does not belong to the future and a method of analysis which does not provide the outlines of the future. Indeed, Picasso is an historic figure, who, while he marked out a new future and is still painting vigorously on the eve of the ninth decade of his life, already has been followed by painters whose mode and subject matter are further removed from Picasso than Picasso is from the artists of the seventeenth century. But an analysis of a painting by an artist who belongs to both history and the modern world, in a subject matter not usual to his palette—"The Crucifixion"—but growing out of his very being, may provide clues to the nature of the arts. There is too much analysis which is not bound to nor grows out of the discipline and context of the art medium at hand.

Great painting has universal significance, but it is never mass-produced or the gift of any but the few. Through great art, reality gives itself to be known beyond, but not without, the gift of the artist, and then only to the disciplined seeing of the beholder. The period of mass art can be justified as self-expression and therapy. In itself, it may disclose much about an age. But the art that transcends an age even as it reflects it, brings profound perceptions and the gifts of an artist to mutual expression. That is why I think the delineation of the work of a great artist is instructive for any time, for it helps us to try to see with the eyes of the artist without the gifts of his palette. But in another sense, it is even to see more than the artist saw, for the artist brought to the work more than he knew. The resources of his being, joined to a great gift, become a source of revealing to us.

The Iconography of Picasso's "Crucifixion"

Almost twenty-five years ago, the Museum of Modern Art held a large exhibition entitled "Picasso: Fifty Years of His Art." On that occasion Alfred Barr wrote, "It is true that Picasso's recent renown does not depend upon his art alone. Picasso's life in Nazi-occupied Paris took on, apparently without the artist's intention, a symbolic character which had little directly to do with what he was painting. And his political stand after the Liberation was in no way specifically reflected in his art. . . ." Barr offered a thoughtful interpretation: "Responsible only to himself, Picasso works out of his own inner compulsion. Take it or leave it, he says in effect, I can and will paint in no other way. In a world in which social pressures—democratic, collectivist, bourgeois—tend to restrict the freedom of the exceptional individual, Picasso's art assumes a significance far beyond its artistic importance."[1]

Since these words were written, the Picasso legend has grown. Fed by the anecdotes of his friends and critics, art dealers and mistresses, and given superb visual imagery by gifted and imaginative photographers, the man Picasso with his "anarchic individualism" has assumed an image of heroic proportions.

Picasso's output is prodigious; in sheer volume—that is, square yards of canvas, pounds of metal and wood and clay in sculpture, lithographic stones and copper etching plates—if all were gathered together it would be a massive physical assemblage. Among these, there is a unique, small painting, the *Crucifixion*, (plate 1) painted by Picasso in 1930 when he was forty-nine years of age. Brilliant in color, crowded in composition, filled with strange images and distorted forms, it communicates a cryptic content.

The subject matter appears unexpectedly within the work of the artist, whose large output up to that time had been concerned with persons, places, and things taken from the visual data that he saw about him: Gertrude Stein in her little volume on her friend wrote, "Picasso knows, *really* knows the faces, the heads, the bodies of human beings, he knows them as they have existed since the existence of the human race, the soul of people does not interest him, why interest one's self in the souls of people when the face, the head, the body can tell everything."[2] But she goes on to say, indeed to deplore: "During this last period, from 1927 to 1935, the souls of people commenced to dominate his vision, a vision which was as old as the creation of people, lost itself in interpretation. What he could see, did not need interpretation but in these years, 1927 to 1935, for the first time, the interpretations destroyed his own vision so that he made forms not seen, but conceived."[3]

It was during this period, 1927 to 1935, that the *Crucifixion* was

---

[1] Alfred H. Barr, "Picasso: Fifty Years of His Art" (New York: Museum of Modern Art), p. 11.

[2] Gertrude Stein, *Picasso* (Boston: Beacon Press, 1960), p. 47.

[3] Stein, *Picasso*, p. 47.

painted, and a series of studies on this theme relating to this painting and to the great sixteenth-century altarpiece of the Crucifixion by Grünewald were done.

Before attempting to decode this *Crucifixion* let us turn to the earlier phases of the artist's work, extolled by his patron and biographer, Gertrude Stein, to see in his earlier work "the faces, the heads, the bodies the artist knows as they have existed since the existence of the human race."[4] With this as a background, we can return to the *Crucifixion* and to the vision Miss Stein describes as dominated by the souls of people, by forms not seen, but conceived.

Picasso moved to Paris from Spain, having already had an exhibition of his paintings in his home city, Barcelona, when only sixteen, and having won a prize with a painting exhibited in Madrid two years later. His father was a competent art teacher at the Barcelona academy who had instructed and encouraged the precocious young Picasso. Barcelona, then a cultural and artistic center, had connections with Parisian artists and writers, and Picasso's friends encouraged him to make the move to Paris. Within a few days of his nineteenth birthday he arrived in Paris, and came to live in a dilapidated old wooden house nicknamed the Bateau Lavoir which housed many literary and artistic persons. It was there that he met Fernande Olivier, a French woman of great beauty and some culture, with whom he lived from 1903 to 1912. She describes her first impression of the artist in her little volume entitled *Picasso and His Friends*: "Picasso was small, dark, thick-set, worried and worrying, with gloomy, deep, penetrating eyes, which were curiously still. His gestures were awkward, he had the hands of a woman and was badly dressed and untidy. A thick lock of shiny black hair gashed his intelligent, stubborn forehead. His clothes were half-bohemian, half-workman, his excessively long hair swept the collar of his tired jacket."[5] She continued, "I was astonished by Picasso's work . . . astonished and fascinated. The morbid side of it perturbed me somewhat, but it delighted me too. This was the end of the Blue Period. Huge, unfinished canvases stood all over the studios, and everything there suggested work: but, my God, in what chaos!"[6]

Fernande was especially intrigued by the combination of intellectuality and human emotion she discerned in the paintings of this period. She writes of one which particularly struck her, of a gaunt and haggard man whose expression was one which "told of his hopeless resignation. The effect was strange, tender and infinitely sad, suggesting total hopelessness, an agonized appeal to the compassion of mankind. What was at the bottom of

---

[4] Stein, *Picasso*, p. 47.

[5] Fernande Olivier, *Picasso and His Friends* (New York: Appleton-Century, 1965), p. 26.

[6] Olivier, p. 27.

this kind of painting? Was the work completely intellectual in conception, as I've come to understand it since, or did it reveal a deep and despairing love of humanity, as I thought then?"[7]

The painting Fernande describes and questions in this passage is not *The Old Guitarist*, (see Barr, p. 28) but yet her words, even her query, apply to the emaciated figure who bends with an exaggerated pathos over his instrument in the familiar painting. It was this work which inspired the poet Wallace Stevens to write his long poem, "The Man With the Blue Guitar." The poem begins with the lines:

> The man bent over his guitar,
> A Shearsman of sorts. The day was green.
>
> They said, "You have a blue guitar,
> You do not play things as they are."
>
> The man replied, "Things as they are
> Are changed upon the blue guitar."
>
> And they said then, "But play, you must,
> A tune beyond us, yet ourselves,
>
> A tune upon the blue guitar
> Of things exactly as they are."[8]

The poem continues exploring the relationship between art and life, the poet and his readers, dream and reality.

The somber and pathetic subjects who people the paintings of Picasso's Blue Period, gave way soon to studies of circus performers and actors. The pervasive blue tones were left for a lighter, rosier palette.

Two years later in 1905 Picasso painted the *Family of Acrobats* (see Barr, p. 36). In this large canvas he assembled a number of circus characters who appeared in his earlier drawings, prints and paintings of the two previous years. The young harlequin, the somber corpulent clown, the leggy adolescent tumbler, and two children, form a group physically near one another, but psychically unrelated, each self-absorbed—dreaming their own individual dreams, as does the charming woman seated at the right who looks out of the picture zone toward the viewer with an unfocused, inward gaze.

For years this painting hung in a private home in Munich where Rainer Maria Rilke, who knew Picasso, lived during the summer of 1915. Grasped by the haunting poetry of the painting, Rilke composed the fifth of

---

[7] Olivier, p. 28.

[8] Wallace Stevens, *Selected Poems of Wallace Stevens* (New York: Vintage Books, 1959), pp. 73–74. © 1959 Alfred A. Knopf, Inc.

his Duino Elegies, according to his own words, while "beside the great Picasso." It begins, "But tell me, who are they, these acrobats, even a little/more fleeting than we ourselves,—so urgently, even since childhood,/ wrung by an (oh, for the sake of whom?) never-contented will? That keeps on wringing them,/bending them, slinging them, swinging them, throwing them, and catching them back—"[9]

A year later Picasso began a portrait of his friend Gertrude Stein (see Barr, p. 50). We have the sitter's account of the creation of this magnificent portrait in Gertrude's *Autobiography of Alice B. Toklas*; "Just how the portrait of Gertrude Stein came about is a little vague in everybody's mind. I have heard Picasso and Gertrude talk about it, and how it came about they do not know. Picasso had never had anybody pose for him since he was 16 years old, he was then twenty-four, and Gertrude Stein had never thought of having her portrait painted, and they do not either of them know how it came about. Anyway it did and she posed to him for this portrait ninety times and a great deal happened during this time."[10]

For those who are not familiar with the *Autobiography* and know Alice B. Toklas only as the inventor of a recipe for brownies which requires hashish as one of its ingredients, the original Alice B. Toklas was a Californian who became the companion of Gertrude Stein and lived many years with her. Gertrude told her companion that she should write her autobiography, teasing her about what a lot of money she could make with a book entitled *My Twenty Five Years with Gertrude Stein*. Realizing that Alice B. never would, finally Gertrude herself wrote the book, but did it as if it had been written by her companion. The book ends with these sentences: "About six weeks ago Gertrude Stein said, 'It does not look to me as if you were ever going to write that autobiography. You know what I am going to do. I am going to write it for you. I am going to write it as simply as Defoe did the *Autobiography of Robinson Crusoe*. And she has and this is it."[11]

Throughout the book we get numerous references, with great affection and humor to Picasso. Following a detailed description of the initial sitting for the portrait of Gertrude, Gertrude wrote: "Finally spring was coming and sittings were coming to an end. All of a sudden one day Picasso painted out the whole head. 'I can't see you any longer when I look,' he said irritably. And so the picture was left like that. Gertrude and Alice B. went off to Italy and while they were gone Picasso painted the face in again.

---

[9] Barr, p. 37. Reprinted from *Duino Elegies* by Rainer Maria Rilke. Translated from the German, with Introduction and Commentary by J. B. Leishman and Stephen Spender. Copyright 1939 by W. W. Norton & Company, Inc. Copyright Renewed 1967 by Stephen Spender and J. B. Leishman.

[10] Gertrude Stein, *Autobiography of Alice B. Toklas* (New York: Vintage Books, 1960), p. 45.

[11] Stein, *Alice B. Toklas*, p. 252.

On her return Gertrude was pleased, but everybody else said that she did not look like that. 'But,' Picasso said, 'that does not make any difference, she will.' And she did."[12]

During the time that the portrait of Gertrude Stein was in progress, Picasso was also concentrating his creative energies on an extraordinary painting, *Les Desmoiselles D'Avignon*, (see Barr, p. 54),[13] which sums up the many pictorial inventions of the previous, very productive year. Although it was only once publicly exhibited in Europe, and rarely reproduced, it was seen by other artists in Picasso's studio, and had an influence way beyond what can be explained by these limited viewings. Now, sixty years later, its power remains undiminished.

Gertrude Stein's alias, Alice B. Toklas, tells of her first seeing of the painting in Picasso's studio on the occasion when she went with Gertrude for the first sitting for the Stein portrait. "Against the wall was an enormous picture, a strange picture of light and dark colours, that is all I can say, of a group, an enormous group and next to it another in a sort of red brown, of three women, square and posturing, all of it rather frightening. Picasso and Gertrude Stein stood together talking. I stood back and looked. I cannot say I realised anything but I felt that there was something painful and beautiful there and oppressive but imprisoned."[14]

Picasso's own recollections about the painting were recorded by his friend David-Henry Kahnweiler as they chatted in 1933 about those early days in Paris, when cubism as a style was born, and Kahnweiler eagerly espoused the cause and became the dealer for Picasso and Derain and Braque.

Picasso in speaking to his friend, said, "According to my first idea, there were also going to be men in the painting—I have drawings for them, too. There was a student holding a skull, and a sailor. The women were eating— that explains the basket of fruit that is still in the painting. Then it changed and became what it is now."[15]

Thus the painting which was intended originally as an allegory of the wages of sin changed. The sailor and the flowers were taken out leaving behind some fruit and what Alfred Barr has referred to as "five of the least seductive nudes in the history of art." Picasso has on occasion spoken of the way the work of art changes during its creation: "A picture is not thought out and settled beforehand. While it is being done it changes as one's thoughts change. And when it is finished, it still goes on changing, according to the state of mind of whoever is looking at it. A picture lives a

[12] Stein, *Alice B. Toklas*, p. 12.

[13] All paintings discussed in this article can be seen in Alfred Barr's book, *Picasso: Fifty Years of His Art*. New York, 1946.

[14] Stein, *Alice B. Toklas*, p. 22.

[15] Herschel B. Chipp, *Theories of Modern Art* (Berkeley and Los Angeles: University of California Press, 1968), p. 266.

life like a living creature, undergoing the changes imposed on us by our life from day to day. This is natural enough, as the picture lives only through the man who is looking at it."[16]

The style of cubism radically changes the way we see the visible world. Gertrude notes three reasons for the making of cubism in her little volume on Picasso: "First, the composition, because the way of living had changed the composition of living had extended, and each thing was as important as any other thing. Secondly, the faith in what the eyes were seeing, that is to say the belief in the reality of science commenced to diminish. To be sure science had discovered many things, she would continue to discover things, but the principle which was the basis of all this was completely understood, the joy of discovery was almost over. Thirdly, the framing of life, the need that a picture exist in its frame, remain in its frame was over. A picture remaining in its frame was a thing that always had existed and now pictures commenced to want to leave their frames and this also created the necessity for cubism. The time had come and the man."[17]

Picasso himself in a conversation in 1923, remarked: "The fact that for a long time Cubism has not been understood and that even today there are people who cannot see anything in it, means nothing. I do not read English, an English book is a blank book to me. This does not mean that the English language does not exist, and why should I blame anybody else but myself if I cannot understand what I know nothing about?"[18]

The later refinement of Cubism is seen in Picasso's portrait of D. H. Kahnweiler (see Barr, p. 71). Picasso, reflecting on this phase of Cubism told Francoise Gilot:

> In those polyhedric Cubist portraits I did in tones of white and gray and ochre, beginning around 1909, there were references to natural forms, but in the early stages there were practically none. I painted them in afterwards. I call them attributes. . . . It was really pure painting, and the composition was done as a composition. It was only afterwards that I brought in the attributes. . . . You know my cubist portrait of Kahnweiler . . . in its original form it looked to me as though it were about to go up in smoke. But when I paint smoke, I want you to be able to drive a nail into it. So I added the attributes—a suggestion of eyes, the wave in the hair, an ear lobe, the clasped hands. It's like giving a long and difficult explanation to a child: you add certain details that he understands immediately in order to sustain his interest and buoy him up for the difficult parts.[19]

Picasso added an interesting comment, showing a recognition of the problem of communication his art presents the viewer; "As Hegel says, they

[16] Chipp, p. 268.

[17] Stein, *Picasso*, p. 12.

[18] Chipp, p. 264.

[19] Francoise Gilot and Carlton Lake, *Life With Picasso* (New York: Signet Books, 1966), pp. 66–67.

can know only what they already know. So how do you go about teaching them something new? By mixing what they know with what they don't know. Then, when they see vaguely in their fog something they recognize, they think, 'Ah, I know that.' And then it's just one more step to 'Ah, I know the whole thing.' And their mind thrusts forward into the unknown and they begin to recognize what they didn't know before and they increase their powers of understanding."[20]

All the cubist artists made contracts with Kahnweiler, and until the war he did everything for them. The afternoons with the group coming in and out of his shop were for Kahnweiler really afternoons with Vasari. He believed in them and their future greatness. Later he wrote a little treatise entitled *The Heroic Years of Cubism;* reflecting on that time, 1907–1914, he wrote:

"What occurred at that time in the plastic arts will be understood only if one bears in mind that a new epoch was being born, in which man (all mankind in fact) was undergoing a transformation more radical than any other known within historical times. The enormous change that took place during these seven years in painting and sculpture went down to the very roots. . . . What is certain is that the direct visual study of the exterior world that European humanity had demanded of its painters and sculptors since the Renaissance ceased to be the aim of the artists. . . . One realises how great a spiritual revolution this was, an *introvert* art after six centuries of *extrovert*."[21]

In 1920 another shift of style and the fragmented flattened forms of cubism gave way to the ponderous volumes of the female figures in the large painting, *Two Seated Women* (see Barr, p. 116). Picasso derives the colossal figures, the stylized features, and columnar folds of the garments for early classical sculpture. The gravity of the mood, the massive forms, their passivity and ponderousness contrast strikingly with the dynamism of the *Desmoiselles D'Avignon* or the poetic, haunting charm of the *Acrobats*. But in this Neoclassic painting, Picasso returns again to "the faces, the heads, the bodies . . . as they have existed since the existence of the human race," to use Gertrude's words again.

A violent change of mood is found in the *Three Dancers* painted only two years later in 1925 (see Barr, p. 142). But between the lyrical naturalism of some of the paintings of this period and the convulsive, dynamism of the *Three Dancers* an event of importance to the artists and writers of Western Europe occurred. In 1924 Andre Breton's *Manifesto of Surrealism* gave formal definition to a movement which had grown out of the post-World War I Dada movement. "I believe," Breton proclaimed, "in

[20] Gilot and Lake, p. 67.
[21] Jane Dillenberger, *Secular Art with Sacred Themes* (New York: Abingdon Press, 1969), p. 14.

the future resolution of the states of dream and reality, in appearance so contradictory, in a sort of absolute reality, or Surreality, if I may so call it."[22] He went on to characterize Surrealism as based on the belief in the superior reality of certain forms of association heretofore neglected, in the omnipotence of dreams, in the undirected play of thought, the absence of any control exercised by reason, and as being beyond any esthetic or moral preoccupation.

The *Three Dancers* confronts us with a vision striking in its physical and emotional violence. Seen objectively as representations of nature, cubist paintings such as the *Three Musicians* of 1921 are grotesque enough, but their distortions are comparatively objective and formal, "whereas the frightful, grinning mask and convulsive action of the left-hand figure of the *Three Dancers* cannot be resolved into an exercise in esthetic relationships, magnificent as the canvas is from a purely formal point of view. The metamorphic *Three Dancers* is, as Alfred Barr remarked, a turning point in Picasso's art almost as radical as was the protocubist *Desmoiselles D'Avignon.* "The dynamism of the left-hand dancer foreshadows new periods of his art in which psychologically disturbing energies reinforce, or adulterate, depending on one's point of view, Picasso's everchanging achievements in the realm of form."[23]

For the surrealists, art was a means of self-expression, an instrument of self-discovery, not an end to be savored. Whether or not a work of art was surrealist hinged upon the methodological and iconographic relevance of the picture to the main ideas of the movement, that is, automatism and the dream image. Automatism was the draughtsmanly counterpart to free verbal association (Miro and Masson) in which improvisational shapes, biomorphic in form were used, these being both ambiguous and suggestive of much, but identifying nothing.[24]

With this brief survey of certain earlier stages of the development of Picasso's art, we turn now to a study of the *Crucifixion* painting of 1930. This study, or *seeing* of the painting, relates to the theme of this volume, as an example of an investigation into religiously significant images in contemporary art.

Within the early "heroic" years of Surrealism (a period William Rubin delimits to the years between the First and Second Manifesto, 1924–1929) Picasso created his first known (that is, published) *Crucifixion* composition (plate 2). It is a drawing which bears the evidence of numerous revisions of form. Here again we see the Surrealist's curving line which arbitrarily swells, defining a monstrous arm and hand like a catcher's mitt, and diminishes to indicate a mere round protuberance for a head.

[22] William S. Rubin, *Dada, Surrealism, and Their Heritage* (New York: Museum of Modern Art, 1968), p. 64.
[23] Barr, p. 143.
[24] Rubin, p. 64.

Though the line itself ebbs and flows with only minor changes in width or rhythmic speed, it has the magical property of suggesting three-dimensional form, as if the drawing were for a bas-relief, rather than collagelike, as we see in Miro's *Personnages with Stars*. So much for the Surrealist biomorphic style of the drawings.

The iconography, that is the reading of the images begins, of course, with Christ. His small head encircled by a crown of thorns and set in an egg-shaped halo is in the center of the upper part of the composition. His bulbous arms stretch the length and breadth of a wide crossbeam, the hand at our right being palm up, with a large ovoid nail at its center. At the left an enormous hand grasps a diagonal ladder, and a swollen foot is tilted forward below. Several figures merge into each other at the left side of the corpus, and at the right a horseman with a two-pronged lance in one hand is about to plunge it into the side of Christ, while holding a shield in the other hand.

This figure, referred to in John's Gospel simply as "one of the soldiers [who] pierced his side with a spear," long ago was given the name Longinus. The name is obviously derived from the Greek word for spear or lance, and so the spearman is called in the Acts of Pilate (from the psuedo Gospel of Nicodemus), and named in early manuscripts (such as the Rossano Gospel, sixth century). One of the curious conflations of Christian iconography is the later interpretation that the soldier who pierced the side of Jesus was one and the same as the centurion who was converted after the death of Jesus, and exclaimed "Truly, this was the Son of God." Trecento paintings most often represent Longinus, as Picasso does here, firmly astride a horse, and among those gathered at the foot of the cross. We shall see that in Picasso's later drawings the horse and Longinus are both present, but that Longinus is no longer astride the beast in the 1929 drawings, but by 1930, he returns to his mount, his lance in his hand in the *Crucifixion* painting.

The most astonishing figure in this drawing is, however, the female figure who bends backwards at the foot of the cross, achieving an extraordinary posture: her head falls back, the hair cascading down toward her curved buttocks, and her massive ankles and feet. Her inflated arms reach upward imploringly, and the acrobatic curve of the body causes the breasts to be seen in profile against the foot of the cross. This is the Magdalene, who in Christian art, often experiences the event of the Crucifixion with a violence of grief that bespeaks a passionate nature, and indeed, in Christian art she is identified with both the woman taken in adultery, and the prostitute who in Simon's house bathed Jesus's feet with her tears, and wiped them with her hair. Another conflation of Christian iconography, this conflation having a poetic and novelistic justification, whereas the Longinus legend perhaps shows the incorporation of opposites —the evil act out of which came conversion.

Picasso's Magdalene is related to a great, early sixteenth-century representation of this Mary in Grünewald's *Isenheim Altarpiece*[25] in which may be seen the small, but passionately arched body of the Magdalene kneeling at the foot of the cross, her head pressed back, her interlaced fingers raised toward the body of the crucified. Her body is tilted tensely backward, in a "sprung" position. Picasso has taken this figure, rotated it so that her back is to us, and drawn her head down even further than did Grünewald.

Two years later Picasso returned to the Crucifixion subject, and this same figure in a series of extraordinary drawings. On the sheet dated May 25, 1929, we see a series of studies again of this bent, sprung female figure (plate 3). Again the arms reach upward and the head falls backward: tubular legs and feet curve in unarticulated contours across the sheet. The breasts remain recognizable, but increasingly their contours serve a design function rather than a descriptive function. The four extra studies of the face rearrange the human features in willful, playful ways.

The next day, another page has two studies of this figure and shows a further departure from the natural bodily proportions and relationships (plate 4). The impulse to design is uppermost, creating a complex of lines bearing only some suggestive clues which relate, often in an abrasive way, with our experience of our own bodies.

Whereas the May 25th page (plate 3) shows the artist's hand, the servant of a mind groping for a visual image for the expression of an idea, the May 26th page (plate 4) shows the image clearly possessed by that mind, and now the image is elaborated consciously as a design. A more exaggerated contortion of the figure is depicted, bringing the nose to the pubic-anal zone. The lines are more purposeful, the elaborations of details like the carefully drawn fingernails and toenails—the reiterated curves which are read as hair or eyelashes, as blades of grass or as contours of the rib-cage—all of these are rendered with a masterful sense for pattern. A tight, self-complete small study at the lower left shows Picasso working with elements which vestigally relate to the human physiognomy and the breasts, but these forms are displaced and designed so freely that they read first as a vivid black and white design, and only secondarily as nose, hair, mouth, eyes.

Twelve days later Picasso worked again with this figure, but now set into a scene at the foot of the cross (plate 5). This study is followed the next day (plate 6) by a similar grouping and one which may be more easily read since the artist, by adding shading, has assisted identification of the images many of which are to be read doubly.

By studying the drawings together we are able to see that the first

---

[25] For illustrations see Plates 52–53, Jane Dillenberger, *Style and Content in Christian Art*, New York: Abingdon Press, 1965.

undulant line at our left is the contour for the arm and hand of a man who is much larger in scale than any of the other persons or objects. We suddenly sense him to be very near us, his armpit visible, but the palm turned away from us as he grasps the ladder and turns his head with open mouth to the nightmarish scene where we see the legs of the cruci-fied, the Magdalene, her face bent back to her buttocks.

Several female faces, some seen Picasso-wise, that is simultaneously in full-face and profile, others Janus-like, are at the right of the legs of the crucified. Longinus reappears wearing a Greek helmet and carrying a shield and lance. But in the first drawing the lance is thrust vertically in front of him, while in the June 8th drawing it seems to be held at his side, and has become the staff which holds a flag—a flag which has a double profile upon it, a white classical head with open mouth, whose profile creates a complimentary interlocking negroid profile. Just below this image of the flag, we find a similar double profile, dark and light, and a reminiscence of Grünewald's Magdalene with her interlacing fingers is to be seen in the undulating lines with fingers and fingernails carefully indicated. The June 8th drawing has two iconographic additions—center front a drumlike structure with upturned top on which we see a single dice and at the center right an arm and hand with pointing finger, which certainly is related to Grünewald's John The Baptist of the *Isenheim Altar-piece*, with his large hand with its insistently pointing finger. Below a crowd of spectators are seen in profile, and Longinus's horse, far from bearing his master, munches amiably on a turf of grass. Both drawings show a slight indication of setting, several Roman arches.

Two days later another sketch (plate 7) and further transformations and additions. The great man at the left holding the ladder undergoes another metamorphosis as his profile now can be read both as the boundary line of his lips and chin and as the toes of a foot—a foot which presumably belongs to the crucified figure who is seen only partially in these drawings. The Magdalene has been even more cruelly transformed, a long phallic-like nose again pressed against her buttocks, the eyes set one over the other, the mouth in profile surrounded by teeth which enframe a sharp triangular tongue. The hand with the pointing finger which has come to look more like a directional sign than like the hand of Grünewald's St. John, has acquired a head and suggestion of garments. This profile seems a kind of prophet type, grave of expression with one all-seeing eye, a large nose and a flowing beard.

A rather charming, imaginative addition is the filling of the space between the horse's neck and thigh with a woman's head—she seems to peer outward toward us, though one eye is in profile and the other full-face. The inclusion of this face and the turning of the horse's hoof so that we see the horseshoe with its nails, are both gratuitous additions of this mind forever in ferment, creating and recreating—a strange and fascinating mix of forms taken from traditional iconography, from other masters, and from his own repertoire of created images.

Nine months later, on February 7, 1930, another *Crucifixion* was painted (plate 1). Not large in size (20×26 inches), it was painted on wood, and it is one of a group of works which the artist has never sold, retaining it in his own possession. It has been exhibited a few times in the large surveys of the artist's work, but most of the 40 years since its creation, it has been in Picasso's own hands.

The painting must have a special significance for Picasso himself. But what is its meaning for us? With the drawings in hand, we can find the figure on the cross with its flat round head and mere dots for features, its paddle-like hands upon the crossbeam. A pinlike figure standing on a ladder is hammering a nail through one palm. At the foot of the ladder two crumpled figures are perhaps those of the two thieves, whose Tau-shaped crosses are seen, very small in size at the lower left and upper right. In the foreground a figure wearing a helmet holds across his shoulder the "tunic without seam, woven from top to bottom," and watches the throw of the dice, by a monstrous creature who is casting lots with him.

Above at the right, the arms which reach upwards with clasped hands surmount a strange triangular flow of garments. From this, or from behind it, emerges a grotesque sculptural monstrosity, beaklike nose and dots for eyes, jaws with teeth which close vertically rather than horizontally. A great praying mantis, and indeed this strange insect which still inhabits the twentieth-century world, yet seems to come from a prehuman era, is an insect which has fascinated Picasso. Its form may have inspired such a strange painting from 1929 as *The Woman Bather on the Beach* (see Barr, p. 163) which is certainly related to the *Crucifixion* of a year later.

Another antecedent in Picasso's own painting which assists us in understanding the development of certain forms is the strange, demonic *Woman in an Armchair* (see Barr, p. 161), also painted in 1929. Her great yawping mouth with its teeth like nails, in a pincerlike jaw is the prototype for the strange head which seems about to close its jaws about the wound in the side of the Crucified, just as the Longinus—here a tiny figure on his horse—withdraws his spear.

A kind of counterpart to these jaws is to be found in the wide, crescent-shaped form just above Longinus with two round eyes. Is this the moon, as Juan Larrea suggests? We saw a moon and a sun in the 1927 drawing. Are they recreated here? Larrea's suggestion is that the strange masked figure with rays about it at the right is the sun. Alfred Barr and Ruth Kaufmann[26] identify this latter figure as the Magdalene—an identification that I think our studies of the drawings support. The strange realistically three-dimensional object levitating in the upper right is usually

[26] Ruth Kaufmann, "The Burlington Magazine," September, 1969.

interpreted as the vinegar-soaked sponge.

Mary the Mother may be the figure with the vesicle-shaped face at the right of the cross. Her profile is turned to the right but it has again an interlocking profile, with blunt nose and protruding lips. The triangular dark-light zone which encloses both of these faces locks them together in a play of opposites, but the resulting image has an archetypal gravity.

It is quite certain, simply from the evidence of the drawings which have been published, that Picasso made many more studies. And when these are all known, we may have a record of the genesis of the painting, and the step-by-step metamorphosis of the imagery in the painting which will clarify some of the perplexing problems of identification which remain.

Not only will Picasso's drawings now still unpublished provide further insights into the meaning of the imagery, but his writings may help as well. We know from Picasso's friends and associates that during the heyday of Surrealism, he did a great deal of writing. His published Surrealist play *Desire Caught by the Tail* is one known example, but it is reported that there is much more written material. Gertrude Stein said that he stopped painting at intervals between 1927 and 1935—the period when these Crucifixion compositions were done. She goes on to say that since "it was impossible for him to do nothing he made poetry but of course it was his own way of falling asleep during the operation of detaching himself from the souls of things."[27]

But, in another sense, to fall asleep is to dream. And the dream was the great primal source of subject matter for the Surrealists. But whereas Picasso's contemporaries dreamed of and painted metamorphic subjects from nature like Miro's *Snail Woman Flower Star* (1934), or oedipal desire, as did Dali in his *Oedipus Complex*, or the passive voyeurism seen in Delvaux's painting, Picasso's most surrealistic painting is this intense, complex, brilliantly colored, puzzling, suggestive painting of the *Crucifixion*.

Gertrude Stein, in her little monograph on the artist remarked that, "All ages are heroic, that is to say there are heroes in all ages who do things because they cannot do otherwise and neither they nor the others understand how and why these things happen. One does not ever understand, before they are completely created, what is happening and one does not at all understand what one has done until the moment when it is all done. Picasso said once that he who created a thing is forced to make it ugly. In the effort to create the intensity and the struggle to create this intensity, the result always produces a certain ugliness, those who follow can make of this thing a beautiful thing because they know what they are doing, the thing having already been invented, but the inventor because he does not know what he is going to invent inevitably the thing he makes must have its ugliness."[28]

[27] Stein, *Picasso*, p. 47.
[28] Stein, *Picasso*, p. 47.

Picasso himself must have the last word: "How can you expect an onlooker to live a picture of mine as I lived it? A picture comes to me from miles away: who is to say how far away I sensed it, saw it, painted it, and yet the next day I can't see what I've done myself. How can anyone enter into my dreams, my instincts, my desires, my thoughts, which have taken a long time to mature and to come out into the daylight and above all grasp from them what I have been about—perhaps against my own will?"[29]

Conclusion by John Dillenberger

For me to comment on paintings may not be as recent or strange as it seems, having been among those at Union Theological Seminary in the forties who encouraged Tillich to lecture on art. In recent years, I am sure I have seen as many paintings as many art historians and more than any theologian I know. Having tried to take seriously the natural sciences[30] and the world of art, I have become acutely aware of various modes of apprehension and of the diverse but complimentary sensibilities our potentially rich humanity demands. Today we are enriched by participation in many styles of apprehension, more than was the case when all disciplines were unified or translatable one into the other. Our illuminations through so many avenues have become incredibly rich, partly because they do not fall into any overarching scheme, and probably because they make facets of reality apparent not otherwise available. How interesting the old idea of the art of politics might become, were artful people involved.

There is danger in talking about paintings, namely, the danger of explaining the meaning of paintings. In essence, a painting discloses a new level of reality. So it is not just another medium or universe of discourse or another way in which the old reality is disclosed. Great painting increases the illumination, for nothing could substitute for it.

Picasso has written and talked a good deal about art; yet his talking never violates his painting. Barnett Newman was a volatile contemporary artist whose speech and writing was sheer eloquence. In conversations with him I noted that he never transgressed. Indeed, I think I learned from him what the word "transgression" means. His voluminous language was only a pointer, never a passing beyond the barrier.

Picasso has indicated that there may be need for aids, as in his throwing in a few clues to the untutored eye. This procedure may be an analog to the old theological idea of accommodation, but unlike accommodation, or perhaps accommodation at its best, it is meant to carry one

[29] Chipp, p. 272.
[30] John Dillenberger, *Protestant Thought and Natural Science* (New York: Doubleday & Company, 1960).

beyond what is apparent—that is, to the reality which could not be apprehended otherwise.

But as one whose profession has been centered in the history of theology, rather than in the history of art, I would raise a few questions without suggesting that they either should, or can, be answered. Suppose that Gertrude Stein was right. Picasso knew the faces; indeed, he knew the faces exquisitely. But she was wrong in one point. Picasso knew the faces so well that they disclosed the souls. In the instance when Picasso painted out Gertrude Stein's face and then painted it in again, Picasso was right. She would look like that and she did, for he painted her soul as it would be expressed in her face. In short, he turned Gertrude Stein upon herself.

But the meaning of his surrealism may lie in that the faces as he had known them, no longer disclosed the soul. Surrealism, which includes the psychological and psychoanalytic depths, brought unknown depths of spirit to the fore. Whether it is the time of Picasso, or the combination of the time and Picasso which creates this surrealism, does not matter. Picasso's being demanded another mode. What he apprehended about himself and his world now demanded a new "thing." He may be right in saying that it brought ugliness with it, the ugliness of the new creative act. What follows these initial acts is not necessarily more beautiful nor made to be beautiful. Rather, our eyes are given, or have been given, to see that what had appeared ugly no longer does. Those who see ugliness in Picasso may not have looked enough, nor seen enough—that is, experienced enough in the depths to know what seeing is. Great art demands something of us, but what it demands of us is not effort or resolution of will, but the gift of being able to see because we have seen enough and, by grace, have been able to open ourselves to seeing in this sense.

What is not clear to me is whether Picasso has executed and returned to the Crucifixion theme at critical junctures of his own life, or whether the return at times has been accidental. Is the subject matter accidental, or does it occur in his Surrealist phase out of an inner necessity, if not a deliberateness? Does it recur by accident or necessity in the Corrida *Crucifixions*? Of course, there is a deep association between the bull-fight theme and the Crucifixion, as Jane has shown in her book, *Secular Art with Sacred Themes*.[31] But that does not say enough about the dynamics of the recurrence. Picasso is a man of deep perception and vision, one in whom the archetypal roots of existence, and his early and continued apprehensions run deep and strong, expressing in delight and in beautiful ugliness, an incredible range of sensitivities and sensibilities.

His *Crucifixion* painting, too, places aspects of the body in positions

---

[31] Jane Dillenberger, *Secular Art with Sacred Themes* (Nashville, Tenn.: Abingdon Press, 1969).

which normally are unnatural, but which should not be seen as unnatural. They do not represent distortion, but ways in which aspects of the body are replaced or reput, to make apparent what cannot otherwise be apparent. Even an acrobat could not do what Picasso does with the body. In such replacing of parts or facets of the body, the body discloses angles of vision and perception which could not otherwise be made apparent. That is why Picasso, in his late eighties, can still develop this technique, purveying in his etching the act of sexual intercourse as an expression of sheer beauty in which the mystery of human existence, male and female, is disclosed. While these have been called his erotic paintings, the situation calls to mind the fact that much Kierkegaard was first sold in English as pornographic literature. Picasso, as Kierkegaard, will have revenge in the sheer excellence of what he is about.

In the remarks introducing Jane's account, I indicated, as she would, that Picasso has been superseded by others who have gone into quite different directions. Picasso now is interesting and important because all that he creates manifests the incredible unfolding of the talents of a lifetime, vibrant and continually expressing anew—not the new—the manifold richness of his life. Commenting on the unbelievable dexterity of this octagenerian in his *347 Etchings*, John Canaday has written: "Here Picasso seems to have attacked the plates with an all out desperate ardor for life. Anything but reflective in character—for they burn and explode—they are nevertheless a summary of Picasso's life and art in fusion with each other. The stylistic manners and the personal iconographical themes that run through the prints in the rest of the exhibition in chronological order are combined and recombined in what appears to be the pictorial equivalent of stream-of-consciousness autobiography. Horseplay, tragedy, poignant remembrance, pornograph, braggadocio, and the tenderest sentiments— they are all here in this brilliant exhibition."[32]

Barnett Newman and Mark Rothko, not to say Pollock, expressed reality in a richness of color and line that vitiated all the traditional forms, but thereby still expressed reality in a new mode. While such painting expressed less in some ways, it expressed more in others. Rothko's last paintings reflected an increasing somberness and seemed to have been forebodings of his tragic end. Newman's last paintings reflect the very rich, joyful life of a man who even in death looked joyful. When one contrasts the paintings of Pollock at his prime and the recently made available materials when he was a mental patient, the difference between his genius and his illness is apparent. His genius carries us into an orbit beyond the rational apprehensions to a new order; his illness takes us into recognizable forms executed with skill, but analyzable and subject to explainable interpretations. They do not purvey the human spirit in all its grandeur and in many ways are second best Picasso, not the genius which carried

[32] *The New York Times,* October 14, 1970, p. 50.

him beyond what Picasso had done. Beyond in this sense is not a qualitative word but a cultural judgment.

Elsewhere I have put the matter of the arts in this way, indicating that the art of the future will have a new shape:

> The radical historicity of all creation may be evident in the deliberate use by some contemporary artists of materials which will not survive, and therefore make their art come to an end. And such approaches are taken by artists of exceptional competence, whose work is not ephemeral. One can also say that major changes have occurred among artists of great discipline and training, whose work is indeed meant to survive. Jackson Pollock and Barnett Newman will stand in the grand tradition of art. . . .
>
> There is a greater affinity between Rembrandt and Picasso than between a painting by Picasso and a painting by Jackson Pollock. There is a connection between Rembrandt and Picasso in that the traditional forms and the ways of conceiving things are still evident. The same techniques and forms are found in both. Picasso's art does not break through the traditional ways of seeing. No new art forms emerged with him; the old forms are still apparent, and the attempt to say something new has been conveyed through distortion, deflection, and disarray. There is an annihilation of bits but not a transformation of the whole. Seventeenth-century theology is like Rembrandt—though I like Rembrandt considerably more than seventeenth-century theology—and Tillich is like Picasso. Indeed, connecting Tillich and Picasso has its own justification through Tillich's insinuation of his views concerning Picasso's *Guernica* into the theological discourse of the modern world.
>
> When one comes to a man like Jackson Pollock, the situation is entirely different. The traditional forms have disappeared. The boundaries do not exist. In music, too, even Stravinsky is like the great classical composers of the past. It is with the music composers like John Cage that the traditional forms have disappeared. The usual boundaries do not exist, and the contours of things are no longer traditional. The new gropings are not without their form, nor without their formative power. But the new form is not yet recognizable or, if so, is not yet one to which we are accustomed. Today there is a randomness which bespeaks life itself with its contours of meaning and of dynamics. We live in a waiting, forming period. The expressions of faith and thought must utilize the vitality of new forms strange to our eyes and to our hearing, hardly familiar or lasting, but somehow speaking in and to our time.[33]

For that to happen, there will be a winnowing process. There is a great waste in creation, but its enduring creations are both historic and universal. Even that which does not endure may serve its time. But great art is both of a time and beyond it, the gift of inordinate perception and artistic ability. The art of the future may serve many purposes; but only some of it will be genuine art.

[33] John Dillenberger, *Contours of Faith* (Nashville, Tenn.: Abingdon Press, 1969), pp. 153–154.

PLATE 1 THE CRUCIFIXION, 1930.
Oil on wood, 20 by 26 inches.
Collection of the artist,
Mougins, France. Permission
S.P.A.D.E.M. 1971 by French
Reproduction Rights, Inc.

PLATE 2 CRUCIFIXION, drawing, 1927. In *Cahiers d'Art*, No. 2:49-54. Permission S.P.A.D.E.M. 1971 by French Reproduction Rights, Inc.

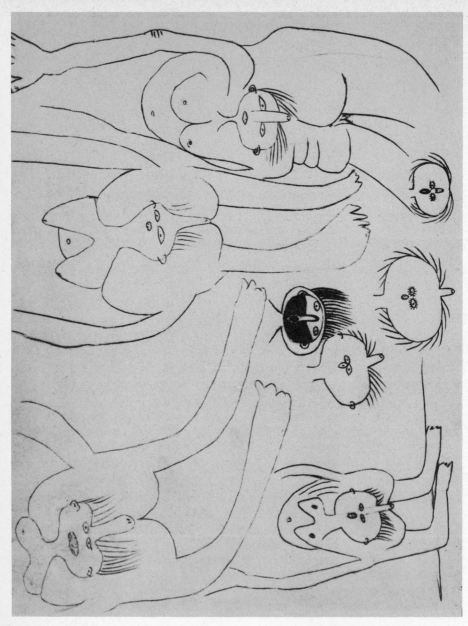

PLATE 3 STUDIES FOR
THE CRUCIFIXION, drawing,
May 25, 1929. In *Cahiers d'Art*,
No. 3–10, 1938. Permission
S.P.A.D.E.M. 1971 by French
Reproduction Rights, Inc.

PLATE 4 STUDIES FOR
THE CRUCIFIXION, drawing,
May 26, 1929. In *Cahiers d'Art*,
No. 3–10, 1938. Permission
S.P.A.D.E.M. 1971 by French
Reproduction Rights, Inc.

181

PLATE 5   STUDIES FOR
THE CRUCIFIXION, drawing,
June 7, 1929. In *Cahiers d'Art*,
No. 3–10, 1938. Permission
S.P.A.D.E.M. 1971 by French
Reproduction Rights, Inc.

9

Images of Significance in the Cinema

Robert Steele

"Plastic Development Corporation Plans Disposable Camera." Under this headline the following news item appeared recently: "The development of an inexpensive disposable plastic camera that will include a film cartridge and processing return mailer is proceeding on schedule, Earl M. Slosberg, president of the Plastic Development Corporation of America told stockholders at the company's first annual meeting yesterday. . . ."[1]

This news has to do with the means of recording a still image. If the disposable camera catches on, movies may be threatened. Five years ago the big news concerning the production of moving images was that the Eastman Kodak Company had finally manufactured an eight millimeter film stock that was so inexpensive that "it was as disposable as a paper cup." Cheapness and disposability are not the objectives that coincide with consequential contributions to cinema.

Alone of the major art forms of our time, cinema has been discovered and developed within the lifetime of many who are still here to enjoy it. Still photography, of course, was the ancestor of cinematography. The many photographic experiments that prepared for the birth of the movies were sufficiently coordinated so that on February 13, 1895, Louis and Auguste Lumière patented the first movie projector.

From 1890 on it was possible to see images that seemed to move, but they moved only when an individual looked into a kinetoscope which

[1] *The New York Times*, July 25, 1970, p. 29.

amounted to a peep-show experience. A projector made it possible to throw the moving images on a wall or screen. On March 28, 1895, a moving picture, some fifty-five feet in length, "Lunch Hour at the Lumière Factory," was shown before the *Societe d'Encouragement de L'Industrie Nationale.* More movies were shot so that by December 28, 1895, a program of movies was presented to a public and paying audience at the Grand Cafe, Boulevard des Capuchines, Paris, in a basement called the Salon Indien. Historians generally accept 1895 as the birth year of movies. Perhaps, we ought not expect too much of a series of images that so recently was an experiment. Yet in this brief span of time movies have been transformed from an experiment and a novelty into a medium of communication and education and a form of art.

Now movies are on their way to such an extent that Arnold Hauser in 1951 in his *The Social History of Art* describes our age as the film age. Scholars like Marshall McLuhan have developed theories that interpret modern man as an extension of the electronic media. Whether one accepts McLuhan's argument or not, it is clear that the film medium appeals more today to the eighteen-to-twenty-four-year olds than books or other art forms. Movies have become an alleged liberal art taught in many institutions of higher education, and for some, they have such great value that they are put into the curricula of secondary and elementary schools. The popularity of movies today must not lead us to believe that they have more worth than literature, theater, painting, sculpture, dance, and music. This is not to say that contemporary films are worthless when compared to a poem of Rod McKuen, an assemblage of Bruce Connor, a painting by Andy Warhol, forty-five minutes of silence in a musical composition of John Cage, or *Coco*, starring Chanel 2, 3, 4, or 5. It is saying that when we take a long view of what we have inherited from other art forms and compare that with our movie peregrinations, movies are still a baby that has yet to learn to walk.

Popularity and newness get confused with worth for those who have little perspective. Because films make money and have been industrialized, they have been given excessive attention. Money power has created what appears to be movie power. Thus, compared to other arts, we are swamped with movies.

Then most of us feel good if we have created something. Making movies satisfies persons sufficiently so that they get a satisfaction that is a surrogate for the satisfaction one gets from having created something. It is possible to make movies even if the maker has no idea, talent, intellect, or purpose other than to make a movie. It is clear to many of us when a novelist, playwright, painter, or musician has not done his homework and has nothing to offer. We are less discerning when we are confronted with movies. An Eastman Kodak company slogan "You push the button, we do the rest" enables a person who has some money to have something before him which "he made." If he has been lucky and the laboratory has done a good job correcting his mistakes, he may have produced a passable picture. With little skill and no imagination, he may pull shots together so that he and his confreres think he has made a movie. He satisfies his desire to create and may make a career for himself without his discovering that he has nothing but a purchased instrument with which to create.

Because of the ease and certainty with which an image may be produced—automation helps the would-be film artist to think nothing, feel nothing, see nothing, know nothing—even ten-year olds can make movies. The shooting of film for educational and therapeutic reasons can be efficacious. The more the better so long as the results are not confused with movies and passed on to an arrested, gullible, and captive audience. It is better for youths to carry cameras than knives when they wander about the streets, and they may be too disturbed to have the stamina to mix pigments or practice the piano. Disposable equipment, paper film stock, and miraculous laboratories for children and tourists are fine. Their preoccupation with movies should not delude us into thinking that our movie age has arrived. Movies are still in infancy. They have attracted and given release and expression to our infantilism.

And movie popularity is to be explained by our being dupes for anything that passes as a story. Because we are lazy a story told in pictures by way of a comic book or movie is a bigger attraction than one that is read. History got its start with the recording of stories we know as myths. Often they have been told by childlike people. Some have tried to give us answers to questions in the absence of facts. Stories in the Old Testament sum up the moral experience of a people. Most stories pass the time of day for persons who have little use to make of their days. Most films have been Westerns, who-done-its, thrillers, romances, and action pictures. Their value is limited to diversion. Most movies are diversions. Stories in pictorial form are bought by persons who would be ashamed to have books of the same stories seen on their coffee tables. A banal story glorified with movie accoutrements is acceptable when the same story in print would be scoffed at and rejected.

Movies do not crawl from the standpoint of technique. They not only walk, they also fly. For the last three decades we have become accustomed to technical finesse and even brilliance. Because of the refinements already accomplished in moviemaking instruments and materials, manufacturers have had to resort to obsolescence and disposal appeals in order to keep up their sales. The development of sound and color in cinema was strongly influenced by economic competition. However, since the twenties and before the sound and color cinema, a few films were made which have the worth, substance, style, and beauty of art objects.

We have had films which were not infantile and were not concocted to appeal to infants when we have had a few persons enter the movie business and triumph over it because they abhorred its being a profit-making business and because they knew how to express themselves through the medium. They created something of worth in spite of the economic imprisonment of the art form.

This has happened so rarely that those few films created by independent and mature artists are like radium. Such films have been the touchstones of fine films that have followed them. They have functioned like "the mystery of a remnant" about which Amos Wilder writes in his *The New Voice*, "which is located in incognito in all levels of society and is free from the avidities and emulations which infect all groups, and whose members, therefore, are all the more enduring in their witness to justice and freedom."[2] Dr. Wilder's statement can be verified even in an industry that has fought its survival hinged on mass appeal, mass communications, mass culture. Those cinematic artists who deserve to be designated members of the "remnant" are strange bedfellows for the run-of-the-mill practicioners of the motion picture industry. Fertilization by the remnants has resulted, however, in occasional births that give us faith and hope that with the passing of time cinema may mature. The cinematic remnant of films and persons has had to have a redemptive power or cineastes could not have carried on.

The history of film makes it abundantly clear that the use of traditionally "religious" subject matter is no guarantee that the film will be worthy of its content. It is well known that the stories of the Old Testament have been a storehouse of raw materials used to make fortunes by way of film spectaculars. It is painful to think of the money and labor that have been spent on research having to do with the Old Testament period in order to get every set and costume to be authentic. Yet it appears all too often that few who worked on films using such research ever had the idea that something might be learned from the Old Testament. One lesson which might well have been taken to heart is the fundamental teaching that sin brings destruction—a pertinent diagnosis of what has been wrong with our film industry.

If sin means an offense against God, a misdeed, a fault, a transgression of the law of God, a vitiated state of human nature, then Hollywood has been the follower of gods other than Yahweh. Hollywood has been the adulterous bride, the target of the wrath of the prophets. Movies in the United States with few exceptions have been guilty of consummate waste and offense against human resources. It has been the world of the profane against which the remnant has pitted itself.

A look at the trade journals today gives ample evidence of current sin and consequences of past sins. The fiftieth anniversary issue of *Box-office* has an article headed "Recapturing Lost Audience Ranks as Top Challenge for Future." The author, Burton Robbins, president of the

---

[2] Amos Wilder, *The New Voice* (New York: Herder & Herder, 1969), p. 15.

National Screen Service, says: "Today, as we all know, the overwhelming percentage of moviegoers are less than twenty-five years of age. Now, I'm not suggesting there is anything wrong with such an audience, in itself. What is wrong—decidedly wrong—is that we've allowed ourselves to lose the over-twenty-five audience—a "mere" one hundred million potential patrons."[3]

Now it is necessary, or at least it is thought to be necessary, to spend as much on advertising of a film as in making the film. Nothing is thought of spending another half-million in order to sell it. Otherwise, no matter how good a picture may be, it dies. "Success" hangs more on advertising and promotion than on the quality of the product.

Trade journals are obsessed with new ideas about making more profits out of snack bars in theaters. Exhibitors concern themselves with revamping cinemas so that impressive lines form outside of a cinema and yet may have access to the snack bars so that the patrons will purchase and eat while they wait.

Executives are not men who know movies or care about the worth of cinema. They may come from the world of high finance directly into the filmmaking industry. The new president of Paramount Pictures Corporation currently is also president of its parent company, Gulf and Western Industries. His academic qualification appears to be his having been graduated from the Wharton School of Finance. The man who is thought to be a financial wizard becomes the king of the industry.

Those who manufacture the product, who would like to be known as film artists, even if they are half blind and deaf and mentally deficient, must be aware of the volume of tragedies and casualties that have littered our brief history of movies. Suffering to the extent of moving from disillusionment through depravity and even premature death characterizes a tragically high number of case histories of those of greatest talent and intelligence who have been involved in the making of films. They have been bought for money and have known they were being harlots.

Those who have not met tragic fates but have metamorphosed themselves sufficiently so that they might survive, have been the donors to tour movie junkyards. They have made livings, which have enabled them to live lavishly, and have sired children. Some of the children may be the remnant that will salvage something out of their parents' wasted lives, but that possibility does nothing to justify those whose lives and films have been ciphers, or, to use the words of Professor Moses Bailey, "ciphers with the rims knocked off."

Were it not for the presence of a few directors and writers who fought producers and front-office executives, who have made a mark as being remnants in the film world, there would be no place in this book

[3] Burton Robbins, "Recapturing Lost Audiences Ranks as Top Challenge for Future," *Box Office* (Kansas City, Missouri), July 20, 1970, p. 44.

for this chapter. We cannot say that the remnant escaped from the film industry, because they would not be true to their cinema missions if they pulled out of the film economy and became recluses living in attics. No one has made a major film on his tips earned from being a waiter at Schraffts or by way of selling produce grown in his garden. But a few have survived long enough to beat the system and to make a film or two. Some films have been made that seem to endure. They may not be known outside of a remnant audience, but the tastes and work of this remnant have rescued some films from being forgotten and destroyed. In the midst of a holocaust, a few worthy men—unfortunately, no women—have made films that have qualities which make them last.

If one is an atheist or agnostic, he has no assurance that the remnants have kept alive a vision of cinema which may initiate new beginnings. But if one believes there is a power of consciousness in the cosmos that is long-suffering, just, good, and loving, then the creations of the remnant may have repercussions by way of more patience, work, and loyalty which will result in a maturing cinema.

What started thirty to forty years ago as a graveyard for the remnants seems today more like a school than Forest Lawn. A few persons were self-driven to do something about preserving film remnants. They did lonely and difficult work in order to found film archives. At the beginning these pioneers were looked upon by the industry as cemetery caretakers. They were salvaging and maintaining films of the past which they felt were worth saving for generations in the future. Now in some large cities over the world, archives developed by these pioneers have become the centers to which pilgrimlike students go to learn from the past. Until the last few years, the enemy of archivists have been the owners of the films—that is, the large studios. Because film bosses are not remnant-minded, even though they find storage space and costs for films a problem because of their declines, they do not give to archives without strings attached. The strings are in the form of loans that expire. After a film has been preserved by a privately financed archive, it may be taken back when the owner has a hunch that a new audience has come into being which may make a re-release commercially feasible.

Despite the youth of the cinema, it appears that some of the most rewarding work of that discerning minority we call the remnant is not that of our newest and most touted filmmakers but rather of those whose films have been singled out by the archivists and the cultivated viewers. They are ones whose commercial lives were thought to be finished, so they have gone into archives and into sixteen millimeter distribution to schools, churches and film societies. Their enduring appeal, however, has made them the kinds of films that studios think of re-releasing commercially.

While it appears that few filmmakers are adults looking for answers to important questions, when one surveys the panorama of films that have been made, a few films can be found that are worthy of being called art objects and works of the remnant. It is these films which will continue to influence the image of man in the future as in the present and recent past. Unlike most films, these films address themselves to questions such as these: What is a viable vision of existence? What should be our vision of the future? What am I doing about my life? Who am I? What does it mean to be? In contrast to the merely popular film in which audiences seek comfort, pleasure, diversion, or escape, these pictures are serious though not necessarily solemn. The work of the remnant in cinema may be found and certainly is not finished.

Remnant films are those that have had some responsibility for giving us stories that reveal an awareness of the important questions to be asked about life. Morality has been their concern rather than romance, adventure, and the examination of history. Films of the latter sort occasionally have been beautiful and lasting, but they are outside the scope of this chapter. Feature films that do not stop with recording man's experience but have a vision of his divine potentiality are more entitled to be recognized as our cinematic remnants.

On June 5, 1967, an American Film Institute was founded. This Institute was the realization of a dream that had been the concern of many film specialists for years. Government support for comparable institutions had been a reality in other major countries for years. The United States was a Johnny-come-lately. A part of the work of the Institute is to salvage lost, little known, unappreciated films. After its work progresses further, remnant films, such as those indicated below, may become more abundant. At this time American films make a minor contribution to the serious cinema of the world. But, appropriately enough, the cinematic situation is never static. The following references are offered as instances of the cinematic art which have characteristics of serious concern, universality of appeal, and high quality of achievement, which make them worthy of being called the works of the remnant. The reader will recognize that the list is only suggestive and certainly far from exhaustive.

A less commercial and more unpopular subject for a film than Kurosawa's *Ikiru* could scarcely be conceived, and yet it is surely a film by a member of the remnant. An old clerk, dulled by thirty years of work in the civil service, finds out that he has cancer of the stomach. He does something to justify his life as his death approaches. Here is a film whose subject is no more or less than life and death.

Griffith's *Broken Blossoms* offers the story of love given freely by a Chinese man to an American girl. He gives by sheltering and protecting her and exacts no reimbursement from her.

Forgiveness that exemplifies Christian grace is the *raison d'etre* for Pagnol's *The Baker's Wife*.

Science and medicine are put down by John, a "mad" man who is able to perform a miracle because of a child's faith in Jesus of Nazareth, in Dreyer's *Ordet* (The Word).

A man and his work meet defeat and destruction until a magician appears and casually says, "We're ready to begin." And a still baffled Guido in Fellini's *8½* . . . says "What is this sudden joy? Why do I feel strengthened and renewed? Forgive me, sweet creatures . . . I didn't know. I do accept you. I do love you. I feel I've been freed. Now everything seems worth while . . . meaningful . . . true. . . ."

In Wickis's *The Bridge* it is a tragic and stupid blunder to perish because one is victimized into believing that it is valiant to die for the sake of his patriotism to his country.

Being totally used up and exhausted by service to the poor and sick is the best life that can be conceived in Cloche's *Monsieur Vincent*. "You will find out that charity is a heavy burden to carry, heavier than the bowl of soup and the full basket. But you will keep your gentleness and your smile. It is not enough to give soup and bread. This the rich can do. You are the servant of the poor, always smiling and always good humored. They are your masters, terribly sensitive and exacting masters, you will soon see. The uglier and dirtier they will be, the most unjust and insulting, the more love you must give them. It is only for your love alone, that the poor will forgive you the bread you give to them."[4]

In *Earth* Dovzhenko celebrates the goodness in life and death when nature's bounties are equitably distributed to all.

In Wellman's *The Ox-Bow Incident* those who are prevailed upon to lynch on circumstantial evidence for the sake of "justice" end their days with bad consciences that torment them.

The loving care for a child which is absent in the boy's life in Truffaut's *400 Blows* is the responsibility of parents and everyone else.

Chaplin's *Monsieur Verdoux* is a thinking man whose logic does not accept mental dividers between violence in murder, violence in war, and violence in private enterprise.

The conscience of an individual, which reflects his ethical code, triumphs over what might be a fulfilled desire but also destruction for others in Lean's *Brief Encounter*.

According to Bresson's *A Man Escapes*, no matter what the obstacles are, a man by his essential nature has to achieve freedom.

Even if the most horrible abuse conceivable falls upon human beings, as it does in De Sica's *Two Women*, it is possible for life to go on, even though it has to go on differently. Even though it means abandoning a family in need and perhaps death, a man has no choice but to act against evil when it threatens, as it does in Ford's *Grapes of Wrath*.

Despite measureless hardships and suffering, including the death

---

[4] *Monsieur Vincent*, Brandon International Films, New York.

of an only daughter, the mother, the father, and Apu, the son, survive in *Pather Panchali*, the first film of Satyajit Ray's trilogy. Only Apu survives in the second part, *Aparojito*. Apu's bride dies in childbirth in the third part, the *World of Apu*, and he hovers between being and nonbeing. For the sake of his baby son, Apu picks up his life again.

Dellanoy in *Symphonie Pastorale* shows the inevitability of tragedy when the psyche of one moves into the body of another and circumstances bring about the rejection of that incarnation.

The verdict in Bourguinon's *Sundays and Cybelle* is that two "ill" persons may achieve mutual healing if we do not blunder into their lives by asserting our judgment about the health of their relationship.

Roemer and Young's *Nothing but a Man* shows that the love of a good wife and having a job are not enough to enable a black man to be himself when he is denied respect for his manhood.

Even if the parents are aged and thought to be a nuisance, according to Ozu's *Tokyo Story*, they should be given loving care by their sons and daughters, their wives and their children.

Rather than let their husbands shoot it out and risk destroying their homes and villages, sagacious and hospitable women in Feyder's *Carnival in Flanders* welcome and thereby disarm the alleged enemy.

Wars can delude persons into making separations exist when in reality they do not, as shown by Renoir in *Grand Illusion*. When expectations of a small and corrupt man are made in Rossellini's *General della Rovere*, even though they are made in error, this man can become heroic.

Misery can be born better, as shown in De Sica's *Bicycle Thieves*, if a poor man remains honest rather than being less poor by being dishonest.

Purpose exists in the cosmos for Gelsomina and even for a stone in Fellini's *La Strada*.

Our fashionable great-gloom films have been omitted from this listing. Some are sincere but others, thought to be sincere, are capitalizing on a vogue. It is regrettable that some church people who care about religion and theology are taken in by them. Some of the genre of the past decade have made worthy investigations of the state of contemporary man. These technically impressive and sober films have analyzed and dissected our predicament and then stopped. It is as if they threw up their hands in despair. They get high praise for their recreation of Dante's "Inferno" and "Purgatorio," but are forgetful that Dante wrote *The Divine Comedy* which concludes with "Paradiso."

When we already know our condition, it becomes wearisome and destructive to have it flung at us again and again as if it were news hot off the press line. (Perhaps the discovery *is* news for film boys who are sometimes described as today's geniuses. They are film babies who have grown up in a narrow and provincial film domain, and they are ignorant of observations that have been propounded for years by historians and poets, philosophers and theologians.) The moral preoccupation of the remnant in cinema sets it apart from those who simply show us where we are and what we are. The remnant cinema shows us this much but does not stop with mirroring culture. The remnant film artist holds up a mirror to us to show us that he sees more about us than we see ourselves. With him we step behind the reflection in order that we may face the reality of our predicament which he perceives.

Because the remnant accepts moral responsibility, it is in that sense affirmative. The remnant, in fact, has to be affirmative or else it is no true remnant. It is the intention of this essay to point to images of affirmation within the works of the "remnant."

Something needs to be said, however, about the physical properties of the cinema which exist even when the form, subject matter, and content of films do not make a place for themselves as vital remnants. If our senses do influence our lives, cinema by its nature can sensitize us to what we have missed and where we are going. Cinema reaches more of our senses trenchantly and simultaneously than other art forms and media of communication. Our heightened sense perceptions can augment our spirituality and begin a redemption of our physical reality.

The physical reality of the image gets at our senses in a different way from an artist's fabricated reality. The man or woman on the screen is radically different from the man or woman created, say, by Picasso or Rouault. The distance between him and a spectator is less and less demanding of his intellect to get close to. The man or woman placed in what is or seems to be a real, physical environment brings him closer to the environment that a viewer knows to be real for him also. The man or woman's being presented in the context of real sound, music, color, and physical, actual movement closes the gap between the reality of the artist's creation and the reality known firsthand by the viewer. The physical properties of cinema have an impact which is different from that of other arts. This difference goes far to explain its easy appeal and popularity.

Cinema is second only to literature in its attempt to take on man's wondering about the meaning and portent of existence. Because it is a vocal art it can portray decision-making and its consequences. The theater can also do this but its appearance of being more artificial makes it remote when compared to cinema. (Cinema may be equally or even more artificial, but it is inherent in its nature to create the illusion of naturalism and easy believability.) The appeal of cinema and its accessibility for masses of people give it a domain which is closed to literature. Unfortunately, we are inclined to bypass the book and wait for the movie. Trashy and trivial films may sensitize us so that if we mature sufficiently, we may groom ourselves for films that grapple with mature interests and concerns.

Will anything come of the plethora of films that exacerbate our senses? Might they make us aware of our loss of a religious dimension in our living? Looking at the bulk of current, popular, and vogish movies, the obvious answer is "no." For example, to read about the New American Cinema, so-called by its makers, makes one feel something new, American, and cinematic is taking place. I wish this were true. Jonas Mekas, film critic for *The Village Voice*, says the objectives of this group are to tell the truth and to present an understanding of man. He says it doesn't matter if artistically the films of the group are good or bad. They are to serve humanitarian purposes. After seeing many of the films one is not certain about their idealism.

The two films which initiated the loudest screaming are *Blonde Cobra* and *Flaming Creatures*. They have been described by Mekas as "the greatest films ever made." They have caused difficulty for the police and censors because they do not see them this way. They have different words to describe them.

The *Film-Makers' Cooperative Catalogue* has a good bit to say in its pitch on behalf of *Blonde Cobra*. The Catalogue says,

An unholy marriage between *Blonde Venus* and *The Cobra Woman*; beautifully dirty-mouthed, sad as sad can be. I don't want to sound heretical, but I insist that the only revolution in form and content is going on in the American Independent Cinema. Rice's *The Queen of Sheba Meets the Atom Man*; Jack Smith's *Flaming Creatures*; Ken Jacobs' *Little Stabs at Happiness*; Bob Fleishner's *Blonde Cobra*—these are four works that, I think, are the real revolution. They are illuminating and opening sensibilities and experiences never before recorded in the American arts: a content which Baudelaire, Marquis de Sade, and Rimbaud gave to world literature, just a few years ago, a world of *Flowers of Evil*, of *Illuminations*, of torn and tortured flesh. A poetry which is at once beautiful and terrible, good and evil, delicate and dirty. A cinema which Cocteau tried to reach through intellect alone and failed; poetry to which Kenneth Anger, early Brakhage, and Markopoulos came very close, several times, and stopped, as if afraid to make the final step into the terrible freedom. The *Blonde Cobra*, probably, is the masterpiece of Baudelarian cinema and it is hardly surpassable. Larger audiences will, no doubt, misinterpret it, misunderstand it. As there are poets appreciated only by other poets, so now there is a cinema of the few, a cinema of the film poet, too terrible and too decadent for an average man in any organized culture. But then if everybody would dig Baudelaire and Marquis and Burroughs, my God, where humanity would be![5]

The film *Blonde Cobra*, is new in that half of the time there is nothing to see. One looks at a blank screen while he listens to the dirty-mouthed sound track, and it is dirty—laboriously dirty. One does see, the other half of the time, a man trying on women's hats and scarfs, and carry-

[5] *Film-Makers' Cooperative Catalogue*, New York.

ing on antics that are repetitious, tiresome, and ludicrous. The film seems to add up to being an attempt to blaspheme, but it fails to do it with power. Sitting through it is a chore.

About *Flaming Creatures* the same Catalogue says: ". . . a most luxurious outpouring of imagination, of imagery, of poetry, of movie artistry, comparable only to the work of the greatest, like Von Sternberg. *Flaming Creatures* will not be shown theatrically because our social-moral guides are sick. That's why Lenny Bruce cried at Idlewild Airport. This movie will be called a pornographic, degenerate, homosexual, trite, disgusting, and so on, home movie. It is all that, and it is so much more than that."[6]

I cannot help but wonder, after reading this kind of endorsement and seeing these films, if a big part of the intention of a "new American cinema" filmmaker is his wish to shock for the sake of shocking (he doesn't seem to have anything to say or show for its own sake) and to put himself on the side of the "misunderstood" which he hopes may promise martyrdom. The trouble is the films do not really shock, such as a Dali painting or Buñuel film manages to shock, and there is no cause at stake that is worthy of martyrdom.

There has to be quality about films, which these films lack, in order to make them sufficiently serious to be shockable. They are slovenly slung together by persons who are not able or who do not bother or care to learn some craftsmanship. Real skill and talent are not discernible. Matters like exposure, controlled focus or out-of-focus images, and editing couldn't be cared about less. They look as if they were made in someone's small room in a rooming house without thought or finesse. They do smack of home movies, but suggest someone was at the end of his rope in knowing what to do with himself at home. They are like a last resort hit upon because of excruciating boredom with one's self.

Mekas feels *Flaming Creatures* succeeds where others have not: "Cocteau failed, and Anger, early Brakhage, and Markopoulos came very close and stopped as if afraid to make the final step into the terrible freedom."[7] Probably, he is talking about their stopping at the exposure of genitals. They do want to show but dodge by way of two-frame shots and shadows. We need not have objections to the exposure of genitals provided they are made interesting, erotic, or beautiful, and the exposure is made with imagination and dramatic potency. Instead, they are shown so badly in *Flaming Creatures* and other films that a gauche recording rather than a "terrible freedom" results.

Most of the films are not new, interesting, or anything to get in a furor about. We should try to understand the reason for his hoped-for rebellion. Most of the films coming from this group seem to be outpourings of human beings in misery. Probably, there are good and sad reasons for

---

[6] *Film-Makers' Cooperative Catalogue*, New York.
[7] *Film-Makers' Cooperative Catalogue*, New York.

their misery. One feels they wish above all to strike back at something, and hit anything that might be, even slightly, considered conventional, and above all, to shock. Striking back, hitting convention, and shocking may be understandable needs of a generation—particularly adolescents, but why is it done by way of a mania for expression through film? It takes some work and money to make even a crude film. These filmmakers are spending their own money, and they can have no expectations of getting any tangible rewards. But, instead of doing it for the love of it, they seem to do it for the hate of it—hate for themselves and hate for life as they know it in big cities in the United States. They express themselves in a way that is safe and masochistically satisfying. They would be at the top of lists of talkers about the evils of segregation, war, Wall Street, Hollywood, Puritanism, and censorship; but they do not get themselves into situations where, because of their convictions, they might get shot at, or where imagination, maturity, and judgment might dissolve some of the evil in the country.

These filmmakers are outsiders and far more so than the outsider described by Colin Wilson. They are outside film because they do not make films that are lookable. The mechanics of the medium are too demanding for them—they would probably not admit this by denying there is anything that you need to know. They are to be pitied because, evidently, they are intent upon using the medium, and our film schools are so costly, some of these filmmakers can't be blamed for not having had the opportunity to learn how to handle a camera and bring off a production. Film schools can give some help, and are an alternate way to the ideal way to learn something about filmmaking—that is to serve as an apprentice to a fine filmmaker. They are a cult, outside of films, and this explains the embarrassing extent of their ecstatic, mutual appreciation. More sadly, they are outside their human beingness, despite the protestation in their writings that their films have to do with the understanding of man. They are children trumping up tantrums. Underneath, they want fame, success, and to be somebody, and something happened in their early days which confirmed disinclination to work hard for these "rewards" of the twentieth century. They are victims of a psychological black plague, and we all are the worse for it because we need and want some new American cinema.

If you know or care too little about the nature and technique of film production, as is the case particularly with Stan Brakhage, Charles Boultenhouse, Herb Danska, Storm DeHirsch, Ken Jacobs, George and Mike Kuchar, Bob Fleishner, Jack Smith, and others, the difference between an experiment that works and one that is a disaster is not overly apparent. Audiences know less than the filmmakers, so when a film is put on the screen, for which an admission has been paid to see, despite their being bored and feeling cheated, they don't know enough to boo it off the screen.

Only by experiments will we get new form and subject matter in film. The more the better. The history of film is the history of experiments.

Both Cocteau and Von Sternberg, mentioned by Mekas, destroyed rather than exhibited and sold tickets for their experiments which failed. Maya Deren, the filmmaker upon whom creative cinema depends more than anyone else in the United States, the "high priestess" of neophyte filmmakers of the underground today, also did not show her failures. (One film in which she used Marcel Duchamp and the Guggenheim Art Gallery seems to be totally lost.) Taste comes with judgment and knowledge, and in time if many of this group of filmmakers continue, we can expect improvements not only in taste and style but in technique.

Underground or independent filmmakers, unfortunately, get some kind of satisfaction from encounters with censors and police. Hostility equates "success." Why bother structuring a film so that it is bound to offend, I ask? Always we will have some persons who are prurient, but they are not the persons whom we care about when we make films. After two evenings the Boston Cinemathèque was closed. It closed so abruptly that persons could not be notified in time to prevent their coming to the auditorium for the complete works of Bruce Connor and Andrew Meyer. The endeavor opened and closed in November 1966, after having shown Andy Warhol's *Chelsea Girls* and the complete works of Peter Kubelka. The Warhol film so bored the audience that many left, and I encountered no one who was not negative about the experience. But there was no trouble. At the second program, featuring Kubelka, I suspected that the venture might fold—or, certainly, that the audience would fall off so much that it would have to move from its large auditorium to a coffee house or basement. Kubelka's longest film and the *pièce de résistance* of the evening looks like the trims and outs from an 8mm film that a retired Gimbel's department store executive shot with a Keystone the afternoon he was taken big-game hunting on his grand tour of Africa. The members of the audience had paid $1.50 a head. They were ready to see something different and probably hoped to have a wild and outlandish experience, but they were bored and they booed. They felt cheated, so it seemed to me, and only a handful of persons showed up for the repeat screening of the films. The Kuchar brothers' film, *Hold Me While I'm Naked*, could not save the evening, and for some it caused even more disappointment.

The police and censors didn't have a chance to get around to scrutinizing the programs—perhaps they weren't interested. The owner of the auditorium and the sponsor, the Institute of Contemporary Arts, felt the programs were too shoddy to be cooperated with.

Propagandizers on behalf of this film movement, who seem to be without taste and style in their own works, for whom "anything goes," if it has a chance of offending and possibly stunning someone, talk a lot about Arthur Rimbaud. I have not heard or read references to Rimbaud that suggest these apologists know much about Rimbaud. His name is used as an endorser for all that is sloppy, wayward, and degenerate. We have yet to have a film from many of the would-be filmmakers mentioned in this article that evokes a response comparable to that we feel when read-ing Rimbaud. Films that hope to be black, violent, demonic, sadistic, and erotic are associated with Rimbaud. Yet where is one film that is worthy of comparison with Rimbaud?

It is a sacrilege to mention Rimbaud in the context of this kind of cinema—or Baudelaire or de Sade. These men worked on their writing. They did not make sport at an audience's expense. *Season in Hell* may be a short literary work, but Rimbaud hibernated for five months to write and rewrite it. Because these men had talent, knew literature, and enslaved themselves to hard work, we have masterpieces from them. No doubt, they filled waste baskets before they released manuscripts to publishers. If they wish to entertain or even infuriate sophisticated persons with their films, this lesson many so-called filmmakers will have to learn.

A big difference between many of these filmmakers and Rimbaud is that they appear to be lazy, and Rimbaud was not. Also, there was no self-indulgence, bohemian posing, or willy-nilly "sinning" in him. His vio-lence, degradation, and "sinning" were rational and purposeful. He eschewed bohemianism and could not be bothered with opposing conven-tionality for the sake of opposing conventionality. He did not give con-vention an unmerited importance.

The greats among artists, Rimbaud, Apollinaire, Gide, Rilke, and Picasso are like the greats among filmmakers. Their opposition to conven-tionality is based on the destruction necessary in order to create new beings and new art. There is purpose, reason, intelligence, talent, and technique, in our bona-fide *maudits* which drives them to discover and originate. The boring and outlandish for the sake of boredom and outlandishness do not enter their works. The absence of love and purity and the presence of hypocrisy are driving forces for maturing artists. If they are great enough, their works become metaphysical. They do not horse around and indulge in melodramatic antics for the sake of their own swinging egos. Zaniness, filth, degradation are means to something else. The nonexistent "some-thing else" in the movie games, played by Brakhage, Jacobs, Warhol, Jack Smith, and their imitators, brand them as opportunists and charlatans.

The popularity of these films with certain groups is to be explained by the lostness, sickness, and infantileness that has taken over so many of us. An artist or filmmaker would begin with us as we are and create in terms of who we are and what has happened to us. He is a part of his times but he manages not to be consumed by his times or to be a rubber stamp of them. He changes and even twists reality into becoming art. He combines form with his respect for reality. He transforms reality by way of his art.

Because of the faddishness which this kind of film has achieved, because of the cheap publicity it has managed to get from persons who use it to try to shock and amuse in order to sell newspapers and maga-zines, some fine film artists have gotten on this film wagon. Many were making films before the underground was heard of. Its being the "in cinema" results in its being hard for them to stay out and still be in vogue. Shirley Clarke is a prime example. Her films have artistry and technical virtuosity. She is no underground filmmaker, but she allies herself with the group and endorses Warhol's *Chelsea Girls* because it helps to keep her *avant-garde* image intact.

Hillary Harris, Stan VanDerBeek, Ed Emshwiller, and Robert Breer were all making films before the current wave of publicity having to do with *outre* cinema set in. None of them play at cinema, and they are not lazy or sloppy. They are hard workers and genuine innovators. Bruce Connor said he edited *Cosmic Ray* at a rate of two seconds per day for four months. His films are funny, to the point, short, original, and artistic. This can be said also about some or portions of the films of Kenneth Anger, who to his credit, gets the finest cameraman he can; Bruce Baillie, whose latest film, *Tung*, is breathtakingly beautiful, Carl Linder, and Harry Smith. Markopoulos certainly is not to be lumped along with these film-devotees who have yet to discover they do not have what it takes to make a film. His films are pretentious, arty, and overly intellectual, but they do not bore or insult the film sophisticates by their bumbling.

The easy and suspect notoriety underground films are receiving shows that something is lacking in our movies. Therefore, we welcome even the bumblers in case accidentally they give us something. New form and subject matter is needed—as well as honesty, audacity, and originality. If we keep going, some self-indulgence, artiness, and tedium in film can pass. In time the film medium itself exposes frauds and juveniles. Many of the juveniles are committed to film as well as to their hoped-for notoriety, and if they have talent and tenacity, as they gain film skills and sense, we can be on our way to a better and independent American cinema.

The answer to our volume of empty and lost films, reflecting our empty and lost lives, is given in the apocalyptic conclusion of Antonioni's *Zabriskie Point*. This film of despair, which was intended to be about Antonioni's vision of American life today, ends with an explosion. Buildings with people in them blow up, fall, and burn. From the point of view of cinema remnants, the "now" movies, the big-money makers, the adored movies that have cultish followings, and most of the movies given awards by the Academy of Motion Picture Arts and Sciences and the New York National Society of Film Critics are not worth the space they would take up in archives.

Probably we will not escape the apocalypse projected in Revelation unless we learn quickly to see, admit, and wrestle with our massive debauchery and evil as remnants down through history have done. Remnants are remnants because they are not listened to, believed in, or followed. But if remnants escape extinction, they are the architects of a new age.

10

Emerging Images in Teaching Religion and the Arts

Roger Hazelton
Dorothy A. Austin

In this essay we shall be exploring the steadily growing interest in the arts within theological education at the present time, asking what we believe are pertinent questions about its motivations, resources, and potential effects. That such an interest has indeed emerged is indicated by the noticeable increase in courses, exhibitions, and performances given in the seminaries. Yet it cannot be denied that it is mostly sporadic, local, and marginal in character. Piecemeal proliferation and haphazard additions to an already overtaxed curriculum do not constitute a new or significant approach. This interest in the arts, however, is already beginning to elicit more substantial reflection among faculties and students. What it may portend for the life of the church, the changing shape of its ministry, and the theological enterprise itself—these are large, long-term questions which deserve to be seriously considered in decision making now.

Our inquiry will not be primarily concerned with assessing trends, weighing pressures or recommending specific techniques in this increasingly important field. Rather, our orientation is chiefly theological in attending to what the arts may contribute toward a deepening of Christian vision and action. What is at stake today, as perceptive seminarians and their teachers realize, is more than the updating of a viewpoint or the renovating of an institution. It is the question whether any meaning that is recognizably Christian can be given to the circumstances and categories which make up contemporary secular experience. Can any sense be made of living in today's world by reference to the ancient landmarks, the well-trodden paths, of Christian belief and behavior? If such theological work is to be done, it will require the help of many collaborators besides professional theologians and churchmen. In particular it will need to enlist the energies of those who are fashioning symbols, parables, and prophecies within the arts of our own time.

At all events the question about the purpose of the arts in theological education is both lively and pressing. When a whole way of thinking and being is threatened by extinction, one must ask whether it can be reinvigorated or reexpressed.

I

This question may be answered in several ways, of course. It is probably common knowledge that today's theological students, like their contemporaries in other professional schools, have generally no more than a passing acquaintance with works of the creative imagination either classic or contemporary. An undergraduate "liberal arts" degree is no proof to the contrary in most instances. This cultural lack not only impoverishes a student's personal resources for a maturing faith but also actually endangers the full, effective exercise of his future ministry. Not to know, not to have been stirred or shaped by, what our cultural traditions have found valuable and illuminating is a very real liability when one's own vocational promise it at issue. Therefore it is not surprising that seminary faculties have been led to add some elective courses or provide some incidental experiences in the arts.

Or it is argued, in the second place, that the contemporary arts are especially necessary to give the student an "inside" view of the kind of world in which he is preparing to serve. As opposed to factual and statistical data or to conceptual hypotheses regarding issues and institutions, the arts harbor possibilities of humane, humanizing insight which the ministry neglects at its peril. The tensions and lesions of "a world gone awry" are better rendered through images than by propositions. Since man's anxious yearnings and ambiguous loyalties form so much of the texture of present-day novels, plays, painting, sculpture, music, architecture, or the dance, should their emphatic witness be neglected? Can we really speak of an education for the pastoral and preaching ministry in which a student's sympathies and sensibilities are largely left untouched? Or can we presume that preparation for this ministry has been given without taking into account the perspective on contemporary experience made available through metaphor, symbol, story, and vision?

These are good reasons for including some exposure to contemporary art within the seminary experience; but there is a further reason to which the second part of this essay will be devoted. It has to do with a minister's own self-image, his or her identity as a professional person. Men and women preparing for the various kinds of ministry are, by their own admission, troubled about what "being a minister" involves and requires. Very often they come to the seminary not because they are sure but just because they are unsure. Whatever else it may come to academically or vocationally, a seminary experience is chiefly one of trying on "the ministry" for size, weighing its demands and opportunities against the student's personal needs and goals. The fact that this is largely an extracurricular process does not mean, however, that courses or teachers can remain impervious to it. Lifelong vocational commitment surely requires that a style of ministry should be discovered capable of absorbing one's abilities and concerns, surviving disenchantment, and echoing the deepest tones of one's selfhood.

Wisely used, the contemporary arts can bring an exceptional kind of clarity and support into a student's search for identity-in-ministry. One thinks at once of T. S. Eliot's plays or of the stories of André Gide, Georges Bernanos, and Graham Greene, for example. Also there is a remarkable array of Christ figures in both literature and the plastic arts of the present and the recent past, which raise similar issues in a less direct but perhaps more compelling way. And more generally, the virtual preoccupation with "the self, terrible and constant" among most contemporary artists may be drawn upon for a whole variety of purposes both educational and theological.

To be sure, any work of art has an integrity of its own which the reader, viewer or listener must learn to respect. It should not be raided for theological meanings or faulted for theological failures unless the artist himself has chosen a subject or offered an interpretation that invites such use of his work. Yet this is not to say that a theologian must simply stand mute when confronted by an art work not avowedly or explicitly religious. If his categories are challenged or maybe shattered by it, that too is for him a theological event. And if the work sets up sensuous or visceral reverberations rather than purely intellectual ones, its power to do so must finally be taken into theological account. "It is the heart, not the reason, that experiences God," wrote Pascal; and this is a truth of enormous theological import which ought to have much to tell us about the materials and methods of theology.

Obviously the word theology is being stretched here far beyond its usual departmental, academic meaning. It is well that there should be a traditional discipline devoted to the comprehensive, coherent setting forth of what is true in Christian faith, but its boundaries are now admitted to be more fluid and far-ranging than was formerly thought. Nothing human is alien to it. The zone of the arts is strikingly close to its interests, if only because the arts deal so manifestly with the "I questions" that also form much of the experiential basis of theological reflection. Theology has its undismissable content, memory, and task; it can never become the mere extension, or attenuation of psychology or phenomenology. But unless theologians choose to be frozen into their own past, performing operations which are merely habitual and repetitive, they must stay humbly open to the solicitations and urgencies of changing human experience which is always the raw material of creative art as well. Since theology is committed to the proposition that "God is the meaning of human existence," in Berdyaev's words, it is concerned with showing that it is this experience as presently felt and known, endured and enjoyed, which demands precisely that meaning.

If we insist upon considering artistic and theological endeavor as two kinds of territory, possibly adjacent, between which some sort of semantic-conceptual bridgework needs to be constructed, we forget that their relationship is not external but internal. Both have their roots tangled in the rich subsoil of man's feeling and awareness. Each is vulnerable to and acted upon by the other, whether consciously or unconsciously. Man the maker and man the thinker are not two kinds of man but elementally one. In this respect as in others we must beware of what Whitehead termed "the fallacy of simple location." Undoubtedly there are significant differences in our ways of seeing and shaping a humanly lived reality, but their convergences are no less significant—and often far more interesting.

Some art works, in any event, have overtones or intimations which may fairly be recognized as theological in character. This does not mean that they must illustrate or instruct; works with an announced churchly or religious purpose may or may not deserve serious theological consideration, depending first of all upon their artistic worth. The only condition for theological attention and reflection is that a work of art should embody and express dimensions of ultimacy, of mystery, as these are grasped in a fully human existence. The work may be ambiguous or open-ended with regard to "the faith." It may evoke dread or wonder, radical doubt or sublime assurance concerning God. Its subject may be religious or secular. Indeed it may seem to transcend all such distinctions by including them. But any artist who shows in his work that he has thought with insight and passion about what it means to be a man or a woman in a fundamentally unmanageable, awesome environment can be said to be a theologian *malgré lui*. If not all artists accept this remark as the compliment it is intended to be, that may only indicate that they are unaware of the greatly broadened contours of present-day theology.

What Christian theologians and creative artists have in common, then, is a concern with what may be called the human mystery. Such an interest is not greatly nourished by psychological techniques or sociological analyses unless these have themselves been informed and responsive with respect to the power of images, stories and myths to reflect and to shape man's condition in the world. Jung's work on archetypes and Robert Bellah's work on transcendence show impressively that this is entirely possible without losing the perspective and consistency of the discipline involved; and many similar examples can be given for the encouragement of artists and theologians alike. Yet there is no real substitute for the work of art itself in developing a sense and taste for what is after all unfathomable and inexhaustible within the life of man. Rembrandt's self-portraits, the sculptures of Henry Moore, the mime of Marcel Marceau, are instances of this mysterious quality, at once enigmatic and paradigmatic, which is the *sine qua non* of all humane learning and achievement.

Probably this is not the place for lamenting the grave atrophy of the imaginative powers in contemporary education, especially at its "higher" levels. Nevertheless the arts have a potential contribution to make to educational development which ought to be more generously acknowledged than it is. Everyone knows that the arts can be taught in such a way that their humane, liberating value is factualized or categorized away; hence simply to include the arts in the curriculum is scarcely what is needed. However, many theological students are unfitted in advance for the work of the ministry because they have been victimized by a dominant school mentality that equates intelligence with value-free neutrality and simulated objectivity, even in the presence of art works that should be profoundly moving to them. They will never be able to grasp, much less make their own, those questions of reason and faith, freedom and grace, law and gospel with which theology must always be engaged. How could they be expected to, when they have been subjected all through the educational process to ways of reading human existence which deliberately rule out whatever is mysterious or ultimate concerning it?

Mystery and meaning are the poles between which all theology, like all art, constantly moves. Man's "little life" as Shakespeare called it is never self-contained or self-explaining but requires interpretation—and participation—in a far more spacious context. This "more" in which man lives, moves, and has his being may be viewed as threatening to him, like the absurd of Albert Camus; or it may be regarded as benign and favoring to him, as in the thought of Teilhard de Chardin. But man is more than he knows, and somehow he knows this too; and he is more than he can say, but he must create symbols capable of suggesting this as well. The common enemy of art and theology is literalness, triviality, the drive toward a confined, thingified experience cut off from its roots in mystery and therefore also in reality. But both theology and art are sustained by a kind of hope that meaning can be found in the midst of mystery, can be bodied forth in such fashion as to call forth response, whether conveyed by image or idea.

Sir Herbert Read has often emphasized in his writings the priority of image to idea in personal and cultural development. This raises the question whether image making and idea forming are activities as different or opposed as they are sometimes taken to be by artists and theologians in their vocational separateness. The visitor to Chartres Cathedral, before he begins his inside tour of the windows, is met by a sign admonishing him that if he has come for purely esthetic reasons he is not to forget that the church is after all a religious edifice designed for prayer and worship. Certainly the warning is well meant and on the whole well taken. While a service is in progress it is generally free from interruption by tourist groups, and sightseers circle the church without giving the worshipers more than a curious glance. It would seem then that a practical distinction can be made and kept which maintains order and insists upon the priority of ecclesiastical over esthetic concerns. But a sign like this raises other more far-reaching kinds of inquiry. Are the purposes of art and faith so very different? Do religious and esthetic modes of experience proceed by separate paths to incompatible goals? Such questions are not settled by directives from the clergy, nor for that matter are they to be resolved by arbiters and critics speaking for the arts. Instead they point toward a profounder realm of meaning and mystery where faith and art appear to merge as images and ideas reach out in mutual recognition.

Questions of this kind are coming more and more into the open as the study of works of art within the theological context gains momentum. One seminary course, for instance, focuses upon visual perception and the shaping of belief; another, on the theology of culture, uses symbols drawn from the contemporary cinema to explore religious and ethical themes; still another endeavors to understand imagination and creation in the arts with clues derived from man's experience of the holy. Such probes or ventures indicate a basic shift of perspective that is both more esthetic and more theological. They proceed on the assumption that artists and theologians share the task of illuminating mystery with meaning, and prophesy at least the possibility of greater collaboration and communion in fashioning a more humane culture for the world's future.

Enough has been said to show that theological education is taking the arts with greater seriousness and precision than formerly. Even more important is the fact that the current *rapprochement* goes well beyond the use of artistic media for brightening the church or freshening the Christian gospel; no longer do illustration and instruction, or decoration and diagnosis, exhaust its theological possibilities. What is new in the situation, as will be noted in the further sections of our essay, is an acknowledgement that works of art have much to offer by way of clarifying the purposes and methods of theology itself. Better ways of reading, seeing, or listening must first be found and used, of course; and this may be one significant result coming from this emerging field of study. At the moment, an intensified desire to grasp and be grasped by works of art in their immediacy and on their own terms is surely much in evidence. It is as if the theological student or teacher, like Jacob wrestling with the angel, declared to the artist, "I will not let you go until you bless me."

II

It has been more than a decade since H. Richard Niebuhr and his colleagues defined the theological seminary as "the intellectual center of
the Church's life" and described its goals as "genuine Church-thinking."
Such thinking, in Niebuhr's view, is not to be taken as meaning purely
rational criticism or conceptual abstraction. These have their obvious place
in theological study and no special case needs to be made for them. But
the word "intellectual" as Niebuhr used it signifies not detachment but
attachment, not suspended but intensified involvement in the corporate and
spiritual life of the Church. It requires tautness, rigorous attention, and a
real capacity for excitement over the presence of truth claims and value
standards, as these pertain to the experience of faith. Niebuhr's definition
was welcomed enthusiastically as a correct and plausible interpretation of
the seminary. It was bravely repeated by those who hoped against hope
that it might be true. At the present time, however, it represents more
a wish than it does a real state of affairs.

The typical present-day seminary lacks the settled, focussed atmosphere that is necessary for cooperative intellectual endeavor. Its relations
with the churches are troubled and unsure. Antiintellectualism still exists
within the churches, and antiecclesiasticism in the seminary. Some members
of seminary faculties deplore the dissipation of their energy into field work
projects, counseling sessions, and political maneuvering—energy which
might better be channeled, they think, into biblical, historical, or theological
scholarship. Other professors believe that the traditional or classical seminary curriculum is manifestly off-center when it comes to providing the
contemporary minister or church administrator with an adequate foundation for his work. Consequently faculty and students find themselves caught
in the crossfire of opposing pressures—scholarly and political, professional
and academic, ecclesiastical and "secular." In such a situation it becomes
almost impossible to build any kind of consensus—discussions of "purpose"
and "community" are fruitless as well as interminable.

It is clear that the shaping of the seminary after Niebuhr's model is
not an easy task, for its subject matter is the forming of human destiny
by the mystery of the Being which lies beyond being. Such an effort must
include the tragedy and magnificence of man, the destructive power of
evil within personal, social, and political spheres, the longing for physical
and spiritual healing and wholeness, and the painful but patient unfolding
in history of the means of Grace and of the hope of glory. The attempt to
comprehend all of this, to wrest order and meaning out of it and to communicate it to the world, keeps the theological institution in turmoil and
torment. It therefore comes as no surprise that academic theologians,
clerics, and theological students subject themselves to constant self-
examination which demands that the very substance of their discipline,

as well as their own faith, be made justifiable and "relevant." Those involved in theological endeavor do not enjoy a place set apart from the difficulties of the world where theological questions may be contemplated at leisure. Seminarians and their teachers struggle with familiar problems of life-style and ultimate meaning, as do all their thoughtful contemporaries. Their added burden is derived from the fact that they operate within an entire mind-set and a community which rests on the precarious affirmation that there is an actual reality at the crux of man's existence, and at the heart of the universe itself, which is to be adored, celebrated, and obeyed. In a problem-prone, object-producing technological society the "offense" of the Gospel staggers the mind as it never did before. And the academic road to hearing, interpreting, assimilating, and proclaiming the Gospel is a singularly difficult one, particularly so for a student population full of unrest and anxiety about the future of the world, their individual futures, and the meaningful survival of the human race. Rightly or wrongly, these students demand that the seminary should provide them with a mind-altering, perception-clearing experience, or vision, to pull together their lives and to give them personal and professional identity. They look there-fore to the seminary for clues, models, styles which will allow them to express meaning and caring, ways to change and heal their society. Unlike the scholastically oriented or clerically motivated seminarians of the past, who heard God's call to the ministry and accepted it forthwith, today's theological students are restless, disaffected, yet seeking intellectuals.

All this presents a two-pronged theological question to the seminary: the question of God (essentially, how can one "know" God?) and that of theological method (how can one speak responsibly and intelligibly about God, if at all?). Obviously it is impossible to separate the substantive question from the methodological, as the *necessity* to speak of God must be accompanied by the *possibility* of speaking about God if one is not to fall into Kierkegaardian despair. On the one hand, a student can become so emotionally involved in his theological work that reflective analysis and criticism are no longer really challenging to him. On the other, the intense intellectual activity required in theology, that of keeping the object of ultimate concern at the edge of awareness, may tend to isolate a student from his rightful heritage in ancient writings and the history of ideas. Indeed, the perils encountered in theological education are frightening.

Before the substantive question of the reality of God can be pur-sued, a student should have participated in some form of authentic religious experience. To be sure, theological education cannot guarantee such an experience for any student, but it can provide conditions and incentives favorable to its happening. Spiritual formation and growth are not per-ipheral but central to the seminary; Christian nurture can hardly be con-fined to the church school. This means that opportunities must be provided for members of a seminary to confront their Lord. All the latest techniques and models of ministry, whether they be social, political, educational, or psychotherapeutic, are but empty forms if they merely beat around the burning bush. It may be that much of the present stress upon new forms and specialized roles in ministry has actually obscured or postponed the hard empirical and systematic wrestling with the meaning of God which no one who belongs to a theological community can long escape.

In an essay on "The Relevance of the Ministry in Our Time and Its Theological Foundation" Paul Tillich warned against the likelihood that specialization and novelty in ministry might easily become "pseudorelevant." The fashioning of new skills and styles, he went on to say, is important, but in themselves they do not make the ministry relevant as *ministry*. That kind of relevance depends upon the ability to communicate the message of the new reality known in Jesus Christ as answering the boundary situations of human existence. One who would truly minister, said Tillich, must point with inward authority to the eternal. But this will not happen unless the minister himself is conscious of experiencing the eternal and is capable of articulating to others the nature of this experience.[1] The warning is still valid.

To judge from the large amount of contemporary work on "transcendence" it would seem that theologians have decided to face the substantive God question squarely. Much work is also being done at present on the nature and function of religious experience, after a long and sterile interlude. The new empiricism is revealed further in the preoccupation with mystical elements of Asian religions, consciousness-expanding drugs, and disciplines of meditation, all of which indicate a widespread desire for religious experience among university and college students. In addition, autobiography has now become an acceptable form of theological expression. Such books as Sam Keen's *To a Dancing God* may be cited as indicating not only a relaxation in academic scrupulosity but also a theological honesty that seems peculiar to this time.

For many of us, therefore, questions like these become urgent: What forms and methods lead most surely to a recovery of authentic religious experience, what academic approaches yield the best and richest opportunities for participating in genuine theological exploration, and how may the Reality known and celebrated in faith break through layers of cultural indifference to crack open the hardness of men's hearts? The few among us who are grasped and moved by the spiritual power of Being are profoundly committed to responding with creative vigor to the obduracies and potencies of the present situation.

Precisely where a recovery of the religious experience and breakthrough to faith's reality become possible, we discover that the arts possess

---

[1] *In Making The Ministry Relevant*, Hans Hoffman, ed. (New York: Charles Scribner's Sons, 1960), pp. 17–35.

a significant power to awaken, provoke, and motivate the human spirit. It is recognized that the esthetic mode of experience is marked by an immediacy, by direct and whole acquaintance, which may not be qualitatively different from the vision of God. Certainly there is this evocative power in a Toccata and Fugue of Bach, mediating the sublimity and splendor of divine transcendence far more truly than most Sunday morning polemics can claim to do. Le Corbusier's pilgrim chapel at Ronchamp is a magnificent illustration of the architectural fusion of religious with esthetic insight. And a twentieth-century seeker after God may be led to see himself and realize his life's dilemma in Flannery O'Connor's *Hazel Motes*, whose integrity lay in his inability to get rid of that "ragged figure who moved from tree to tree in the back of his mind."

If we are to understand and value the place of the emerging image in the teaching and learning of theology, we must ask ourselves just what it is in the experiencing of works of art which moves man in the depths of his personality. Sensing this, Tillich was prompted to say of early Christian art, "What no amount of study of church history had brought about was accomplished by the mosaics in ancient Roman basilicas."[2] Today it may be protest art that reaches theologically-minded people with particular effect, because such art quickly establishes a common ground of prophetic concern and determination. Poetry, film, the theater have for many of us this kind of compelling and confronting power. Artists and theologians alike are aware of being alienated from the dominant culture of our time, and their alienation may paradoxically become the needed impulse toward a new community of insight and effort.

III

From the viewpoint of a theological teacher working with the arts, there are several matters pressing for consideration and decision. Some are more practical and administrative, others more theoretical and normative; but these are basically inseparable and must be faced together. An example of the former is the current discussion as to how the field may be defined, which inevitably arises as a new course is planned or an exhibition or performance scheduled. Can this burgeoning if rather random growth be given a name, treated as a substantial part of the theological curriculum, made to fit into the spectrum of academic expectations? As pressures mount and programs are initiated this kind of question becomes increasingly prominent in faculty counsels. Some attempt at answering it needs to be made if only to lessen the haphazard, fractional character of present offerings.

Courses having to do with the arts have grown up chiefly in three

---

[2] Quoted in James Luther Adams, *Paul Tillich's Philosophy of Culture, Science, and Religion* (New York: Harper & Row, 1965), p. 66.

previously established fields of study: systematic theology, usually in relation to an emphasis upon the theology of culture; practical theology, joined normally to "skill" courses and the media of communication; and liturgics, which is frequently put under the professional disciplines but now and then appears within the historical or systematic departments. In every case, study of the arts seems to represent an extension of areas in the curriculum once more tightly defined; and in most cases it is made available because an individual teacher has the requisite aptitude or interest. Such a study is seldom if ever included in a catalog description of the school's corporate aims and programs, although there is some reason to hope that this may soon change.

The gratuitous, unstructured look of work in the arts across the seminary board may in fact be something of a blessing in disguise. It could signify that the present divisions of the seminary curriculum are antiquated and in drastic need of being redrawn. If so, then one might give thanks and get on with the revising job. Surely it should be possible, in the curriculum of the future, to provide solid blocks of academic time facilitating sustained concentration upon experiencing and evaluating works of art. Do not drama, painting, sculpture have an equal claim on the Christian imagination with "church architecture" or "religious music" as they are taught presently? It may certainly be argued, however, that these claims are better met by courses offered in more than one department or field. This should not eliminate the possibility of concentrating in the arts in an interdisciplinary program of some kind, which would necessitate the sort of academic bridgework that in one sense violates the unity of truth and knowledge while in another sense, given the departmentalizing that still reigns supreme in most situations, it is indispensable to the "integration" which all faculties profess to care about and seek.

One aspect of the problem of defining the field is more intriguing theoretically. It is the fact that exposure to the arts is likely to generate a wish for creative expression on the part of students. Recently an instructor teaching an introductory course in the arts was amazed to receive from his class, instead of the expected book reviews and theme analyses, two plays, an architectural model, several groups of poems, a triptych, some drawings, and three short stories. Needless to say, the teacher found himself at a loss when this work had to be graded according to customary academic standards, and called on artist friends to give him a hand. Yet the experience was salutary in bringing home to the teacher the fact that exposure to works of art may not only prove to be contagious but may release pent-up creative ambitions of one's own. Can we foresee the time, perhaps not too far off, when studio courses manned by artists-in-residence are offered in the seminaries alongside those which stress receptivity and interpretation? If so, it would represent one further sign of the shift from passive to participant learning which is already much in evidence.

Probably the demarcation of an academic field for instructional and

administrative purposes will not be feasible for quite a while. In the mean-
time one may hope that experiments will go forward in the direction of
creative work and interdisciplinary study, and that they will meet with
increasing faculty favor and support.

The individual teacher who commits himself to working theologically
with the arts is faced with other matters than those pertaining to curricular
reorganization and administrative arrangement. One of the things he finds
particularly engrossing on the job is the relation of style to content in any
art work. He is sure to realize in his more honest moments that he naturally
tends to find more theological suggestiveness in a work than the artist
intended to put there. Once his attention is captured he becomes concerned
with communicating what has come through to him as the meaning content
of the work. It is a rare theological teacher indeed who can resist successfully the temptation to verbalize and thematize, singling out for emphasis
those features of a work that speak to him with greatest force. Therefore
he may be normally less sensitive to stylistic or formal considerations than
a competent art critic would be.

Nevertheless, the teacher's native bent toward content analysis may
actually benefit the fuller understanding and appreciation of a specific
work. Not that he chooses to regard it as a communicative parcel with a
"message" wrapped up inside; but he insists, and rightly, that all creative
art has something to say or show concerning man's being-in-the-world, and
this is what he hopes to identify and consider in theologically fruitful ways.
He would also wish to be the artist's ally in defending him against critics
who might try to reduce all meaning content to questions of style or
provenance, and so the teacher would bear tribute to the need for taking
the creative arts with full human seriousness. That could be a real gain in
the present state of esthetic criticism.

It is a general principle, or should be, that style is not to be studied
in isolation from content. This has been well demonstrated by Nathan
Scott, Jane Dillenberger, and John Dixon among others. Why did Matisse
in his "gay chapel" choose to render the stations of the cross in roughly
drawn black lines on a bare white wall? Or why have composers like Bach
and Stravinsky borrowed dance tunes and jazz rhythms for music written
with devotional or biblical texts? Such questions as these are pertinent both
esthetically and theologically, and they illustrate the unity of style with
content in the arts. Or, to take an example from theology, why did Karl
Barth object strenuously to interpreting the Mass as having a "dramatic"
structure, while he did not hesitate to speak of the "saga" of the biblical
record of God's mighty acts toward the people of ancient Israel? Here again
the style-content question is being raised, albeit inadvertently. The manner
and the matter of a literary document, musical composition or mural drawing are far easier to distinguish verbally than experientially. They are given
together and it often becomes impossible to say which is which.

The words "style" and "content" obviously refer to aspects of a work of art which are different and ought to be discriminated for provisional purposes at least. But these words are only rough approximations of artistic reality, like Aristotle's "form" and "matter" or Sir Herbert Read's "image" and "idea." At all events, how an artist does it is inseparable from what he means to do. The "Tree of Jesse" window set into the front wall of Chartres Cathedral may perhaps be admired, but scarcely understood, apart from the fact that it presents the royal ancestry of Christ as given in the Bible. Here, it does not seem too much to assert, the color of the glass and the placement of the panels represent the working out of what is basically a theological conviction, namely, Christ's real yet God-given humanity within actual history. As the tree lifts the eye from the bottom to the top of the lancet window, it contains in succession four kings, the Virgin Mary, then Christ with the seven doves symbolizing the gifts of the Holy Spirit. The prophets who proclaimed the coming of Christ are pictured to the left and right of the central tree symbol. By adopting the biblical image of a tree the stained-glass craftsmen rendered in two-dimensional space the upward thrust of time itself, woven of the mystery of human continuity. Still more, they gave unparalleled expression to their own faithfulness as stewards of the Christian revelation as it had nurtured them and their forefathers.

Or one may take another example from contemporary abstract painting. The large canvas by Alfred Manessier titled "The Resurrection" hung in the Musée de l'Art Moderne in Paris gives no pictorial details of the event recorded in the gospels. There is no perceptible tomb, no body rising, no guardian angel. The painting is done in tones of red and black, interspersed in such a way that they contrast almost explosively. The brighter color, however, seems to be irradiating and breaking up the darker, which may be seen as foreground or background depending, one might say, on the theology of the beholder. The abstractness of the style, coupled with the definite title, universalizes the Resurrection, giving it cosmic as well as historic significance. Hence, Manessier's painting is no mere repristination of Christian tradition, but rather a renewing at its source.

Our examples thus far have been selected from art that is explicitly religious, and so may seem to support the idea that religious or theological factors are primary while esthetic or stylistic factors are derivative and "merely technical." But this is clearly not the case. An artist may be so wedded to a particular style, so absorbed in exploring its possibilities for his work, that it may even decide his choice of subject matter. Neither are these examples meant to prove that whereas content belongs to faith, style pertains solely to art. Such a distinction is most difficult to draw precisely in the greatest religious art. A Giotto fresco, Bach cantata, or Blake drawing does seem to repel and finally to transcend all such attempts at analytical division. What has to be said is that a work of art, whether called religious or not, can be rightly known and valued only as an experienced whole—hence as a unity of style with content shaped by an artist's own intent and patience.

Teaching the arts theologically, then, involves us with the style-content principle in at least two ways. First, the work in its wholeness forbids isolating technique from meaning except for highly specialized interests which are not likely to be theological. But secondly, factors of style may be important in determining content. The way a brush is held or a cadenza is introduced sometimes makes all the difference between banality and originality. The teacher must therefore be wary of extracting meanings capable of being stated in his accustomed propositional manner, but also equally on guard against a kind of philistinism that does not honor virtuosity when it appears or will not stay with a work of art long enough to let its whole impact be felt.

A third area of growing interest for the teacher is built up around the recognition that art works may be valuable not only intrinsically and humanely but in helping him to know his own theological enterprise better. Is it not true that esthetic aims and methods enter more emphatically into theological speaking and writing than is usually supposed? Every theologian is an artist, or at any rate a rhetorician, *malgré lui*. The way he organizes a chapter or plans a lecture is germane to his vocation and may carry meanings of its own. If he decides, as Barth did, to "throw the Gospel like a stone" at his contemporaries' heads, that is a rhetorical as well as a theological decision. Actually, however, no one does his theology in quite this peremptory and violent manner. We do, after all, want to persuade others of the truth of what we are saying, for the sake of that truth itself. In order to achieve this we must employ some rhetorical devices of which perhaps we are partly unaware. A "plain, unvarnished statement of the truth" is itself a curiously rhetorical accomplishment; naturalness in speaking or writing professionally seldom comes naturally to anyone. Some day a doctoral candidate will probably write a dissertation exploring the amazing rhetorical world of Barth—his controlling images, techniques of emphasis and repetition, hyperbole, and long asides—and then his theology will certainly be better understood.

The word "rhetoric" as everybody knows has fallen upon evil days. At the moment it generally signifies the verbal packaging in which a bid for power clothes itself. Nonetheless it is an old and honorable term having to do with something other than propaganda or publicity. Amos Wilder has examined with careful and deft insight the rhetoric of the New Testament. Similar criteria and procedures may be used to disclose the theological process of reflecting on the Gospel, traditioning it, and persuading men and women in any age of its essential truth. This kind of examination, furthermore, does not divert us from the main business of theology. Every theological statement is at bottom a proposal that intends to persuade, which means to elicit loyalty and trust in the God who is spoken about whether directly or indirectly.

To regard theology as consisting somehow of propositions, declarative sentences organized in a consistent fashion, will not do, despite the penchant of linguistic philosophers and media men for simple, unequivocal assertions. Indeed, it is not assertion but affirmation that makes a statement theological. The very standards of comprehensiveness and coherence in theological work are as much esthetic as they are rational. They point toward a unity of truth in God which always lies beyond language and logic even as it employs them for expressing it. Taking our cue for the moment from painting, do not perspective, highlighting, composition have as much importance in the doing of theology as definition and argument have? The standard of coherence, often taken as the mark of rationalism in theology, gains much of its force from metaphors or models of part-whole relationships. And the standard of comprehensiveness or system is plainly based on symbols of inclusion arising in experiences of security and identity. One is never very far from image and myth even in his most logical, rational efforts.

This shaping of theological discourse by the esthetic consciousness needs recognition and celebration among theologians. Just as mathematicians speak of the elegance of a proof so theologians may refer to the rightness of a belief or doctrinal statement. Thus we express, however unknowingly, our dependence upon the age-old esthetic criterion of *fitness* without which our work could be neither performed nor judged.

All this amounts of course to saying that theology is as much a matter of style as it is of content. It is mistakenly identified with hard-core propositions, largely definitions, arguments or summations, which can be extracted from it. The Inquisition tried to do just this for the purpose of detecting suspicious deviation or heresy in the sermons, treatises and lectures brought to its attention. In one celebrated case of this kind, that of the condemnation of Jansen's *Augustinus* in the seventeenth century, only one of the five propositions said to be found in the work could actually be located there; the others were the reductive efforts of hostile critics. Whitehead once observed that the disease of philosophy is the itch to express itself in syllogisms—"all S is P, no S is P"—and the same ailment threatens theology too. It is impossible truly to teach any man's theology, least of all one's own, without due regard for the form and fashioning in which it presents itself. For instance, the fact that Tertullian and Calvin were trained as lawyers explains the brieflike nature of their writings. And the fact that Chrysostom and Athanasius were Greek speaking gives to their work a conversational fluency which one does not find in Hilary or Duns Scotus who wrote in Latin. Style always determines content in theology in the sense that ways of seeing and speaking give rise to ways of believing and thinking which are noticeably different and elicit different kinds of response.

We have Paul Tillich to thank for his reminder that "style" has also a wider, cultural reference. It may mean the web of presuppositions which a given epoch takes for granted as above dispute and not needing defense. Some of these are more like idioms than axioms. Thus an attendant at Vatican II observed that the council members seemed to have a doctrine for everything except what was happening to them; there was no doctrine for the development or changing of doctrine. No teacher of theology can afford to be without the comfort, challenge, and correction such a doctrine might be able to give him. To accept the relativity, that is the style, of one's own formulations of the Christian faith is not to betray or abandon the truth of other, past formulations. And to engage in conscious departure or novel utterance may prove to be the most responsible way in which one can keep faith with tradition, rather than by mere reiteration. Just as an artist tries on different styles in order to discover and set free his own talent, so a Christian thinker is free to experiment with modes of discourse, persuasion or behavior which can make his truth clearer and more convincing.

IV

To sum up, it cannot be disputed that the arts have entered into theological teaching and learning and are likely to remain. Perhaps we should speak of a reentry, as former generations of students and professors were generally familiar with the classic imaginative expressions of their faith such as the works of Dante, Milton, or Bunyan. That same heritage needs to be repossessed in the present generation for the reasons noted in this essay. It might speak again with power and grace to a cultural epoch floundering between pseudoabsolutes on one side and a devouring nihilism on the other.

Yet the new, emerging use of the arts in theological education is not classical but contemporary. Their imaginative illumination of man's mysterious condition in a very present world is what students and teachers look for and discover. This is as it should be since the mystery of our humanness has been the perennial matrix of the Christian faith, and whatever alerts us to this mystery must be welcomed as fundamentally favorable toward the creation of loyalty and trust in it. Whoever dares to call the mystery by the name of God is caught up forthwith in mysteries of his own, venturing and risking his life in ways of hope and love that are appropriate to it. No guarantees of safe conduct can be offered either theologically or artistically today. However the ironies and negativities of contemporary art, as well as its occasional affirmations, may serve the theologian well in recalling the distance that always separates actual circumstance from ideal fulfillment, and therefore demands patience in the face of promise.

11

Mona Lisa
and Melchizedek

Walter Wagoner

The notion that a seminary is a kind of professional dancing school where, during the years of a preordained state of grace, the future clergy may be "improved" by the arts may be a worthy idea for salesmen of rotogravure bibles but it must be quickly disavowed here. However, there are many valid ways by which, during the seminary years, the arts can effect a life-long civilizing influence on the clergy—not perhaps as canonical means of supernatural grace—but certainly as redeeming works of joy and catharsis. In this chapter, and with a vivid sense of the standards of Amos Wilder, I should like to outline some fruitful relationships between the arts and the more technical and professional preparation for ordained ministry.

The chief axiom in all this is that the clergy are human and that most of them are men and women of more than average sensitivity to the shades and coloring of human existence. The fine arts have helped to humanize and to civilize people in all walks of life. Therefore, *mutatis mutandis*, there is every reason to press for a consistent and sophisticated exposure to the arts during and after the seminary years, especially since the clergy ought to be even more resonant than most to the grace of the arts. The peculiar mission of the clergy is, from the perspective of Christian insight, to keep the world human, to love, to chasten, and to quicken the joys of Creation. The correlation of the arts with such purposes is so demonstrable as to be past argument.

There is one healthy reservation to be voiced about the relationship between the mission or role of the arts and that of the ministry: namely, no simpering romanticism about the impact of the arts. Some seminarians and some clergy, as with all other groups of human beings, are apparently tone deaf to the music of the arts. Not all, however stimulating the artistic environment, can or wish to respond. And most of us respond much more to one form of the arts than to another. The arts have no built-in, guaranteed, messianic function. One of the worst forms of snobbery and preciosity about the arts is, with "arty" pride, to take umbrage if someone doesn't respond to one's artistic convictions. "Up from Chautauqua" is no motto for a seminary.

What follows, then, is put before the readers as if they were a representative committee of seminary students, faculty, and lay trustees which has asked for an *apologia* or a position paper on the role of the arts in theological education. Let us assume, so that we don't waste time on passé parlor games, that this committee is composed of the cultured sympathizers of the arts—persons who do not need to repeat Menckenish satire about Sallman's *Head of Christ* and related forms of ecclesiastical philistinism. The committee is also beyond the stage of sniffing at church-art junk with all the self-satisfaction of those who took an art appreciation course in college and once wrote a paper on "Tachism, Pollock and the Modern Spirit." That stage, with most seminarians and seminaries, is behind us.

There are four distinctive ways the optimal relationships between Christianity and the fine arts may be encouraged during the seminary years.

1. *An effort must be made to acquaint seminarians with the history of the church's relationship to the arts.* The seminary is not a graduate school of the fine arts, but no educated Christian can neglect both the awesome and awful performances of the churches in the history of art. Whether the Haggia Sophia or the Cathedral at Albi, whether a Byzantine icon or *The Peaceable Kingdom*, whether Sutherland's "Pantocrator" Tapestry or Corita Kent's posters, whether a Bach *Magnificat* or a folk mass, the enormous bulk of Christian symbolism is in art forms: music, windows, missals, statuary, architecture, painting, mosaic, tapestry, poetry, novels, woodcarving, ceramics. Only the most appalling and narrow view of Christianity—restricted to bibliolatry and mimeograph machines—would not seek an historical and artistic understanding of the faith. Such a familiarity should go beyond the apologetic or homiletical appropriation of the Christian heritage. It should, hopefully, even go beyond the necessary knowledge of the facts of Christian art history. In the course of the study there should be intensive reflection about the interrelations between theology, art, and culture. Let seminarians, for example, consider what Panofsky has done with Dürer, or Tillich with art history; or, in a most engaging way, what Horton Davies has done in correlating nineteenth-century English church history with architecture, music and liturgy; or what Amos Wilder has done with poetry and theological reflection. Why is it, for

example, that varying theological assumptions result in varying art forms? Can there be a high religion without an elevated use of the arts? Which types of symbols (artistic or verbal) convey or distort theological truths? What is the total message of a Mt. Saint Michel or the Church Center at 475 Riverside Drive? A seminary which does not open doors into such areas of reflection certainly must be judged to be failing lamentably. This is the type of educated intellect that, with a sure tropism of its own, turns the Christian heart and mind toward the great liberating forces of Christian art history.

However one approaches it in seminary, as General Art History, as Christian Art, as Theology and Culture, as Christian Esthetics, there ought to be a serious attempt to deal with some of the major figures and artistic creations related to the Christian Church and to initiate discussion of the more theoretical, cultural, and esthetic correlates and questions.[1] To a few of the latter I shall turn in what follows.

2. *Opportunities need to be provided for growth and development in the arts for seminarians with artistic promise of accomplishment.* If a seminary of reasonable size does not contain at least a few students with marked abilities in music, or painting, or drama, or dance, or another of the arts, the admissions committee should be fired. Let us assume, as basic to this argument, that the admissions committee has encouraged students with artistic promise. Once admitted, they have singular potential as human beings and as church leaders. The stewardship of their talents must be encouraged by providing space, equipment, and curricular status. Since most seminaries operate with a guild system of credits and other merit badges, the artistically competent students should not be made to feel that the time and effort which they give to artistic expression is merely tolerated by *noblesse oblige* administrators, or in any way judged to be outside the pale of theological respectability. It is just barely possible that a jazz trumpeter working on a new hymn, or a student who knows the difference between a Gabo construction and a Sunday School flannel graph might be as important to the future of the church as safe-and-sound Johnny Seminarian taking the Canterbury Club on a hayride or Sammy Seminarian studying Ugaritic.

These artistically inclined students should be encouraged to take leadership roles in seminary committees and planning groups having to do with the arts. Insofar as possible, funds should be made available for programs.

The aid and comfort given to such students does not in the least assume that the arts, any more than any other seminary discipline, are beyond criticism and critical thought. Muses are not to be tampered with

---

[1] A very strong case can be made that the Christian Gospel is, *sui generis*, more of an esthetic than a logical or ethical phenomenon.

and mutilated, to be sure, but neither are artistic poseurs or dilettantes to be encouraged. Artistic leanings do not excuse the neglect of the basic ingredients of theological education: biblical, ethical, historical, theological, and professional studies. A theologically naive Christian artist is bad news. One can never unfailingly know, much less legislate, the boundaries between a dilettante flailing about in the arts and a student who is willing to discipline himself in the arts. But the difference finally shows.

These are days of careless artistic expression, much of it used as decor for ideological causes. Peer group pressure, in revolutionary times, exerts strong temptations on the young artist either toward social realism or toward labored attempts to be radically different from prevailing art forms (as in giving ontological status to a Warhol soup can). Revolutions are probably even more artistically philistine than the bourgeois art which prevails in the galleries and museums of the establishment.

It is probably true, as Germain Bazin, Chief Curator of the Louvre, has written, "that the modern Sodom displays its obscene ugliness before our eyes with indecent complacency; but any artist who wishes to maintain integrity must submit himself to the martyrdom of discipline, silence, and the risks of not being with the crowd." The peroration of Monsieur Bazin, while a bit purple, is true enough:

"Every genius, before being raised upon the altars must be crucified . . . 'thrown to the wild beasts', as Delacroix put it. 'O Multitude!', cried Vigny in *Stello*, 'nameless multitude, you were born an enemy to names!' . . . deprived as they were of witnesses to sustain their judgement, and surrounded by contempt and indifference, these men had to find the principle of their strength in themselves alone."[2]

All this is to say that seminaries, like society at large, will do well to encourage the artistically creative student, even as no impression is to be given that creativity is cheap, easy and wholesale.

3. *The relationships between theology and art, or between theological education and the artist, need to be honest.* The art form and the artist are not to be manipulated. Artistic expression has its own dignity and autonomy. The church is not to build up a "stable of artists" to be run in a competitive derby. Nor, to change the figure, is the artist to be the victim of an ecclesiastical triumphalism which treats artists as prize converts, cups on the church mantelpiece. An honest relationship, for the Church and seminary, demands that clergy, particularly, help the artist to do what he really wishes to do, and not in any way, however well motivated, tempt him into artistic deformity.

The real problem here is subtle and deep, and goes beyond the more obvious forms of commercialism, censorship, or the church's search for prestige. The real problem rises from the fact that the articulate clergyman

[2] Germain Bazin, *The Loom of Art* (New York: Simon and Schuster, 1962), p. 263.

and layman are hypersaturated in the *quest for meaning,* are determined to express the meaning which Christian theism gives to life. Christians, and seminarians with special and understandable intensity, search out scripture, history and tradition for every evidence of God's self-revelation. One common illustration of this will help: the way most clergy read books, a Faulkner or Peter de Vries, not to mention the latest volume on the problem of evil, is to scan them for "meaningful quotes," for teleological hints and redemptive footnotes. That a clergyman should have a keen eye for the hand of God in history is laudable enough; but that this attitude should degenerate into a Christian *meaning mania* which is unable to deal with works of art on their own merits is to permit one good to ruin another.

Another of the curious and dangerous parallels between cultural art trends and theology is suggested by the following words of Gaston Diehl: "Success in the arts has also brought with it excesses caused by fear of being behind the fashion. All over the world we have seen in the past few years the most astonishing bid for primacy, and the bitterest competition for the roles of martyrs and pioneers exhumed from oblivion."[3]

The parallel, of course, to what Diehl is referring to is faddism in theology and studied *avant-gardism.* Seminaries which study these parallel phenomena in arts and theology cannot help but to be more alert to silliness in each camp.

The seminarians and the clergy will be kept honest, and the arts autonomous, if works of creation are accepted without the desperate attempt to find the Creator in every burning bush. Protestantism easily slips into hasty moralizing and into homiletical theology. It is a trait which does not keep good company with the arts, and which thus often imposes categories of meaning on art forms which do not require program notes written by hard-breathing theologians eager to capture every ideational clue to God's whereabouts.

Tillich, for all his enormous services to arts and the culture, ruined the *Guernica* mural for many with his sermonizing about its Protestant qualities. I can think of several literary critics who have been so eager to Christianize *King Lear* that the play, *qua* play, disappears behind a fog of ideological or theological pleading. Even Camus has been baptized by over-eager proselytizers. This is dishonest. It is a habit which can be fought off during the seminary years, if the arts are presented on their own terms. We who are Christian are incurably imperialistic. In the artistic sphere this means that we have an insatiable lust to wear as theological talismans the poetry of Eliot and Auden, the music of Bach, the paintings of Wyeth and Van Gogh, the stories of Melville and Conrad. The arts, unless expressly shaped as propaganda for God, should be allowed their

[3] Gaston Diehl, *The Moderns* (New York: Crown Publishers, 1966), p. 6.

own dignity. Living on the edge of mystery, as Christianity does, it should be more than willing to grant that right to the arts, and to be humble about it.

Reiteration at this point may help to avoid misunderstanding about the best relation between the artist and the self-conscious evangelistic Christian who wants commissioned art to "carry a message" or to "testify to the Glory of God" so that all may see and believe. Are there not several commandments sanctioned by Christian art history? *First*, the artist shall create his own meaning. He is not the exegete of the patron. *Second*, the medium is the message—which in this context means that good art both *is* and *acts*. The being, the isness of good art is not exhausted by any simple message or act of symbolization. There is also both mystery and many messages in a work of fine art. *Third*, good art's message is never translatable into a literal symbolic paraphrase of the patron's intention. If it were, we would not need it.

Considerations of the above sort, subject to debate and dialogue, will very much help the seminarian arrive at a more responsible understanding of Christian patronage of the arts.

The prior warnings about a triumphalistic and manipulative use of art and the artists by the church should not mean withdrawal of the church as a patron of the arts, any more than the abjuration of political colonialism need imply political irresponsibility or isolationism by the former colonial power. The church and churchmen can grant a *sui generis* dignity to the arts without forswearing them. It is also true that no other institution in the West has both so used and abused the arts. We must work toward eliminating the abuse. Seminaries can help.

It is egregious abuse for the church to say to an artist: "We will pay you for reflecting our piety in your next work." After all, Dürer's praying hands have been manufactured as bedroom night lights. Nevertheless, such obscenities must not be allowed to produce the conclusion that the church must stay clear of the arts. What we need to do once again is to encourage the church to commission, to seek out, to buy, to applaud good and great art.

A proper sense of honesty about the affinity for the arts by seminarians can be enhanced by exhibitions, by courses, and by using the metropolitan-cultural resources. Visiting artists and artists-in-residence will be of great help. Since seminarians are graduate students, the arts are demeaned by any packaged "art-appreciation-picture-of-the-month" pedagogy more befitting junior high school students. The constant assumption and reminder should, again, always be that the arts have their own integrity and autonomy. This dignity can be accorded the artist by the Christian and by the church employing the artists only insofar as the understanding is that the artistic creation is carried out primarily on the artist's terms. If the artist has no feel for the Christian church or if the artist is non religious by conviction, he or she will probably not accept any commission for church work. Purism is not expected—that is, the artist need not *fully* agree with the viewpoint of the church in order to contribute a work which makes an honest statement in a church environment.

It would be a pity beyond tears, were Christians to heed only art forms that have immediate, obvious relevance to the religious life, either having been commissioned for church use or bearing an overtly religious or ethical theme. Religious conviction has produced such bankruptcy, just as political ideology had done. Such people have been made blind by eyes which can only read and see homiletically.

The caveat works both ways, of course. What obligations may fairly be asked of the artist by a Christian patron? Or, more obliquely, what kind of art is not appropriate to the symbolization of the Christian gospel? It goes without saying that often the most "un-Christian" art is the prettified junk sold in stores of "religious articles": golden rule teacups and pink plaster virgins. Generally, any art is beside the point here if it demeans the human, expresses only cruelty or nihilism, glories in the trivial or is otherwise not consonant with the spirit of Christ. Christian art, in this sense, can express the whole range of tragedy, comedy, joy. But despair cannot be unrelieved; the statement cannot mock the Christian revelation of God. It certainly may, however, raise the question of Job and the agony of the world.

Christian patronage of the arts, then, can talk in the generalities above; it can say beyond that only, "We need an anthem for this occasion or a window for this wall." Having done that, the main obligation of the patron then is to choose a good, sympathetic artist—and let him alone. Seminarians as future patrons (builders and furnishers of churches, persons of influence in church circles) very much need to think about this dimension of the church's relationship to the arts.

One concluding disclaimer: it is manifestly true that the Christian's (the seminarian and the layman) relationship to the arts is not only, perhaps not even primarily, to be conceived within the specialized context of the seminary, the institutional—the overtly Christian use and patronage of the arts. Art, whether secular or Christian, is of course a creation of the human spirit, and *all* art should be of concern to those human beings who are also Christian. The parallel which comes immediately to mind is "secular theology," as it explores everything under a Doctrine of Creation. But for purposes of focus and limitation this wider interpretation is here neglected.

4. *Seminary communities, when exposed to and involved in the arts, can empower the language and mythology of Christianity.* Theological language, if it is to carry meaning and impact, must essentially be formed by the major currents and crises of its society. This is essential to a viable and persuasive Christian vocabulary, since Christianity is an incarnational

—not an idealistic—religion. Its historical nature is sustained and freshened by making sure that its symbols and interpretations are rooted in contemporary soil. The myths, figures of speech, liturgies of our faith resonate when they are deeply and existentially related to the major undercurrents of our life. Otherwise, the gospel will seem archaic, quaint, unreal.

Close association, therefore, with the better artists of our society is bound to have a happy effect on theological thought and evangelization. Such association should ward off preciosity, nostalgia, and angelism. How can any theologian conversant with the better drama of our day, Genet's *Blacks*, for example, permit his writing to flow off into vapidity—"very beautiful and twenty miles from nowhere." How could any wide-awake liturgists not be strongly sensitized by the folk music of our present culture? Let it be granted that our times are imbalanced, toward the Dionysian, toward the "God of the Dance," toward a sensate culture. We could too easily lose touch with the logical, the rigorous, the disciplined. But it is the theologian's task to realize these imbalances as they occur, without slighting either side of the scales as he weighs his ideas. Furthermore, as is now a truism, the genuine artist "sees ahead." He—the poet, the painter—has an early warning system which the more prosaic of us must rely on to comprehend what is heading in our direction.

The arts, it must be argued, best serve the church by expanding the humanity and sensitivity of those human beings who call themselves Christian, in this case, seminaries and their faculties. "Art is a weapon. After millions of well aimed blows, someday perhaps it will break the stone heart of the mindless cacodemon called Things as They Are."[4] If fine art did not make its impression on substantial numbers of clergy, at least an influential minority, what a bleak and barren landscape the church's leadership would occupy. The arts profoundly sensitize us, add depth and wisdom to our human and ethical judgments, and give "experience a greater intensity." The tide of interest should run as much to the arts for art's sake as from art to the Gospel. The arts, even if one can hone his competence to deal intelligently with a few of them, open up new universes of meaning and rhetoric.

Talking about the painting of Morris Graves, Rexroth also writes with a perception that is very persuasive:

> The function of the artist is the revelation of reality in process, permanence in change, the place of value in a world of facts. His duty is to keep open the channels of contemplation and to discover new ones. He can bring men to the springs of the good, the true, the beautiful, but he cannot make them drink. The activities of men endure and have meaning as long as they emanate from a core of transcendental calm. The contemplative, the

[4] Kenneth Rexroth, *Bird in the Bush* (New York: New Directions, 1959), p. 8.

mystic, assuming moral responsibility for the distracted, tries to keep his gaze fixed on that core. The artist uses the materials of the world to direct men's attention back to it. When it is lost sight of, society perishes.[5]

According to Cicero, Democritus blinded himself so that he could concentrate the more on his philosophizing. That blindness is one of the darkest fates possible for the clergy. The clergyman, of all professionals, needs eyes in the back of his head, needs the widest peripheral vision, needs all the sight he can muster ... and not merely to observe, but to see into, to peer, to perceive. Theology that is true to Christ's eyes must, at all costs, avoid a *trompe l'oeil* view of the human scene. Anything which insulates, which fakes, which misrepresents (which mere representational art forms often do), is the declared enemy of the artistically sensitive clergyman. The seminarian who is exposed to the insights of the artist is developing traits which will make him a much more keen pastor and accurate prophet.

Christianity lives, furthermore, on the edge of mystery. Mystery is the atmosphere, the reality, in which the roots of faith are planted—not as obscurantism, but because the God whom Christians worship rules over a universe of fathomless mystery. God himself is finally a mystery, however confident Christians may trust that what Christ has revealed of that mystery is crucial. Therefore the vision and the agony of the great artist should be cherished by the minister. There is a cognate relationship between the two strivings—that after God, and that after beauty or meaningful symbolism. One may, of course, acknowledge mystery without acknowledging religion or Christian faith. But how can one who does claim to be Christian *not* acknowledge the necessary companionship of the artist?

The above thesis is valid, I believe, for the most rigorous type of theological thought, for the most disciplined and logical forms of religious discourse, and is no excuse for sloppy romanticism, for formlessness. The hope, however, is that the best religious thinkers and the more thoughtful pastors will move closer to the heart of things when in the company of the artists. It is esthetic fundamentalism to claim that "Jesus did not need artists" or to try to build an antiartistic or nonartistic rationale from the New Testament documents. The point, rather, to be discussed is how art can help not only seminarians, but all Christians to appropriate the glories of existence, how to sound the depths of humanity, how to touch the hem of ultimate mystery.

Seminarians, in the midst of all their wrestling with the effects of a secularized culture on theology and evangelism, will come here up against the insulating, defusing effect which our nontranscendent, nonsupernatural culture has upon Christian symbolism. These days, even in the hands of

[5] Rexroth, *Bird in the Bush*, p. 57.

the finest artists, it is terribly difficult for the conventional symbols to speak, to convey; just as it is for theological language.

Christian esthetics, faced with this cultural nonconductivity, immediately faces the danger of becoming cultically ingrown, sectarian, and defensive. Certain Christian theologians, uncritically eager to penetrate the surrounding culture, will either distort the Gospel into faddish forms or will go (dragging the seminarians with them) on one of those symbol safaris which seeks to find Christian meaning in everything from *Peanuts* to Updike. One of the curious and constant parallels between cultural art trends and those in theology has been the fear of being behind the fashion of the times. This fear brings with it a tendency toward excess in competition for being thought most "successful." It is these temptations, in Christian esthetics, that the seminarian needs to be acquainted with as he thinks through the role of the arts for a minority religious culture, as Christianity now is. This challenge should lead to new insight.

Finally, the humanizing effect of the arts is crucially important to religious professionals. Christian professionalism, that is, the making of one's livelihood by being paid for religious expertise, is a necessary but very dangerous business. The guild mentality, orthodox brittleness, pontifical power, ascribed status: these are the sworn enemies of Christ just because they are constant temptations to serious discipleship. Such temptations may be counteracted by humor, by humaneness, by loving criticism, by prayer. The arts, too, can make a key contribution to maintaining the sanity and humanity of clergy. The symbolism of art, with its openness, its beauty, its glorious stimulation, goes far to avoid professional atrophy and sterility. Susan Sontag implies this redeeming function when she writes: "Art adds great and deep experiences of life which must be used as sensuous evidence when one is forming a religious world-view."[6] It is precisely the world-view of the seminarians, their ability to see life with all its colors and shadows, which seminaries are concerned to enhance. The attention given to the arts and the esthetic sensibility must, therefore, be both serious and sustained.

Appendix: The Arts and the Seminary Curriculum

What is actually being taught for credit in the field of the arts in American seminaries?* A quantitative and statistical survey of the current catalogues of eighty-eight Protestant and Roman Catholic seminaries, at the professional degree level, gives a fairly accurate profile of the main interests. The crucial caveat, of course, is that such a survey discloses little about the quality of the course and the competence of the instructor—a study which

---

[6] Susan Sontag, *Against Interpretation* (New York: Delta, 1966), p. 8.

* Acknowledgment is here made to Mr. Ronald Reed, the Episcopal Theological School, for his research assistance in this summary.

would be well worth doing. The following data has been compiled only from course descriptions in catalogues, with the further qualification that only those courses are categorized which evidence more than a dilettante or superficial approach. No course is categorized more than once.

In order: (one semester courses)

Theology and Painting   1
Religion and Dance   1
Directed Study and Research   2
Arts in the Black Religious Heritage   2
Non-Christian Religions and Art   3
Theology and Architecture   4
Arts and Creative Communication   10
Theology and Poetry   10
Esthetics and Art Criticism   11
Theology and Film   15
Worship and the Arts   15
Arts in Church History   16
Theology and Culture and Art   17
Theology and Drama   33
Theology and Church Music   34
Theology and Literature   67

There are a few observations/conclusions worth venturing from a study of the catalogue evidence: (1) A serious study of the arts is very much a minor part of seminary curricula. (2) A three year comparative study of catalogues indicates, however, that the field is growing steadily. (3) Seminaries in cluster/university contexts are much the stronger in this field. (4) "Film" as a genre is the fastest growing. (5) Most of these courses apparently are still relying heavily on the teacher-lecture method, with relatively few courses involving student creativity. (6) The courses related to literature (novel, poetry, drama) are in the overwhelming majority— about 70 percent.

12

Jerusalem's Wall
and Other Perimeters

Stanley Romaine Hopper

It would be appropriate now to gather up the central threads of the fore-going essays and wind them into a ball, confident that they would lead us in at some new heaven's gate set in Jerusalem's wall. But our topology of being has changed since Blake: "heaven" is not where we thought it was, and "Jerusalem's wall" has a parochial (if not alienating) ring to it. The traditional symbol systems have been sprung, and the images that emerge in the arts today bear witness to this difference. It is a difference that has become radical to the Western consciousness.

If we concur in this (that a radical change has come over the Western consciousness, and that our arts bear witness to it) it is essential that the questions we ask of it be radical too. If we ask, what images of affirmation may be seen emerging from the arts today?—we must question the mode of our questioning, lest it surreptitiously reinstate the *status quo ante* of the very modes of thinking and feeling that have been called into question. If I ask for images "of affirmation" am I, perhaps, asking whether the arts show evidence of a reinstatement (in modified form, of course) of former affirmations, thereby neglecting the poet's adjuration:

> Throw away the lights, the definitions,
> And say of what you see in the dark
>
> That it is this or that it is that,
> But do not use the rotted names.[1]

[1] Wallace Stevens, "The Man with the Blue Guitar," 32, *The Collected Poems of Wallace Stevens* (New York: Alfred A. Knopf, 1954), p. 183.

Do I, even in the act of *observing* the poet's warning necessarily *stand apart* from it, thus exempting myself once more from the time's dilemma and entering once more into complicity with the assumptions of the Western consciousness, the fructifying springs of which have today run dry? Must we not go one step further and concede that this very speculation as to the adequacy of our mode of questioning *is itself specious*, being already compliant with the objectivizing mode of the Western consciousness. To "understand" our cultural dilemma analytically or intellectualistically is not to understand it. Or, to put the paradox in the language of Martin Heidegger: "Thinking is thinking when it answers to what is most thought-provoking. In our thought-provoking time, what is most thought-provoking shows itself in the fact that we are still not thinking."[2]

This means, at the very least, that we must enter into the problem quite differently: that is, *we* must enter into it; *we* must *enter* into it; we must enter into *it*—and it is precisely that which has not yet shown itself. It is the undisclosed; it is that which still remains hidden within and behind the manifold expressions of our modern and contemporary arts. What I would suggest is this: that if we wish to discern in what way or in what direction our arts are pointing, we must become attentive to that which remains unsaid precisely *through* what is overtly uttered in the work of the artist; we must recognize at the outset the extent to which contemporary works are ciphers of the "collective unconscious," that as such they are highly indicative, but must be "read"—must be "interpreted" in terms of that which is made to appear behind and beyond and through the work's specifics of articulation. There is, in short, something internal to the work which is the secret of its "meaning" which speaks "over and above" (under and through) what is spoken overtly. Especially is this the case in a time when the traditional systems of reference have dropped away and we are thrust radically upon the primary enigmas of existence. It is here that all authentic "thinking" (in Heidegger's sense) must begin.

I

Certain initial dilemmas and/or paradoxes will at once come clear.

If we return for a moment to Blake's poem of the "golden thread" we discover in our response to it an important ambivalence.

> I give you the end of a golden string;
> > Only wind it into a ball,
> It will lead you in at Heaven's gate,
> > Built in Jerusalem's wall.[3]

[2] Martin Heidegger, *What Is Called Thinking*, Fred D. Wieck and J. Glenn Gray, trans., intro. by J. Glenn Gray (New York: Harper & Row Publishers, 1968), p. 28.
[3] From "Jerusalem," *The Poetical Works of William Blake*, John Sampson, ed. (London: Oxford University Press, 1928), p. 403.

We respond to it pleasantly and with good feeling, but are not deeply moved. The terms which petition the informing myth structure show clearly that the supporting myth, as something believed in and therefore validating for the poem's utterance, has dropped away, leaving only metaphors (now conventional) to carry the argument. These metaphors are not "grounded," as we say, in anything beyond their (emptied) relation to one another. They remain "rhetorical," the conceit being progressively enervated by the withdrawing myth; but as the myth withdraws the continuing presence of the metaphors seems increasingly arbitrary and even artificial (as "Heaven's gate" and "Jerusalem" fail to engage in any depth the contemporary psyche). What was pleasant at a superficial level will become irritating at a deeper level.

On the other hand, behind and beyond the images as such is the movement of the poem itself. There is something archetypal in the image of the thread placed in the hand—the thread or string, let us say, of existence: which we are then to wind as we follow it, with the assurance that it will lead into the heart of the mystery. We speak easily of the "thread of life" (to be cut one day by the shears of Atropos); there was the thread into the Labyrinth; there was also Arachne's thread, and Penelope's thread, and even the "thread of thought" of which we speak so lightly, but which may be prone to all of these (and innumerable other) hazards. There is, in short, beneath the surface metaphors the deeper and relatively unspecified metaphor or archetype) of the journey, together with the assurance—the poem's deeper witness—that by undertaking the journey we shall arrive at the heart of the unknown and find it sustaining. The topology of "heaven" was apparently surrogate for the topology of inwardness.

It is interesting to juxtapose to Blake's verses a near contemporary poem (published 1958) in order to note (a) the striking differences in imagery and structure, and (b) the underlying archetypal similarity of plot and metaphor:

> Kafka's Castle stands above the world
>> like a last bastille
>>> of the Mystery of Existence
> Its blind approaches baffle us
>>>> Steep paths
>> plunge nowhere from it
>>> Roads radiate into air
> like the labyrinth wires
>>> of a telephone central
> thru which all calls are
>>> infinitely untraceable
>> Up there
>>> it is heavenly weather
> Souls dance undressed
>>> together

                    and like loiterers
                            on the fringes of a fair
            we ogle the unobtainable
                        imagined mystery
            Yet away around on the far side
                    like the stage door of a circus tent
        is a wide wide vent in the battlements
                        where even elephants
                                waltz thru[4]

A detailed analysis of the poem is not to our interests here. Nevertheless, let us observe that the poem is not "difficult." It elaborates a simple analogy. Its language and its grammar are conventional. It is didactic as Blake's was didactic. The lines, to be sure, are cut up and placed in such a way as both to assist and impede the reading. They control the reader's eye, requiring the mind to give full value to the intentional units of the poem's argument, and preventing the eye from running ahead to the climax without going the way of the poem itself.

Our concern lies at quite a different point. Kafka's "Castle," we perceive, is a more realistic and durable myth, at this moment in our history, than "Jerusalem's walls." Ferlinghetti knows that Kafka's parable takes hold and that it is sufficiently perdurable in the contemporary consciousness to support a further parabolic addendum based upon it. Kafka's world, as Theodor Adorno puts it, "is a parabolic system the key to which has been stolen."[5] The reader, like "Joseph K" in *The Trial*, feels somehow accused. Despite the fantastic movement of narratives one reads them with the same literalness that one confers upon the imagery of a dream; and with the same involvement also, for the "contemplative relation" between the reader and the narrative is broken down. In like manner its myth is reflexive, at once omnipresent and nonexistent: it returns the reader perpetually to himself already convicted. "As long as the word has not been found, the reader must be held accountable."[6] Adorno intends here, I take it, the talismanic word, as in a fairy-tale—the clue, the open sesame, the three jewels, the unrecognized secret, the incognitoes of release, whereby the spell of the negative is broken. In Kafka's parables the enigma remains; in Ferlinghetti's parable on Kafka's parable the enigma is strikingly appeased.

Ferlinghetti offers us Kafka's Castle as "a last bastille of the Mystery of Existence." This is precisely what we observed above in relation to this time in which the traditional systems of reference have dropped away and

[4] Lawrence Ferlinghetti, *A Coney Island of the Mind*. Copyright © 1958 by Lawrence Ferlinghetti. Reprinted by permission of New Directions Publishing Corporation.

[5] Theodor W. Adorno, *Prisms*, Samuel and Shierry Weber, trans. (London: Neville Spearman Limited, 1967), p. 246.

[6] Adorno, p. 246.

we are thrust radically upon the primary enigmas of existence. He introduces also the symbol of the labyrinth via the "wires" of the telephone exchange. Our frustrated attempts to reach the castle are effectively dramatized. The Castle "stands above the world"; it is "heavenly" and "unobtainable," yet "away around on the far side" is a door, a wide vent that one can waltz through quite easily.

Our question can be put in two ways. Negatively, it is the question whether, in this poem, we have in any real sense gone beyond Blake. For "Jerusalem's wall" we have "Kafka's Castle." For "Heaven's gate" we have "a wide wide vent" in the battlements. If Kafka really stands between, we have a difference. But is not Kafka's realistic myth translated into metaphor in such a way as to delete what is persistently enigmatic in Kafka's parable? Kafka's parable leaves me holding the enigma in my hands: the spell of the myth *as refuge* is broken. I must win *in reality*, as he reminds us in his parable *On Parables*; in parable (as the myth of refuge) I will lose.

Positively, the account stands otherwise. What was archetypal in Blake's poem (namely, the assurance that winding the string will lead us into the heart of the mystery of existence) is present here also. In Ferlinghetti also an access is possible, though it be away around on the far side.

It is difficult to say whether Ferlinghetti understands this. At least it is not clear from the poem. When he says that "we ogle the unobtainable *imagined* mystery," he seems to be saying that the entire surround—from Castle to roads to heavenly weather—is an unreal projection. In which case the "far side" of the castle would not be a projection of the far side of the projection! The far side of the projection lies at its source! It is in me. The wide vent is where I already am, and the entry-way is so enormous that even elephants could waltz through. Kafka, as I have noted elsewhere,[7] (and this I take to be dialectical heart of Kafka's wisdom), puts the matter unmistakably: "What is laid upon us is to accomplish the negative; the positive is already given."[8]

What does this mean? This is the paradox toward which much modern and contemporary literature and art has been pointing: ambiguously, perhaps, as the poems above are ambiguous, but intuiting nevertheless that something in the Western way of seeing and thinking must be radically revised.

II

Kafka's proposition that what is laid upon us is to accomplish the negative is obviously compendious: it means many things. Psychologically, it means

[7] Stanley Romaine Hopper, "The Eclipse of God" and "Existential Mistrust," *The Eastern Buddhist*, n. s. 3, no. 2 (October 1970), p. 58ff.

[8] "Reflections on Sin, Pain, Hope, and the True Way," *The Great Wall of China*, Willa and Edwin Muir, trans. (New York: Schocken Books, 1937), 24, p. 284.

a collapse of our unrealistic projections (including the collapse of the Cartesian ego and its rationalistic projections). Philosophically it means the recovery of the Socratic cross-questioning of ourselves out of our supposed fixed knowledge and into a recollection of the "source" from which we come; or, from a slightly different angle, a setting aside of traditional "metaphysics" and intellectualistic presuppositions on behalf of a recovery of what Heidegger calls a "fundamental ontology." Theologically, it means a resumption of the paradox confessed by Augustine at the moment of his new awareness: "For behold, Thou wert within, and I without, and there did I seek Thee; I, unlovely, rushed heedlessly among the things of beauty Thou madest. Thou wert with me, but I was not with Thee."[9]

Our interest, however, is in the arts and their evidences, and we must be wary lest such a calendar of antecedents be construed as fragments we have shored against our reluctant ruin! Yet it is just in the literary arts that the quest for the positive that is already given can be most readily discerned. It is here also that the enigma of existence is today being increasingly conserved and brought into unity with the enigma of thinking referred to above—to the curious fact that what is most thought provoking *shows itself* in the fact that we are still not thinking.

Ezra Pound, for example, is reported to have remarked: "It is difficult to write a paradiso when all the superficial indications are that you ought to write an apocalypse."[10]

What is striking about this statement is that the abundance of factors which should induce the poet of considerable vision to write an apocalypse are appraised as "superficial." Probably we must agree with this judgment, but we should take care not to do so superficially! In the Western religious tradition—Iranian, Judaic, Christian, Islamic—an intimate relation obtains between Paradise and Apocalypse. They form an Alpha and Omega at the "ends" of history and imply a certain equivalence, as in the notion of the Kingdom, which some theologians would regard as being both Paradise and the New Jerusalem. Very likely Pound, in separating them, intends no symbolic violence, but wishes merely to note the depressing "decline" of the West—what Nicolas Berdyaev termed "the end of our time." Modern literature abounds with such apocalyptic announcements of doom. Rimbaud's *Une Saison en Enfer* was doubtless one of these. Delmore Schwartz, in his 1939 translation of that poem, remarks that "the history of poetry since BLAKE ... is the history of men who found the social order into which they were born increasingly inadequate in every *human* respect and wholly deficient in satisfying the inevitable

[9] *The Confessions of St. Augustine*, J. G. Pilkington, trans. (New York: Horace Liveright, 1927), Bk. 10, xxvii, 38, pp. 247–248.
[10] Donald Hall, "The Art of Poetry V: Ezra Pound," *Parish Review*, 28 (Summer/Fall 1962), 22–51, p. 47.

human need for a whole view of life. Rimbaud knew this need . . . ."[11] We know the "falling towers" of the *Waste Land* (1922)—

> Jerusalem Athens Alexandria
> Vienna London

where "London Bridge is falling down falling down falling down. . . ." There was Thomas Merton's *Figures for an Apocalypse,* and the school of "apocalyptic poetry" to which Amos Wilder called our attention in 1952.[12] Thomas Altizer today argues that the Christian theologian is "called to a new task, a task of mediating what he has been given as apocalyptic faith and vision to a new eschatological time and destiny."[13] I also pointed out some years ago (1951) the startling transition in the poetry of Dame Edith Sitwell "from fancy to Apocalypse," pointing to her late poems ("The Shadow of Cain," "Dirge for the New Sunrise," "The Canticle of the Rose") written after the dropping of the bombs on Hiroshima and Nagasaki.[14] In short, there are plenty of apocalyptic sparrows in our literary sky, enough at least to lend credence to a fairly kairotic summer.

It might also be argued that Pound eschews the apocalyptic because he thinks of it in terms of the more literalistic imagery of crude dualisms, with trumpetings and great things descending out of heaven. But I think his attempt to "write a paradiso" points to something more profound, something which lies beyond the reach of Pound's own consciousness and which therefore both instructs and thwarts his skills. Though his intuition often falters, his instinct on the matter points into the heart of our problem.

His most recent Cantos, the *Drafts & Fragments of Cantos CX–CXVII,* are filled with a haunting nostalgia—the nostalgia of the backward look over the journey, when the time has run out and the goal not reached nor wholly disclosed.

> The hells move in cycles,
>   No man can see his own end,
> The Gods have not returned. "They have never left us."
>   They have not returned. (CXIII)[15]

---

[11] Arthur Rimbaud, *A Season in Hell*, Delmore Schwartz, trans. (New York: New Directions Publishing Corporation, 1939), intro. page xii.

[12] Amos Wilder, *Modern Poetry and the Christian Tradition* (New York: Charles Scribner's Sons, 1952), pp. 207–216 on "The New Apocalpyse."

[13] Thomas J. J. Altizer, "Inspiration and Apocalypse," *Soundings* no. 4 (Winter 1970), pp. 398–412.

[14] Stanley Romaine Hopper, "The Spiritual Implications of Modern Poetry," *Religion in Life* 22, no. 4 (Autumn 1951), pp. 558–559.

[15] Ezra Pound, *The Cantos.* Copyright 1940, 1948, © 1968 by Ezra Pound. Reprinted by permission of New Directions Publishing Corporation.

There is candor and pathos in his references to his "paradiso":

> M'amour, m'amour
> what do I love and
> where are you?
> That I lost my center
> fighting the world.
> The dreams clash
> and are shattered—
> and that I tried to make a paradiso
> terrestre.
> (Notes for Canto CXVII et seq.)[16]

The tone of this is consistent with his ambivalent sense of success and failure in his project. He says (1) "I cannot make it cohere," and; (2) a few lines later, "it coheres all right/ even if my notes do not cohere" (CXVI). Note again the same ambivalence, with the reminiscence of Browning's *Paracelsus* in the concluding lines:

> Charity I have had sometimes,
> I cannot make it flow thru.
> A little light, like a rushlight
> to lead back to splendour. (CXVI)[17]

Now a poet is not obligated to understand altogether what he is saying, and there is no reason why Pound should be an exception. In fact, it is this culminating ambivalence which is the "rightness" he so much coveted for his epic poem. Here also is the clue to what is unsaid in the poem, as well as the clue to that toward which the poem is pointing.

In order for this to come clear it is essential to note the steady mutation of the poet's experience of his own quest. His poem begins with two analogues—the journeys of Dante and of Ulysses. The mythological backdrops to these are not the same; but both persist in uneasy alignment until the end—Dante by way of the light imagery, Ulysses by way of homecoming. Midway in the quest the "periplum" image appears—the voyage of discovery ($\pi\epsilon\rho\iota$, around, plus $\pi\lambda\upsilon\mu\sigma$, voyage, sail: to circumnavigate). The image, appearing in Canto LIX, recurs throughout the Pisan Cantos. It is initially a different way of seeing:

> periplum, not as land looks on a map
> but as sea bord seen by men sailing. (LIX)[18]

[16] Ezra Pound, *The Cantos.* Copyright 1940, 1948, © 1968 by Ezra Pound. Reprinted by permission of New Directions Publishing Corporation.

[17] Ezra Pound, *The Cantos.* Copyright 1940, 1948, © 1968 by Ezra Pound. Reprinted by permission of New Directions Publishing Corporation.

[18] Ezra Pound, *The Cantos.* Copyright 1940, 1948, © 1968 by Ezra Pound. Reprinted by permission of New Directions Publishing Corporation.

This is not unlike Socrates's distinction in the *Meno* between map knowledge (of "the way to Larissa") and the knowledge experienced directly by *going* there. But here one must picture the ship *at sea,* having left one headland and proceeding towards another—unseen, perhaps unknown. It *appears* that the sea comes toward the ship, passes through, and fans out behind in its widening wake. This is an environment nearer to Ulysses than to Dante; but nearer still to contemporary man's sense of voyaging alone in an expanding universe.

There is here a point of contact with Kafka, as noted above. Theodor Adorno wrote of Kafka: "He wrote the consummate Robinson Crusoe story, that of the phase in which each man has become his own Robinson, adrift with his accumulated things on a rudderless raft."[19] Allen Tate, writing about Pound's early Cantos (in 1936) said, "Mr. Pound's world is the scene of a great Odyssey, and everywhere he lands it is the shore of Circe, where men 'lose all companions' and are turned into swine."[20] But the periplum image changes all of this, as far as the image of quest is concerned. Kafka would never have said, as does Pound, that "The great periplum brings in the stars to our shores" (LXXIV).[21] Analogues must be sought in a quite different direction.

The following poem, for example, of Charles Olsen's is (perhaps surprisingly apposite:

In English the poetics became meubles-furniture-
thereafter (after 1630
& Descartes was the value
until Whitehead, who cleared out the gunk
by getting the universe in (as against man alone
& *that* concept of history (not Herodotus's,
which was a verb, to find out for yourself:
'istorin, which makes any one's acts a finding out
    for him or her
self, in other words restores the traum: that we
    act somewhere
at least by seizure, that the objective (example
    Thucydides, or
the latest finest tape-recorder, or any form of
    record on the spot
—live television or what—is a lie
as against what we know went on, the dream: the dream being self-action
with Whitehead's important corollary: that no event
is not penetrated, in intersection or collision with,

[19] Adorno, p. 266.
[20] Allen Tate, *Reactionary Essays* (New York, Charles Scribner's Sons, 1936), p. 48.
[21] Ezra Pound, *The Cantos.* Copyright 1940, 1948, © 1968 by Ezra Pound. Reprinted by permission of New Directions Publishing Corporation.

> an eternal
> event
>   The poetics of such a situation
> are yet to be found out[22]

Leaving Herodotus and Thucydides out of account, two points are to be noted here: one, that Whitehead is credited with having cleared the classical and Cartesian "gunk" out in order to let the universe back into our awareness; and two, that in Whitehead creative self-action is postulated with its cosmic corollary, namely, that every "event" is an interpenetration of the momentary and the "eternal" (or, in Whitehead's language, God is the principle of concretion, and "the ultimate metaphysical principle is the advance from disjunction to conjunction, creating a novel entity other than the entities given in disjunction").[23] It is quite true that the poetics of this world view have yet to be worked out, but Pound's periplum coincides very well with this Whiteheadian cosmology. Momenta of force are here seen *moving through* each singular occasion on their way towards further concretions. The whole is thus "present in each actual entity, and each actual entity pervades the continuum."[24] There is a radical microcosm—macrocosm relation implicit in this vision. The whole events in every part, moves through it in the process of becoming and perishing. In Pound it is a lonely vision, whether it be the self as the voyaging ship in an infinite sea, or the world being constantly diminished in the wild accelerating burst of the expanding macrocosm.

It is not surprising, then, that Pound's images should change, and that his "paradiso" should persist within this difference. He seeks by way of Confucius to "make it new." The images of a poem become a field of force, and are so placed as to evoke resonances and recognitions. These recognitions aim both to let the particular appear as that which it is, and "to affirm the gold thread in the pattern" (CXVI).[25] The question is, "can you enter the great acorn of light?" (CXVI)[26] and thereby see as God sees: "God's eye art 'ou, do not surrender perception" (CXIII).[27] The rose must be perceived in the steel dust; between "heaven" and "earth" is

[22] Charles Olsen, "A Later Note on Letter #15," *Maximus Poems IV, V, VI* (London: Cape Goliard Press, 1968), V.

[23] Alfred North Whitehead, *Process and Reality* (New York: The Macmillan Company, 1929), p. 32.

[24] Whitehead, p. 105.

[25] Ezra Pound, *The Cantos.* Copyright 1940, 1948, © 1968 by Ezra Pound. Reprinted by permission of New Directions Publishing Corporation.

[26] Ezra Pound, *The Cantos.* Copyright 1940, 1948, © 1968 by Ezra Pound. Reprinted by permission of New Directions Publishing Corporation.

[27] Ezra Pound, *The Cantos.* Copyright 1940, 1948, © 1968 by Ezra Pound. Reprinted by permission of New Directions Publishing Corporation.

juniper—"in the center" (CX).[28] Perhaps the turning point of his vision comes in Canto LXXIV, his version (called "secular" by Hugh Kenner) of the dark night of the soul:

> Νύζ animae?
> is there a blacker or was it merely San Juan with
>   a belly ache
>   writing ad posteros
> in short shall we look for a deeper or is this
>   the bottom?
>
>   .   .   .   .   .   .
>
> Berlin   dysentery   phosphorus
>   Le Paradis n'est pas artificiel
>   but spezzato apparently
>   it exists only in fragments unexpected excellent sausage,
>   the smell of mint, for example. . . .[29]

This is the first of the *Pisan Cantos*. Pound's internment camp becomes symbolic of the modern world. It is a world of darkness. The irony is profound: in short shall we look for a deeper or is this the bottom? John the Baptist in prison sent word to Jesus, "Are you he who is to come, or shall we look for another?" (Mt. xi. 3). Here "San Juan with a belly ache" should be compared with Wallace Stevens' "Saint John and the Back-Ache," in which Stevens appeals from the "back-ache" of Western culture and its apotheosis of the *ratio* to *Presence* as the primal mystery. This is not too dissimilar from Pound, who here begins his move into his Paradiso. Pound begins to find his paradise in unexpected places—in sausage, in the smell of mint. For Stevens, Presence fills our being before the mind can think; and it is prior to our speech, our metaphors about it: "I speak below the tension of the lyre."[30] But even more decisive (for determining the direction of Pound's quest) is the comparison with Eliot, instituted by the verse itself:

> yet say this to the Possum: a bang, not a whimper,
>
>   .   .   .   .   .   .
>
> To build the city of Dioce whose terraces are the
>   colour of stars.
>
>   .   .   .   .   .   .
>
>   rain also is of the process.

[28] Ezra Pound, *The Cantos*. Copyright 1940, 1948, © 1968 by Ezra Pound. Reprinted by permission of New Directions Publishing Corporation.

[29] Ezra Pound, *The Cantos*. Copyright 1940, 1948, © 1968 by Ezra Pound. Reprinted by permission of New Directions Publishing Corporation.

[30] *The Collected Poems of Wallace Stevens* (New York: Alfred A. Knopf, 1954), pp. 436–437. See my essay, "Wallace Stevens: The Sundry Comforts of the Sun," *Four Ways of Modern Poetry*, Nathan A. Scott, Jr., ed. (Richmond, Virginia: John Knox Press, 1965), p. 32.

What you depart from is not the way
and olive tree blown white in the wind
washed in the Kiang and Han
what whiteness will you add to this whiteness,
>   what candor?
"the great periplum brings in the stars to our shore."
>   (LXXIV)[31]

His way is thus not that of Eliot, towards the classical hierarchical gradations of being; rather, it is toward the "suchness" of things (to petition an
eastern term) in which ("quand vos venetz al som de l'escalina") our
"gradations" are "distinctions in clarity" (LXXXIV).[32] He puts it still more
bluntly in his adroit and witty paraphrase of Browning's "How It Strikes
a Contemporary" (beginning, "I only knew one poet in my life . . ."):

> I knew but one Achilles in my time
> and he ended up in the Vatican . . . (LXXX).[33]

III

The ambivalence of Pound points to the paradox of our time. It is, at the
same time, paradigmatic of our own ambivalent quest. The theme of quest
is clear in all our arts; but what this points to remains hidden. It remains
hidden partly because our images of quest point outward, or seem to. But
this is something in the nature of our images that we must unlearn, or
learn to construe differently.

It is much the same with our "thinking," which, as we noted above,
has become identified with the work of the analytical intelligence, with
"science," with "logic," with "reasoning." It is for this reason that Heidegger
has noted that "we moderns can learn only if we always unlearn at the
same time. . . . we can learn thinking only if we radically unlearn what
thinking has been traditionally. To do that, we must at the same time
come to know it."[34] I read this again recently in a poem by Charles Peguy
in which "God" speaks:

> It is innocence that is full and experience that is empty.
>   .   .   .   .
> It is innocence that knows and experience that does not know.
> It is the child who is full and the man who is empty,
> Empty as an empty gourd and as an empty barrel;

---

[31] Ezra Pound, *The Cantos.* Copyright 1940, 1948, © 1968 by Ezra Pound.
Reprinted by permission of New Directions Publishing Corporation.
[32] Ezra Pound, *The Cantos.* Copyright 1940, 1948, © 1968 by Ezra Pound.
Reprinted by permission of New Directions Publishing Corporation.
[33] Ezra Pound, *The Cantos.* Copyright 1940, 1948, © 1968 by Ezra Pound.
Reprinted by permission of New Directions Publishing Corporation.
[34] Heidegger, p. 8.

. . . .

Now then, children, go to school.
And you men, go to the school of life.
Go and learn
How to unlearn.[35]

And it is startling to read in the "Prologue" to *Thus Spake Zarathustra*

Bless the cup that is about to overflow, that the water may flow golden
out of it . . .
Lo! This cup is again going to empty itself, and Zarathustra is again going
to be a man.[36]

The Western psyche has again reached the point where it must empty itself
if it is to move to a new plateau of meaning. Our arts today seem to be
pointing to the necessity of unlearning those formulae and patterns which
have walled us in. We must empty the cup again. We seem to be pointing
towards a further paradox: "To be empty is to be full." This wisdom of
Lao Tzu does not yet appear; but we must discern whether what is unsaid
in our arts is tending.

It is easy to see that images of quest are characteristic of our time.
There are the Ulysses narratives, from Pound to Joyce to Kazantzakis to
Space Odyssey: 2001. There are voyages on land and sea, in Melville, St.
John-Perse, and *Crispin*—setting out "to make a new intelligence prevail."
Tony Stoneburner does well to call his poets of the New Humanism "way-
farers." But it should not be overlooked that a Ulysses voyage is a voyage
of return, a coming home; and where this is not the case, there is the quest
for a "newer world" (see Tennyson's *Ulysses*) or a questing for an earthly
paradise.

There are also resumptions of the Grail motif—in Eliot, in Charles
Williams, in Robert Duncan. There is the hero journey, and the fairytale
journey, and the fable and the parable, in which the journey is a seeking
for or a return upon oneself; and today there is the detective story, a quest
for innocence, or for the missing clue, the key to the unknown, the hidden
secret, the incognito that must be unmasked. Even contemporary dramas,
such as those of Beckett, Pinter, and Ionesco are essentially charades which
challenge the spectators to unmask their riddles—which are, in the most
significant cases, the raw riddles of man in his cosmos.

We also note in much of this what Mircea Eliade calls "a nostalgia
for Eden" or for "Paradise." Behind the so-called "revolution" of our time
this nostalgia appears. That is why there is something ineluctably naive
about so many of its evidences. The search for a lost immediacy is apparent

[35] "Innocence and Experience," in *God Speaks*, Julian Green, trans. and intro.
(New York: Pantheon Books, Inc., 1950), p. 38.
[36] Friedrich Nietzsche, *Thus Spake Zarathustra*, Thomas Common, trans. (New
York: The Modern Library, n.d.), p. 4.

in its appeal to an Arcadian "nature," its penchant for the primitive, its assault on taste through crudities intended to shock and violate the sensibilities of supposed convention-ridden upholders of the status quo. Its apotheosis of "love" and feeling is reminiscent of the Rousseauistic program of some decades ago—of the "good savage" and the "beautiful soul." Its religious afflatus recalls T. S. Hulme's definition of romanticism as "split religion."

But once again, this is not the whole story, and we must look beyond these evidences to what is unsaid in these nostalgic modes. To what do these evidences point? Surely they point to a way to overcome the cultural split between the "mind" and the "body"—the dualism inherent in Western intellectualistic methodology and also in the Judeo-Christian objectivizations of inwardness and mystery into doctrine, dogma and obedience to the historicized myth. "Science" inherits the method and degenerates culturally into technology. Society becomes increasingly depersonalized through organization, administration and our fiscal policies. The earth and the world have been deprived of their mystery, man being commanded to "fill the earth and subdue it" (Gen. 1:28). Christ became the unique event in history by whom all men were to be saved, with a certain arbitrariness on God's part thrown into dispensations of grace. Christianity remained binitarian and divisive: it was easily forgotten that even in dogmatics Christ was in order to the Spirit and the Kingdom. As the life of the spirit is progressively emptied, and the desacralization of earth, man, and the cosmos goes on, and the wedge between life and the spirit drives them farther and farther apart, the compensatory imperatives of the deep psyche break through. It is a dangerous moment in the life of a culture.

It is pointed out by Eliade that our symbols never really disappear from the reality of the psyche: "the aspect of them may change, but their function remains the same; one has only to look behind their latest masks."[37] Modern man is full of "half-forgotten myths, decaying hierophanies and secularized symbols." But a quantity of "mythological litter" still abides in the deep psyche. It is these images, he holds, which offer to man the only possible basis for spiritual renewal. This would appear to be indisputable. I should like to propose nevertheless in this time of the "between," when the nostalgia for a lost paradise risks being a fatal refuge of evasion, that what our images are pointing to (as evidenced in our literature and our arts) requires a further consideration. It is that, faced with the necessity of a radical unlearning, we are moving into the zone of recognition of what is involved in Kafka's paradox about accomplishing the negative, and that, as its necessary correlate, we are pointing towards the myth of nothingness.

[37] Mircea Eliade, *Images and Symbols*, Philip Meiret, trans. (New York: Sheed & Ward, 1961), p. 16.

This is evident in the dramas of the absurd. The charades are not primarily eschatological, as our dogmatic consciousness would lead us to infer—thus leaving us outside the dilemma. It was Voltaire who reminded us that it was wonderful to announce the fall of great empires: it consoles us for our littleness. They lead us rather upon the riddle of ultimacy and confront us with their "nothingness." "Nothing," as Beckett quotes from Democritus, "is more real than Nothing."[38] This is an Eastern term, and signifies that the ultimate nature of things lies beyond our conceptual grasp. "The Tao that can be told of is not the eternal Tao; the name that can be named is not the eternal name."[39]

It is not precisely this, however, that our literature seems to be pointing to. Hugo von Hofmannsthal once wrote, "Nothing stands alone: everything is fulfilled in circles. Much escapes us, and yet it is in us, and all we need to know is how to bring it to the surface."[40] This points to the positive, which is already given. Our poetry especially, from Holderlin to the present time, is seeking this resource.

Our images of quest, when interpreted beyond their manifest images, are reaching into this realm of the paradoxical resource. The contemporary poet also reaches into what is already given:

Maybe I will come
to where I am one
and find
I have been waiting there
as a new
year finds the song of the nuthatch[41]

This verse of W. S. Merwin is comparable in its simplicity and profundity to the Oriental verse:

the wind ceases and yet the blossoms fall. . . .

What the eye lights upon here is the mystery of Being and Nothingness, the mystery becoming apparent in the way in which its presence recedes precisely where it shows itself. Thus we are drawn towards its recession, that is, towards Being, which conceals itself in its mystery; at the same time we are aware of its presence in that wherein we permit it to appear. Poetry today, as pointing into this zone of withdrawal, into the

---

[38] Cited in Martin Esslin, *The Theater of the Absurd* (New York: Anchor Books, Doubleday & Company, Inc., 1961), p. 314.

[39] The tao-te ching, 1: *The Way of Lao Tzu*, Wing-tsit Chan, trans. (Indianapolis: Bobbs-Merrill, 1963), p. 97.

[40] "Andreas," *Selected Prose*, Mary Hottinger and Tania & James Stern, trans., intro. by Hermann Broch (New York: Bollingen Series XXXIII, Pantheon Books, Inc., 1952), p. 81.

[41] W. S. Merwin, *Animae* (San Francisco: Kayak Books, Inc., 1969), p. 23.

realm of the nonnameable, becomes itself a sigh (as Heidegger says, quoting Holderlin).[42] This also is myth, which means *the telling word*.

The ubiquity of the symbol (Eliade) is the ubiquity of the telling word: the telling word today is the myth of God's withdrawal. It is a precious moment, for it is a moment in which *mythos* and *logos* may be reunited and the split in the Western psyche healed; and it is a moment in which the West and the East overlap and meet in the knowledge of nonknowing.

Amos Wilder points out, in two passages from William Butler Yeats which exhibit the locus of Being in the thing as given, that "we learn here to recognize the incognitoes of God."[43] Nevertheless it is not easy (though, by trusting that which is given, nothing is easier). In the book of Chuang Tzu we are told:

> The Yellow Emperor went wandering
> To the north of the Red Water
> To the Kwan Lun mountain. He looked around
> Over the edge of the world. On the way home
> He lost his night-colored pearl.
> He sent out Science to seek his pearl, and got nothing.
> He sent Analysis to look for his pearl, and got nothing.
> He sent out Logic to seek his pearl, and got nothing.
> Then he asked Nothingness, and Nothingness had it!
>
> The Yellow Emperor said:
> "Strange, indeed: Nothingness
> Who was not sent
> Who did no work to find it
> Had the night-colored pearl!" [xii, 4][44]

This also is a quest, though that which is sought is already with us. It is not unlike that other parable:

> Jesus said: The Kingdom is like a man who had a
> treasure (hidden) in his field, without knowing it.
> And (after) he died, he left it to his
> (son. The) son did not know (about it), he accepted
> that field, he sold (it). And he who bought it,
> he went, (and) while he was plowing (he found) the treasure.[45]

Epiphany is not the right word, perhaps, for such disclosures. Since

[42] Merwin, p. 10.

[43] Amos N. Wilder, *Theology and Modern Literature* (Cambridge: Harvard University Press, 1958), p. 131.

[44] Thomas Merton, *The Way of Chuang Tzu.* Copyright © 1965 by the Abbey of Gethsemani. Reprinted by permission of New Directions Publishing Corporation.

[45] From *The Gospel According to Thomas*, edited and translated by A. Guillaumont, H.-Ch. Peuch, G. Quispel, W. Till and Yassah 'Abd al Masih. E. J. Brill, Leiden.

Joyce we have been pleased with this term, which means literally to show or appear upon. What the myth of nothingness points to, however, is not the epiphanous but the diaphanous, the showing *through*. A paradoxical transparency is implied, for that which is appearing is also and at the same time withdrawing: which may also be true deeply within ourselves. "I am never all of me/unto myself" as Merwin puts it; and since we occlude the transparency of "Being" or of "Spirit" by the opaqueness wherewith we pursue the negative, we dwell, as the scriptures say, in darkness.[46]

Christianity has understood this darkness very well. The Cross occurs where transparency is lost. For this reason (from the side of the negative) the Gospel warns: "Strait is the gate and narrow is the way which leadeth to Life, and few there be that find it" (mt. vii. 14). But, on the other hand, Christ is the door which, on the far side of our darkness, provides an access so large that even our elephants can waltz through.

Chuang Tzu also understood this:

> To a man who has achieved the Self of Non-Self, all music, whether from pipes or flutes or the wind through nature's apertures, is Heavenly music. But to the man who has not achieved this Non-Self, these sounds are still heard as the Music of Man and the Music of Earth."[47]

It is just here, it would seem to me, that we should speak with Miss Levertov of relearning the alphabet. Like the tree that pulled up its roots to follow Orpheus so the poet and the artist today has had to unlearn the traditional alphabet. It is a radical uprooting, possible to the poet because he hears the music of the Gods. But the alphabet contains the Alpha and Omega of the human condition. "I am Alpha and Omega!" Yet, as Chuang Tzu says,

> You cannot lay hold
> Of the end or the beginning.[48]

But the Cross also is the Alpha and Omega of the human condition; for what is ubiquitous about Christianity is not its doctrine but its sign, what it signifies and lets appear. What appears is the mystery of the negative, seen and not seen in the abyss of our ultimate antinomies. This also is the Alpha and Omega to be relearned. They are not at the "ends" of history; they are within it.

But today we are still with Orpheus, who, it is said, was dismembered:

---

[46] Merwin, p. 22.

[47] Chung-Yuan Chang, *Eranos Tabrbuch*, "Self Realization and the Inner Process of Peace," vol. 37 (Zurich: Rhein-Verlag, 1959), p. 422.

[48] Merton, p. 86.

his head still sang and was swept out to sea singing.
And it is said
Perhaps he will not return.
But what we have lived
comes back to us.
We see more.
We feel, as our rings
increase,
something that lifts our branches, that stretches our
furthest leaf-tips
further.
The wind, the birds,
do not sound poorer
but clearer,
recalling our agony, and the way we danced.
The music![49]

The Contributors

DOROTHY AUSTIN Minister to Youth, First Parish Church, Weston, Massachusetts

HARVEY COX Professor of Church and Society, Harvard Divinity School, Harvard University, Cambridge, Massachusetts

JANE DILLENBERGER Associate Professor of Theology and the Arts, San Francisco Theological Seminary, and The Graduate Theological Union, Berkeley, California

JOHN DILLENBERGER Professor of Historical Theology, and President, The Graduate Theological Union, Berkeley, California

JOHN DIXON, JR. Professor of Religion and Art, The University of North Carolina, Chapel Hill, North Carolina

TOM DRIVER Professor of Theology and Literature, Union Theological Seminary, New York, New York

ROGER HAZELTON Abbott Professor of Christian Theology, Andover Newton Theological School, Newton, Massachusetts

STANLEY HOPPER Bishop W. Earl Ledden Professor of Religion and Literature, Syracuse University, Syracuse, New York

HOWARD HUNTER Chairman, Department of Religion, Tufts University, Medford, Massachusetts

CHARLES KEGLEY Professor of Philosophy and Religious Studies, California State College, Bakersfield, California

NATHAN SCOTT, JR. Professor of Theology and Literature, The Divinity School, University of Chicago, Chicago, Illinois

ROBERT STEELE Associate Professor of Cinema, Boston University School of Public Communication, Boston, Massachusetts

TONY STONEBURNER Assistant Professor of English, Denison University, Granville, Ohio

WALTER WAGONER Director, Boston Theological Institute, Cambridge, Massachusetts